The Laws of Genocide

The Laws of Genocide

Prescriptions for a Just World

Thomas W. Simon

PSI Reports

PRAEGER SECURITY INTERNATIONAL
Westport, Connecticut • London

Library of Congress Cataloging-in-Publication Data

Simon, Thomas W.
The laws of genocide : prescriptions for a just world /
Thomas W. Simon.
p. cm.
Includes bibliographical references and index.
ISBN-13: 978–0–275–97945–4 (alk. paper)
1. Genocide. 2. Crimes against humanity. I. Title.
K5302.S56 2007
345'.0251—dc22 2007016353

British Library Cataloguing in Publication Data is available.

Library of Congress Catalog Card Number: 2007016353
ISBN-10: 0–275–97945–8
ISBN-13: 978–0–275–97945–4

First published in 2007

Praeger Security International, 88 Post Road West, Westport, CT 06881
An imprint of Greenwood Publishing Group, Inc.
www.praeger.com

Printed in the United States of America

The paper used in this book complies with the
Permanent Paper Standard issued by the National
Information Standards Organization (Z39.48–1984).

10 9 8 7 6 5 4 3 2 1

I dedicate this work to the following individuals for their warm friendship and exemplary activism:

Benjamin Mwangachuchu, a refugee from the former Zaire now living in Washington, DC, who has tirelessly worked to bring the lights of truth and justice to Central Africa and who has brought all who know him warmth and cheer.

Elaine Schmidt, a stalwart organizer from the University of Northern Colorado in Greeley, who has demonstrated what it means to lead a life of social justice and who has always been there for others.

Sol Shulman, an accomplished chemistry professor from Illinois State University, who courageously fought fascism and who lives life to its fullest despite a painful past.

Joep Van West, a Dutch immigrant now enjoying retirement in Normal, Illinois, whose good deeds and citizenship have shown that good humor and noble character can survive terror.

CONTENTS

PREFACE

College administrators like to have faculty members fill out reports that outline past accomplishments and future plans for research. Inhabitants of the dean's office think that scholarly interests must fit into a pattern. According to administrative dictates, yearly reports should take the form "Last year, since I published on topic x, now, naturally, I am working on topic y, which, of course, will be followed by publications on topic z next year." For someone afflicted with intellectual ADD (Attention Deficit Disorder), I have trouble following the natural x-to-z progression. Despite this character flaw, my research somehow has fallen—for reasons known only to scholarly gods—into a recognizable pattern. *Democracy and Social Injustice*, the first book, focused on constitutional means of protecting minorities. A second work, *Differences and Injustices*, expands this analysis to an examination of the ways to protect minorities in international law. While these books focus on discrimination harms experienced by groups, the present study explores not just discrimination against groups but attempts to annihilate groups entirely.

The Laws of Genocide—the third one, the "z" in the "x, y, z" series—follows in a natural progression. It retains the focus of the first two on vulnerable groups. Typically, the *genos* in "genocide" are disadvantaged, minority groups. The harms addressed (the *cide* in "genocide"), however, are far more horrific than the discrimination harms examined in the previous works. The connection between discrimination harms directed at disadvantaged groups and mass killings aimed at vulnerable groups seems obvious. The harms differ in degree and kind, and one may lead to the other. Yet, the international community has yet to adopt this common sense observation. Identity politics contributes to this myopia. I encountered identity politics on an intellectual level during three National Endowment for the Humanities faculty seminars. The power of positive group identity became evident in seminars led by Professors John Bowen on Islam, Valerie Bunce on post-communism, and Crawford Young on ethnic nationalism. Our explorations often revealed cases where the valorization of group identity stood in the way of effectively countering harms directed against minority groups.

The practical consequences of refusing to focus on group vulnerability to harm became more apparent on a more practical level. First, after the Soviet Union imploded, the newly formed or reconstituted nations went through a process of adopting constitutions. Through the American Bar Association's Central and Eastern European Law Initiative, many other academic lawyers and myself engaged in constitutional making for a number of nations. We found that in many of these countries previously oppressed groups faced new problems of how to treat minorities within their own territories. Second, the United Nations Working Group on Minorities continually fights an uphill battle to get nations to recognize and enhance the lives of their respective minorities. The Working Group often concentrates on questions of a group's cultural entitlements and glosses over situations of minorities threatened with serious harm. In both the constitutional and the international law milieu, the focus is on how to enhance minority identity. There is nothing inherently wrong with emphasizing the positive aspects of having a group identity. Rather, the deficiency is more of a matter of emphasizing one thing, namely group entitlement, at the expense of another, namely, group protection. If these projects had given more attention to group harms, they would have devoted more energy to considering ways for minorities to resolve disputes, file grievances, and claim violations of the law.

Group vulnerability took on a new meaning for me at the University of Ljubljana in Slovenia. A Fulbright award at the law faculty in this former Yugoslav republic coincided with the Kosovo war. Later, further experiences with group conflict arose while teaching law at Kosovo's University of Pristina, which faced considerable obstacles enrolling Serbian students into an Albanian university. I generally found groups focused on their own past victimization but largely unconcerned with the fate of other groups. Further, anyone who has worked in the Balkans has had to face the challenge of whether to call the suffering of various groups "genocide." Victimized groups often consider that a refusal to call their suffering genocide demeans it. These examples underscored the practical urgency of attaining a better grasp of genocide.

Academic conferences do not always provide the most conducive atmosphere to increase one's understanding of genocide. Some unsettling politics underlie many academic studies of genocide. Given the contentious state of genocide studies, anyone who has a preordained stake in the status of any group's victimization will find some aspect of this present work troubling. I can only say that I do not have any connections by birth, adoption, or affiliation with any group. Nor do I have any academic or political stake in any group's cause.

Academic conferences on genocide have one notable virtue. They invariably include testimonials from survivors. Firsthand accounts reveal a great deal about genocide. Listeners often find these testimonials shocking and humbling. According to an old adage, if you feel despair about your life, talk to someone who is worse off than you are. The many interviews with genocide survivors conducted for this book certainly had a sobering affect on me. Further, I must admit that continual contact with former victims does put one's own problems in better perspective. However, we should cherish hearing stories from survivors for no other reason than that they have honored us with this rare privilege. I owe a deep gratitude to the survivors who shared their painful memories with me. I am forever indebted to those who arranged the interviews with survivors. The incomparable Alenka Mesojedec Prvinsek of the Interior Ministry of Slovenia arranged interviews with Boris Pahor. Holocaust survivors Sol Shulman and Joep von West generously agreed to open their hearts and souls to my classes. Benjamin Mwangachuchu provided me with an undeserved honor when he asked me to give the plenary address to a commemoration of the Rwandan genocide. I felt humbled and ill suited to lecture a number of survivors of the Rwandan atrocities. Perhaps the inadequacies of what I could tell them is somewhat compensated for by this work.

Writers often have secret voices that help to steady the writing and deserve credit for moving the project along to its completion. Benjamin Mwangachuchu has admirably served the role of the inspiring muse. His family and friends throughout Central Africa have suffered immeasurably. His photo albums contain pictures with most of the subjects now deceased. Despite his burdens, Benjamin represents a model political activist whose gentleness and dignity stand out whether he is questioning Justice Richard Goldstone about the resource gap between the war crimes tribunal seated comfortably in Europe and the other one located precariously in Africa or whether he is leading the pursuit of a minister from his own church accused of genocide. Benjamin personifies the truth-seeker in times of political peril and the peacemaker and lawgiver in situations where force and revenge tend to dominate.

For some time, I searched for a concept that brings order to a wildly chaotic world, an idea that gives purpose to an activist's life. Injustice has come to serve as that new paradigm . Whatever else political activists do, whatever other legacy they leave, they should devote energy to fighting injustices. Once we grant the importance of injustice, it is a short step to demanding action on the worst forms of injustice. We demean those who have suffered grave injustices such as genocide by not finding out all that we can about past cases of genocide. We condemn future victims if we fail to fully support current and future efforts to do something about genocide.

To that end, I have tried to write a book that is many things to many people. In some ways, the work is a straightforward textbook on the legal and historical analysis of the genocide. I have tried to include a wealth of information about numerous cases of actual and purported genocide and about international law. I have made every effort to make each chapter independent. These efforts should excuse somewhat the repetition of a number of facts and issues. Despite the independence of the parts, the book constitutes a whole. I tried to produce a unified work. Further, I have tried to minimize any technical language to make the book readily accessible.

Despite its basis in historical facts and actual cases, this work is primarily normative and prescriptive. It is not a survey or a critique of scholarly analyses or court cases. It proposes ways by which we ought to interpret the laws of genocide. The true test of a book is not necessarily its value as an informative teaching tool but rather its ability to raise questions and stimulate thought. If this work stimulates discussion, encourages dialogue, or leads to reforms, then it will have contributed to honoring the victims and survivors of genocide and other grave injustices.

ACKNOWLEDGMENTS

I would like to thank the University of Northern Colorado for its generous support during my tenure as the Robert O. Schulze Distinguished Chair of Interdisciplinary Studies (2002–2003). Dean Schulze left many marks of distinction on the University of Northern Colorado, especially his promotion of interdisciplinary studies. Special thanks go to a number of people who have tirelessly continued to support interdisciplinary projects such as this one. Sue Schulz became a friend and mentor. The dean's office of the College of Arts and Sciences, including Sandra Flake, Maria Lopez, and especially Rich Trahan provided gracious support and inspiration. Professor Maria Livingston, Director of the Life of the Mind program, went far beyond the call of duty to assure the best. Faculty members Lachen Elleezar, Joonok Huh, Hernon George, Alice Klement, and Grace Sussman and many others provided ample intellectual stimulation to sustain this project. Administrators Carol Lucerno and Karen Dwyer gave greatly needed practical direction. Special thanks goes to the fantastic students at UNC, especially Nathan Havey and Clark Callahan, who demonstrated how to live the fight against injustices. Some of the materials for this book made their first public appearance in lectures presented at UNC. A deep bow goes to Karen Johnson, a former architect and mathematics professor turned artist, who did something while the rest of us talked. Allegedly inspired by a lecture on "Representing Survivors of the Rwanda's Genocide," she took her first trip abroad to deliver goats to needy families in Rwanda.

Sincere thanks goes to the Fulbright Committee for its support during my tenure in the Law Faculty and in the Philosophy Faculty of University of Ljubljana, Slovenia (1998).

Alenka Mesojedec Prvinsek and Mitija Zagar deserve the highest praise for dedicating themselves to helping me through the projects despite my many quirks and foibles. Thanks go to Dean Kranjik, Marjan Pvanik, and Andre Ulje and many other wonderful faculty and students for their hospitality.

Special thanks goes to the Academic Training Association of the University of Amsterdam for their support while I taught in the Law Faculty at the Pristina Summer University, Kosovo, and for its support of trips to Macedonia where we followed the route taken by a student refugee and to the site of the Racic massacre in Kosovo. I reserve a special praise for the generous help and friendship from the program's director and my co-teacher Professor Hajredin Kuqi of the Law Faculty. Volunteers for Peace provided me with an opportunity to work at a refugee camp in the Netherlands where I interviewed asylum seekers.

Through its summer seminars and institutes, the National Endowment for the Humanities has provided greatly needed time and resources for completion of the manuscript. I have benefited greatly from two seminars, one on ethnicity at the University of Wisconsin (1997) and the other on post-communist societies at Cornell University (2001). In 2004, I attended a remarkably lively, congenial, and informative institute on Islam at Colorado College. I could not have asked for better mentors than Professors John Bowen (Washington University), Valerie Bunce (Cornell University), and Crawford Young (University of Wisconsin). The influence of another seminar director Donald Kommers (University of Notre Dame) is evident throughout this work.

None of this could happen without support from a work base in the Department of Philosophy at Illinois State University. Iris Baird and Donna Larsen always provide the most comfortable, efficient, and helpful academic home imaginable. I wish to acknowledge the support of former chair Julie Gowen and current chair James Swindler. Special thanks goes to Roberta Trites, former acting dean of the College of Arts and Sciences, who generously provided release time and under whose watch I received the College's Lecturer of the Year award. Colleagues Harry Deutsch and Kenton Machina read early versions of selected parts of the manuscript. ISU student and current Judge Advocate General officer at Abu Graib Dylan Burch excelled at research for the book. Students at Illinois Wesleyan University 2002 May term presented helpful critiques of earlier versions of some of the chapters.

While my home base no longer remains intact in its traditional form, the loyalty and support of family members persevered. Petra Visscher never wavered in her support. Eva Emmalien Visscher-Simon, daughter and graduate of Mount Holyoke College, has become a dear friend and fellow academic traveler. Nora Visscher-Simon, daughter and now high school student, has become a companion and a constant spark of enthusiasm. Mother Sylvia E. Simon, while struggling to hold onto life, continued with her encouragement until, in her words, "I finally wrote it on good paper." I deeply regret that her death in September 2003 prevented her having the final product to display. I want to apologize publicly to my family for often disappearing behind a bookshelf or a computer screen.

I wish to acknowledge the use of earlier oral and written versions of the following parts of the book: "Cleansing the Concept of Ethnicity: Taking Group Harms Seriously," *Emancipating Cultural Pluralism*, Cris E. Toffolo, editor. Albany, NY: SUNY Press, 2003, pp. 55–78; and "Holocaust's Moral Priority," presented at the Twentieth World Congress of Philosophy, Boston, August 10–16, 1998. Chapters 3–7, "Defining Genocide," *Wisconsin International Law Review*, pp. 243–256. Chapter 6, "Genocide: Normative Comparative Studies," *Remembering for the Future: The Holocaust in the Age of Genocide*. London: PalgraveMacmillan, pp. 90–112; "The Holocaust: To Compare or Not to

Compare?" presented at an International Scholars' Conference on Remembering for the Future 2000: Holocaust in the Age of Genocide at Oxford and London, 16–23 July 2000; and "Early Sanity Wanted: States, Minorities, and Genocides" presented at the Third International Conference on Constitutional, Legal and Political Regulation and Management of Ethnic Relations in Ljubljana, Slovenia, December 8–10. Chapter 7, "Organized Violence and Restorative Justice" presented at University of Cape Town, South Africa, October 2000; "Corporate Versus Individual Responsibility" presented at a conference, New Perspectives on the Shoah and the Third Reich at the University of Wisconsin, La Crosse, September 14–16, 2000; and "Responsibility of Organizations for War Crimes" presented at Society for the Study of Values Conference on Criminal Justice and Responsibility in Tulsa, Oklahoma, April 26, 2001.

Thanks go to readers Elizabeth Bartholet, Sandra Bartky, Helen Fein, Hurst Hanum, Richard Haynes, and John Roth. As these critics know, refusal to incorporate suggestions proves my obstinacy and not their inadequacies. The following have provided hospitality and friendship at critical junctures: Penny and Barclay Adams; Allyson Barrett and William Stephenson; Arthur Frank and Mary Kay Dawson; Amy Hoch; Eileen and Marguerite Lykes, Pete Richards, and Melissa Revell; Elaine and Don Schmidt; and Andrew Ward. Finally, to many friends and acquaintances neglected over the years, I hope that this final product somewhat compensates.

LIST OF ABBREVIATIONS

AUM	*Aum Shinrikyo* ("Supreme Truth")
CDR	*Coalition pour de le Défense de la Républic*
ICC	International Criminal Court
ICJ	International Court of Justice
ICTR	International Criminal Tribunal for Rwanda
ICTY	International Criminal Tribunal for the Former Yugoslavia
KDP	*Kommunistische Partei Deutshlands* (German Communist Party)
NSDAP	National Socialist German Workers Party (Nazi party)
OAU	Organization of African Unity
PCA	Permanent Court of Arbitration
PCIJ	Permanent Court of International Justice
PKI	Indonesian Communist Party
POWs	Prisoners of War
RPF	Rwanda Patriotic Front
RTML	*Radio-Télévision Libre des Mille Collines*
SA	*Sturmabteilung*
SD	*Sicherheitsdienst*
SS	*Schutzstaffel*
UK	United Kingdom
UN	United Nations
US	United States
WMDs	Weapons of Mass Destruction
WW I	World War I
WW II	World War II

Introduction

> And there were American guards. I came to see them and... ah... I spoke English and asked them if I could get over. "But who are you?" I said, "I'm a French political prisoner." "Well, I'll ask the captain for that. I haven't got any instructions for you. We just have instructions to pass over the prisoners of war." The captain came back and told me, "I'm extremely sorry for you, but so far I haven't got any instructions for political prisoners, just for prisoners of war." I said, "What shall I do? I haven't any money. I haven't got any papers. I have got nothing to eat. Couldn't you take me over? I have a bad foot and I need a doctor." "I'm extremely sorry, I can't. I can't. Come back tomorrow. Perhaps I'll have such instructions by then."[1]
>
> —Nelly Bundy

> We are in the presence of a crime without a name.[2]
>
> —Winston Churchill

Today, we would call Nelly Bundy a Holocaust survivor. The crime she survived now has a name—genocide. In 1946, while describing the traumas experienced during the war, Nelly Bundy could not call herself a *Holocaust survivor* as the label was unknown at the time. The term *Holocaust* did not come into use until after 1957, but Nelly Bundy needed a label in 1945. On January 18, 1945, the Nazis evacuated Auschwitz, a death camp. Nelly Bundy escaped from the Nazis and sought refuge with American troops, but they demanded to know her identity before they could act on her behalf. By "identity," the Americans wanted to know how to classify Nelly Bundy. Into what category did she fit? She told them she was a *political prisoner*, the only relevant identity she knew. However, as the guards from the United States army only had instructions for *prisoners of war* and the classification *Holocaust survivor* and *genocide victim* did not exist yet, they sent her away.

The linguistic process of giving "victims without a name" a legal classification plays a critical role in the humanitarian process of recognizing a type of harm, a form of injustice. The words "Holocaust" and "genocide" have become familiar, but these now commonplace terms did not exist before World War II. In a case of language chasing reality, cases of genocide preceded the invention of the word "genocide." We will trace refinements in the meaning of genocide since it first became part of international legal language in 1948. Further, we will see how jurists have come to recognize genocide as distinct from other humanitarian crimes. *Holocaust survivors* marks a very different group than *political prisoners* or *prisoners of war* (see Chapter 6). It would have made a difference to Nelly Bundy's life if she had known what to call the crime committed against her and if she had been able to demonstrate the importance of her status relative to other victim classifications. Present and future Nelly Bundys would benefit enormously from a clear and refined understanding of genocide and related crimes.

The twentieth century distinguished itself as compiling more deaths from war, massacres, and genocide than any other century. While thinking about global horrors can depress even the most optimistic person, a study of global horrors provides insights into human nature and into our individual natures. This study offers a mix of realistic hope and guarded optimism. In Chapter 1, erring on the side of hope, we survey legal responses to hate, evil, and grave injustices. The analysis of the laws of war in Chapter 1 uncovers a long-standing and deep-seated humanitarian tradition. While in Chapter 1 we place genocide in the context of the development of international humanitarian law, in Chapter 2 we put the laws of genocide in a utopian global context. In Chapter 2, we envision how we would go about creating an international criminal code. While legal and ethical analyses reinforce one another throughout the study, the remaining (Chapters 3–7), serve, in part, as a textbook on genocide laws as well as a source of information on grave injustices throughout modern times. The book seeks to inform the reader about the Armenian massacres, the Soviet famine, the conflicts in Bosnia and Kosovo, and the Rwandan genocide. A detailed examination of the elements of the crime of genocide illuminates the seemingly incomprehensible. More importantly, by carefully specifying the type of act, intent, motive, victim, and perpetrator needed for a charge of genocide, we lay a firm foundation stone for constructing a more meaningful system of international justice and a more viable framework for a universal morality.

In the spirit of laying the conceptual and institutional groundwork for building a better tomorrow, two questions motivate this admittedly sweeping introductory overview. First, how have humans employed reason to confront injustices? The law has offered one way to apply reason and ethics to injustices. Today, international public law effectively recognizes three main types of grave injustices: war crimes, crimes against humanity, and genocide. Historical surveys (dutifully followed in Chapter 1) typically begin with the first of these injustices, namely war crimes. Even a cursory study of human brutality and barbarism, past and current, may engender despair. The history of the laws of war (undertaken in Chapter 1), however, reveals a progressive evolution beginning with the formulation of legal principles in ancient times through the legal codification of the principles and finally to contemporary institutionalized structures for adjudicating the laws.

These developments deserve high praise as ethical achievements for human kind. The institutionalization of international courts to address war crimes represents a remarkable humanitarian achievement that helps to counterbalance the sordid history of injustices.

A pattern has emerged, particularly within the recent history, as to how international law has responded to two types of injustices, namely, war crimes and genocide. Historically, those transgressions that occur within the relatively structured context of war have received considerably more legal attention than brutal genocide slaughters. Recently, the trend began to reverse when the international community gave more attention to the crime of genocide than to war crimes. For the first time in history, a court (the Ad Hoc International Tribunal for Rwanda) sentenced an individual for the crime of genocide. Further, the newly established International Criminal Court (ICC) has begun to hear cases involving charges of genocide. However belated, we should celebrate these developments as large steps along the road of humanitarian progress.

The establishment of the ICC alone stands as a remarkable humanitarian achievement. Nevertheless, some more recent developments may upset the historical trend finally to "give genocide its due." Since September 11, 2001, the world community has moved towards treating genocide not as the gravest crime but as a lesser one. Suddenly, we find ourselves in a world with an overwhelmingly dominant focus on terrorism and destructive weaponry. Within international law, terrorist attacks fit under the heading of *crimes against humanity*, and terrorist strikes, under *war crimes*. The international community now gives priority to injustices other than genocide. If genocide is the gravest of the grave injustices, then these recent developments signal backward steps on the road of humanitarian progress. This work represents an effort to redirect the movement in a more progressive direction.

The analysis undertaken in this work follows the dictum that the "conceptual and ethical angels lie in the legal details." However, detailed legal analyses carry the danger of swamping the larger ethical lessons and dampening responses to the overwhelming horrors of genocide. After all, according to one sentiment, we should deplore and prevent genocide, not analyze and distinguish it. My initial response to this charge will become vulnerable to the criticism that abstract, formal reasoning commits the sin of hypostasizing. Hypostasizing occurs when theorists treat Reason and other concepts as if they were real. The capitalization of the word "Reason" turns it into a proper noun like Osama. However, it helps my defense to see the situation as a battle between two named forces, Reason and Hate. Explicitly and implicitly throughout the book, Reason battles its nemesis Hate. Reason protests against and dialogues with Hate. Most importantly, we shall find Reason taking Hate to court. The basic thesis is that Reason should use the tools of law to confront Hate's genocide weapons.

Reason needs the help of philosophy and law to win its fight against Hate. Given the horror, hurt, and emotion connected to the crime of genocide, a dispassionate, abstract, legalistic approach helps Reason tame and cage Hate.

A legalistic/philosophical approach does not ignore the human elements connected to genocide. The stories of genocides from survivors and others need a wider audience. Although legal proceedings manage to distort these narrative accounts, legal cases on genocide contain invaluable but admittedly filtered narrative accounts of genocide. Retelling the excruciatingly painful stories that I have had the privilege of hearing from genocide survivors will not do them any more justice and might unintentionally demean them. Retelling some survivor accounts that I know would violate a deeply private space, and the intensity and depth of private versions of some other survivor stories exceed any attempts at a public rendition. With a few exceptions, this work does not contain stories of those who survived genocide. In Chapter 1, we trace the success law has had over the centuries in establishing a fortress for Reason to win battles against Hate on its own turf. In Chapter 2, we demonstrate the advantages of using law as Reason's primary weapon against Hate.

After we provide an overview of the elements of the crime of genocide in Chapter 2, in each of the subsequent chapter, we focus on a different element of the crime of genocide. To convict someone of murder a state prosecutor must prove each element of the crime "beyond a reasonable doubt." National criminal law systems require two basic elements for a criminal conviction. National prosecutors must prove that the accused had the requisite mental state (*mens rea*) in the commission of a criminal act (*actus reus*). The elements for the crime of genocide include act and intent, but international jurists add, or perhaps specify more explicitly, some additional ingredients as well. Besides act and intent, we propose that for the crime of genocide prosecutors need to prove something about the motive, the victims, and the perpetrators. In Chapters 3 and 4, we examine the peculiar nature of act and intent, respectively, for the crime of genocide, and in Chapters 5–7, we examine the three additional ingredients: motive, types of victims and perpetrators.

We take some liberties with the labels used by the drafters of the international criminal code to specify the elements of the crime. The following brief outline of the elements and proposed interpretations of them should help frame the overall project. First, in Chapter 3, we make the case for taking massive killings as the central act of genocide. Second, in Chapter 4, we argue for replacing individual intent with something called "corporate intent." Third, in Chapter 5, we propose adding a motive requirement in the form of institutional hatred. The crime of genocide also involves certain types of victims and perpetrators. In Chapter 6, we reformulate the nature of genocide victims as targeted groups defined by the perpetrator. Finally, in Chapter 7, we take a novel look at the agents of genocide, and we defend the claim that organizations and not individuals are the primary agents of the crime of genocide.

The diagram below brings together the general categories used in national and international criminal law and shows how the interpretations proposed in this book fit under each element for the crime of genocide.

Elements of the Crime of Genocide

Type of Law	Criminal Act	Criminal Mind	Motive	Victim Type	Prepetrator Type
NATIONAL CRIMINAL LAW	Act (*Actus Reus*)	Intent (*Mens Rea*)	[Motive]	[Victim]	[Accused]
INTERNATIONAL CRIMINAL LAW	Conduct Element	Mental Circumstances	Contextual	Consequences	Individual Perpetrators
GENOCIDE LAWS	Massive Killings	Organizational Policies	Institutionalized Hatred	Groups, Perpetrator Dfd.	Organizations and Individuals

For example, what national lawyers call "criminal act" and international jurist refer to as "conduct" becomes, in the analysis proposed here, the specific act of massive killing for the crime of genocide. The differences among these labels reflect the policy recommendation that international law should interpret criminal elements in organizational terms. We propose to reconfigure the concept of individual intent carried over to international law from national law as organizational policy (corporate intent). Similarly, we interpret the motive element ("contextual circumstances" in international law), often bypassed in criminal law, as institutionalized forms of hatred. Further, in determining the nature of genocide victim types, we recommend that courts adopt the perpetrator's perception of the targeted group. Our emphasis on organizations results in a de-emphasis on individual accountability in favor of organizational responsibility.

The avowedly normative analyses offered here do not entirely reflect current legal formulations. However, the chapters not only contain legal arguments to support the proposed interpretations but also suggest viable ways for incorporating the recommendations into international law. Similar to the way changes come about in common law systems, the ICC's formulations can be changed legislatively and judicially. Representatives of ratifying nations will have opportunities to modify some aspects of the original codifications. More likely, changes will occur through the eventual interpretations given to the original text by the ICC. Judicial opinions already have begun to play an interpretative role, and I shall make ample use of cases from past and current tribunals. The overall effect of past jurisprudence on new ICC rulings remains controversial. Nevertheless, I have incorporated evaluations of the jurisprudence produced by the International Criminal Tribunal for the Former Yugoslavia (ICTY) and the International Criminal Tribunal for Rwanda (ICTR), the two primary predecessors to the ICC. Our project fits into a genre that has become routine in many national legal systems. In most countries, scholars and jurists routinely recommend interpretations for their courts to adopt. Scholarly normative recommendations are an influential staple in most national legal systems. While a similar situation exists in international law, it has not firmly taken hold in the discussions and debates over the codifications of the international criminal code. This work represents one of the first voyages into the sea of normative international criminal law. It should help stir more interest in the fascinating interplay between international law and global ethics.

Part I

GENOCIDE IN CONTEXT

Chapter 1

Genocide: Legal Context

All is fair in love and war.[1]

Sweet romantic love often turns bitter, as any divorce attorney will attest. No one would seriously offer a defense of the proposition that "All is fair" throughout all of love's phases—romance, consummation, and dissolution. After all, we have an entire body of family law to correct some of love's unfairness. While some people would disagree that "All is fair in love," many people would readily accept the proposition that "All is fair in war." However, a few pointed examples should convince people that certain kinds of behavior have become unacceptable even in times of war. We can find more agreement over injustices committed in wars than we might think.

The Nazis provided humanity with a range of morally reprehensible acts from the well-known Holocaust to lesser-known reprisal killings. Consider one of countless examples of reprisal killings carried out by the Nazis. On May 27, 1942, Czech partisans mortally wounded Reinhard Heydrich (one of Hitler's most brutal butchers), chief of the Reich Security and the SD (*Sicherheitsdienst*), which was the intelligence service of the SS (*Schutzstaffel*, German for "Protective Echelon"). A few months earlier, on January 2, 1942, Heydrich had convened the Wansee Conference that had designed plans for the "Final Solution," a code word for the complete extermination of all Jews. On June 4, shortly after Heydrich's death, German soldiers and police carried out reprisal killings. They murdered hundreds of adult men and women from the Czech villages of Lidice and Lezaky. They sent hundreds of others to concentration camps where few survived. Our moral intuitions (I trust!) would tell us to condemn these acts. We feel that these senseless acts must be morally and legally wrong. We probably would be convinced that these reprisal killings violated some moral and legal codes somewhere. Yet, where would we find these ethical and legal codes? Fortunately, we could easily find laws governing this kind of conduct in war. There are laws that prohibit reprisal killings. Thankfully, the international community has not accepted that "all is fair in war."

Killing prisoners-of-war (POWs) is another type of act that we should readily condemn. On December 17, 1944, during the second day of the Battle of the Bulge, known as the bloodiest battle of World War II, German SS troops captured American soldiers. Presumably, the 1929 Geneva Convention protects POWs such as these captives from the US military. According to the Third Geneva Convention, POWs "are entitled in all circumstances to respect for their persons and their honor" (Article 14) and "must at all times be protected, particularly against acts of violence or intimidation and against insults and public curiosity" (Article 13). German soldiers herded the American POWs into a field near the Belgium town of Malmedy and then killed all one hundred of them. At a trial held at Dachau, a former concentration camp, the prosecution claimed that the German command had ordered the defendants to disregard the laws of war in the same way that Germany's enemy, the Soviet Union (which had not signed the Geneva Convention), had violated those laws. Survivors testified that they heard orders to kill all the prisoners. A US military tribunal, however, convicted all seventy-three of the accused and sentenced forty-two of them to death by hanging. The United States never carried out the executions and eventually released all of the prisoners.

Indeed, all sides committed atrocities during World War II. Germany also accused US soldiers of killing German POWs. In the *Webling Incident* (named for the town on the outskirts of Dachau), US soldiers executed members of the German Home Guard, which consisted mostly of young boys and older men forced into service to defend local communities after they had surrendered. General George S. Patton, Jr., commander of the Fifteenth Army in American-occupied Germany, reputedly destroyed the papers containing a court martial of the soldiers. In any war, no one side has a monopoly on the commission of atrocities, but one side almost always stands out as having committed more and worse crimes than the other side.

These World War II cases highlight just a few of the many atrocities committed during war. Most importantly, they represent the moral and legal boundaries that presumably we would not cross in thought or deed. Admittedly, we do not know what we would have done under similar circumstances. However, we should have no compunction about condemning the slaughter of unarmed POWs who pose no threat whatsoever. Whether the victims come from the ranks of our soldiers or from the ranks of the enemy's soldiers, the murder of POWs belies the claim that "all is fair in war." Our moral intuitions tell us that these deeds violate some moral principles and that if we do not have laws against them, then we should have some laws in place to punish individuals who commit these types of crimes.[2] In this chapter, we shall become familiar with the laws that do govern war.

War has a notoriously long, bloody history. The regulation of war also has a long, venerable but lesser known history. History provides notable examples of the moral and legal condemnation of certain wars and of particular ways of fighting wars. The classification *war crimes* doubles as a general and as a specific legal category. The general term "war crimes" includes the specific category "war crimes" as well as three other types of international crimes: crimes against peace, crimes against humanity, and genocide. In other words, the ambiguous phrase "war crimes" has a general and a specific meaning. As part of the general war crimes' classification, genocide shares a history with these other international crimes. The story of how these classifications of international crimes developed is a story well worth telling because it is a story of hope, a story of moral and legal progress. We shall see that establishing the laws of genocide marked the latest progressive step in this development.

LAW AND WAR

The phrase "laws of war" may sound like an oxymoron (contradictory words) to some people. An oxymoron ("fighting for peace," "holy war," "civil war," "peace force," "reality TV," "jumbo shrimp," "banker's trust," "military intelligence") combines two ideas that seem incompatible. To some, war seems far removed from legal rules. Further, according to the skeptics, why would any country put its military at a disadvantage by making it follow some rules? After all, nations fight wars to win, not to be lawful.

Surprisingly, however, war has a long history of being treated as a rule-governed activity. Even more surprising, the rules of war include moral as well as legal rules. These rules govern two different aspects of war, the initiation and the conduct of war. The Latin phrase *jus ad bellum* (justice of war) signifies the rules that apply to decisions about whether to engage in war. According to these rules, some wars qualify as just ones while other ones do not. *Jus ad bellum* standards distinguish between *Just and Unjust Wars*, to use the title of Michael Walzer's seminal work. Some analysts, for example, place World War II into the "just war" category and put the Vietnam War into the "unjust war" category.

Once a war has commenced, another set of rules applies to the means used to fight it. The phrase *jus in bello* (justice in war) designates the rules of warfare. *Jus in bello* rules sanction actions otherwise prohibited in peacetime. War conditions allow nations to put some of their citizens in harm's way. Nations use conscription to force their citizens to risk their lives. The rules of war not only permit but also encourage, or more accurately command, combatants to kill one another. The rules of war override peacetime rules that prohibit the killing of humans. Indeed, "a war fought in compliance with standards and rules of laws of war permits massive intentional killing or wounding and massive other destruction that, absent a war, would violate fundamental human rights."[3] Nevertheless, *jus in bello* rules are not entirely morally permissive. Article 22 of the Hague Convention (1907) proclaims "the rights of belligerents to adopt means of injuring the enemy is not unlimited." Article 2(c) specifically forbids belligerents "to kill or wound an enemy who, having laid down his arms, or having no longer a means of defense, has surrendered at discretion." Warfare marks a glaring exception to some of the basic moral rules that underlie civilized society. Still, we do not jettison or throw out all morality when we fight a war.

Both types of rules (*jus ad bellum* and *jus in bello*) fall within the purview of just war theory. This tradition traces its lineage back to ancient Greece and Rome, but it has its primary roots in medieval theology. The just war tradition has guided the codification of the principles of war in international law. The just war tradition stands between realism and idealism. Realism comes in many forms, but in all its variations, we find a dismissive attitude toward attempts to apply legal and moral rules to war. Political realists, for example, reject appeals to morality in international relations; military realists find no role for legal or moral rules about war. For military realists, *inter arma, silent leges* ("in war, laws are silent"), or, more familiarly, "war is hell."

Opposite to realism lies idealism, with pacifism serving as its best-known offshoot. In the literature, you will find just war theorists constantly battling realists. For some unexplained reason, however, they pay scant attention to idealists in general and to pacifists in particular. Michael Walzer's *Just and Unjust Wars* contains only a brief "Afterword" devoted to pacifism. "War moralists" like Walzer walk a middle path between realism and idealism. Oddly enough, they seem to become realists when they analyze pacifism. Walzer wrote a classic attack on realism within the just war tradition, but he speaks as a realist when he examines (however briefly) pacifism. He sees Mahatma Gandhi's nonviolent movement against the British as a limited, strategic form of pacifism. Walzer finds Gandhi's pacifism historically limited to a particular political situation in India. While nonviolence proved effective during India's independence movement, Walzer claims that it would not have functioned effectively during the Nazi reign in Germany. Walzer (a realist in regard to pacifism) finds those who preached nonviolence to Hitler's potential victims, at best, naïve. Pacifists (according to even temporary realists like Walzer) have unrealistic perceptions of the aggressors' humanity.

Given the shortcomings of realism and idealism, the moral realism adopted by Walzer and other just war theorists seems like the only sensible position left. Moral idealists supposedly ignore political reality while realists unsuccessfully dodge moral questions. Moral realists supposedly use common sense to apply moral principles to issues of war and warfare. It is difficult to argue against a moral thesis that has defensible practical applications. While the analysis developed in this book operates within a framework of moral realism, we need to acknowledge, at the outset, that the moral realist perspective has two shortcomings. First, moral realists underestimate the converging progressive developments of law and ethics on issues related to war. Second, they fail to see these developments on war issues as part of the construction of a more encompassing approach to injustices in general.

A brief historical survey, addressing the first shortcoming of realism, demonstrates progressive applications of law and morality to war and warfare. "War might be hell," but even this hell has rules and moral limits. The use of law and morality to address war and warfare may seem as unrealistic as the use of nonviolence to face the Nazis. History, however, demonstrates how we tend to underestimate the effective application of law and morality to war and warfare. Whether this historical trend continues depends on mustering the political will to place international institutions like the International Criminal Court (ICC) on a solid legal, ethical, and political foundation. Whether the application of law and morality will continue to expand to include the worst atrocities and their perpetrators lies within the realm of human choice. To put this point more dramatically, how we choose to apply law and morality to issues of grave injustices will mold the very idea of humanity.

LAWS OF WAR

Historically, law, morality, and war have gone through various phases in their relationships. Before specifying the historical phases and describing increasingly important developments within each phase, we need to issue some cautions and make some confessions. Historical surveys notoriously contain Western biases. Histories of war often pay homage to other civilizations as long as the subject falls within ancient history.[4] Further, authors draw conflicting lessons from each period covered in their surveys. Unfortunately, the analysis below stands guilty of these charges. A more specific description of our aims may aid in their defense. We intend this historical survey to demonstrate that the regulation of war has a long history. Further, the survey should establish that this long history of dealing with warfare has been overall a morally progressive one. The final aim of the survey is best described metaphorically. The survey should provide the reader with a picture that begins vaguely in focus and ends with distinct outlines of an intact legal and ethical structure.

The development of the laws of war breaks down into six historical periods. First, beginning in ancient times, we find legal and moral principles regulating war becoming increasingly specific over time. Second, during the Roman Empire, specific procedures governing the declaration and conduct of war came clearly into view. Third, the Middle Ages marks the time when religiously inspired moral principles supplanted secularly based legal ones. Fourth, a secularized approach to law and war reemerged during the seventeenth and eighteenth centuries. Fifth, the late nineteenth century became inundated with detailed codes regulating the conduct of war. During that period, for example, we find the first national codes as well as the first international codes. Finally, during the twentieth century, courts designed to try war criminals moved to the forefront.

These historical stages lay the foundation for the construction of a global criminal law system. Will the generally progressive historical trend continue into the twenty-first century? The answer lies in how the international community develops the laws of genocide and incorporates them into the overall scheme of international criminal law system. As noted in the sections following the historical survey, developments since September 11, 2001 have posed major but surmountable obstacles to these progressive developments. In this survey, we emphasize the rules and avoid in-depth analyses of the theoretical justifications for these rules.

History of Laws of War

1. *The Ancient Times.* Modern theorists often look back to the distant past with a paternalistic disdain. They assume not only that knowledge has accumulated over time but also that moral consciousness has progressed. Yet, contrary to these modernist sentiments, moral concerns about war emerged very early in human history. Humanitarian rules governing war reach far back historically, and they appeared across the globe. The ancient Egyptians and Babylonians appealed to humanitarian principles in warfare. In the fourth century BCE, the Hindu civilization produced the *Book of Manu* that contains rules of warfare. On the other side of the globe, the Aztecs had strict rules of battle. These ancient sources and examples have more than a historical interest. Apparently, principles developed in ancient times affect the conduct of modern warfare. One commentator, for example, introduced Sun Tzu (sixth century BCE) as a

> Chinese soldier and philosopher who has been highly influential in the development of Chinese military doctrine and who has had (and continues to have) tremendous influence on U.S. military doctrine.[5]

Within different ancient philosophical and theological frameworks, we find descriptions of forbidden weapons that range from types of armaments to designations of particular weapons. Lao Tzu warned against the use of lethal weapons (the ancients' Weapons of Mass Destruction, better known by its acronym WMDs):

> Fine weapons are instruments of evil.
> They are hated by men.
> Therefore, those who possess Tao turn away from them.[6]

The more elaborate the theoretical frameworks, the more specific the descriptions of forbidden weapons. Within the elaborate religious framework of Hinduism, we find relatively specific prohibitions such as the following from the *Book of Manu*:

> When the king fights with his foes in battle, let him not strike with weapons concealed in wood, nor with such as are barbed, poisoned, or the points of which are blazing with fire.

Jumping across many centuries, clear and highly specific descriptions of forbidden weapons appear prominently in the nineteenth century with the use of contract language. According to the *St. Petersburg Declaration of 1868*,

> The Contracting Parties engage mutually to renounce, in case of war among themselves, the employment by their military or naval troops of any projectile of a weight below 400 grams, which is either explosive or charged with fulminating or inflammable substances.

Overall, then, these examples map out a progressive trajectory. Earlier expressions of moral principles set the framework for later formulations set in the language of contractual negotiation. These nineteenth-century specifications, then, in turn, lead to the codified laws of war developed mostly in the twentieth century.

2. *The Roman Empire.* Just war theory traces its roots to ancient Rome. The Roman orator Cicero said, "A war is never undertaken by the ideal state, except in defense or safety."[7] The Romans had an elaborate procedure for dealing with a state before it would declare a war. They deemed unprovoked attacks and ones that did not follow proper procedures as unjust wars.[8] Further, the Romans also distinguished combatants from non-combatants. The dichotomy between combatants and non-combatants remained unquestioned until the Bush administration introduced a third category of enemy noncombatants.[9] A recognition of ancient Rome's contribution to just war theory adds a chapter to a historical survey designed to show that sophisticated versions of regulating war go far back into history.[10]

3. *The Middle Ages.* According to some commentators, the medieval period marked a radical change from previous attempts to justify war.[11] Saint Augustine (b. 383) led the way by breaking rank with the ancient Greek and Roman just war doctrines. The punishment of sin began to supplant "defense and safety" as the primary justifications for war. Nevertheless, while the justifications changed, an increasingly powerful Church began to devise relatively stringent rules of war. The Church placed restrictions on the who (Peace of God, 989), when (Truce of God, 1027), and what (Second Lateran Council, 1139) of warfare. The Peace of God protected clerics, monks, and Christian women from the ravages of war. The Truce of God restricted war to certain days of the weeks and seasons. It first prohibited fighting from 9:00 PM Saturday to 3:00 AM Monday and then expanded the prohibition from Wednesday evening until Monday morning. The restrictions left only about eighty days scattered throughout the year for fighting.[12] This certainly marked an improvement over the previously enacted Muslim designation of the month of Ramadan as a month of peace. Of course, many civilizations, including the present one, have not managed to set aside even a few days devoted solely to peace.

The medieval laws of war had teeth as evidenced by the prosecution of soldiers for war crimes. The Church punished violators of its laws with excommunication. Perhaps, the first war crimes trial occurred in 1305 with the trial and execution of William Wallace, a Scottish insurrectionist. Later, in 1474, twenty-eight judges, representing states of the Holy Roman Empire, tried and convicted Sir Peter von Hagenbach for murder and rape of civilians as well as for perjury and other crimes against the "laws of man and God."[13] The tribunal stripped von Hagenbach of his knighthood and then executed him.

4. *The Modern Period.* Attempts to secularize the just war tradition distinguish the modern period. While imprisoned, Hugo Grotius (1583–1645), the Dutch founder of international law, wrote a treatise in reaction to the devastation of the Thirty Years War (1618–1648). In *On the Law of War and Peace*, he derived

thirteen precepts of law from nine general concepts of law to use to judge the actions of nations. He accepted natural law theory, which melts morality and law together, but he rejected a Christian interpretation, which placed everything virtuous within natural law. Grotius successfully laid the theoretical foundations for a modern, secular version of just war theory in the seventeenth century.

At the turn of the eighteenth century, treaties between nations began to include sections with rules governing possible conflicts between the contracting parties. A 1785 treaty between the United States and Prussia assured protection of "all women and children, scholars of every faculty, cultivators of the earth, artisans, manufacturers and fishermen." The United States incorporated these provisions in its 1848 peace treaty with Mexico. The more widespread means of applying secular natural law through military trials had to wait until the eighteenth century. A trial held for the British soldiers who killed five Boston citizens as they protested the quartering of British troops symbolized what was to come.[14] The Jay Treaty of 1794, designed to settle an on-going dispute between Great Britain and the United States, ushered in a "tribunal century." While the eighteenth century saw theories turned into rules of warfare, the nineteenth century saw the establishment of over two hundred international arbitral tribunals culminating in the establishment of the Permanent Court of Arbitration (PCA).

5. *The Nineteenth Century.* Concerning the laws themselves, the latter half of the nineteenth century witnessed a burgeoning of new laws governing *jus in bellum*. Jurists addressed issues of warfare before tackling the issue of war itself. Developments of *jus ad bello* had to wait until the early twentieth century. The *jus in bellum* rules first covered the military, then, prisoners of war, and, finally, civilians. Although "the great person theory of history" has its flaws, humanitarian law owes whatever strength it has to "a few good people."[15] The *jus in bellum* hero award should go to Jean-Henri Dunant. The Swiss born Dunant had a history of social activism. He joined a movement to help unify Christians and Jews and became a member of organizations designed to help the disadvantaged. However, nothing had prepared him for the carnage he witnessed while on a business trip to Italy. In 1859, he arrived in Castiglione della Pieve in the midst of the Battle of Solferino. He found the French and Austrian armies,

> trampling each other under foot, killing one another on piles of bleeding corpses, felling their enemies with their rifle butts, crushing skulls, ripping bellies open with saber and bayonet.[16]

The cavalry galloped by, "crushing dead and dying beneath its horses' hoofs," while runaway horses "kept trying to pick their way so as to avoid stepping on the victims. . . ."[17] As horrifying as Dunant found the devastation within the heat-of-battle, he became even more "seized with horror and pity" by the unnecessary suffering he witnessed after the battle. Forty thousand died, for example, during the "Little Italian War" while another forty thousand died from wounds and other factors after the war.

In 1863, one year after the publication of his account of the battle, Dunant organized a conference to establish the International Committee of the Red Cross, a voluntary relief society. In 1864, the Diplomatic Conference proposed the *Geneva Convention for the Amelioration of the Condition of the Wounded Armies in the Field.*[18] Shortly thereafter, Dunant ran into financial difficulties and lived out his remaining days in obscurity and ill health. In 1895, a journalist discovered him in a remote Swiss mountain village. In 1901, the Nobel committee sent him its first Peace Prize by post.

Contemporaneously with these developments in Europe, President Abraham Lincoln authorized Francis Leiber, a law professor at Columbia College (later Columbia University), to develop a code of military engagement. Leiber, a German immigrant who had fought against Napoleon, personally felt the pangs of the Civil War. His eldest son died while fighting for the Confederate Army, and his younger son lost an arm while fighting for the Union Army. Leiber drafted General Orders 100 (*Instruction for the Government of the Armies of the United States in the Field*). During the Civil War, the Union Army governed its conduct by the Leiber Code. These regulations remained in effect for nearly fifty years. One commentator called the Leiber Code "the most impressive code that has guided any military force up to that time."[19] Although Leiber had codified already existing customs and regulations, his efforts "marked the first time in Western history that the government of a sovereign nation established formal guidelines for the conduct of its army in the field."[20]

The principles of the Leiber Code played a pivotal role in the *St. Petersburg Declaration* (1868). This one-page document, signed by twenty nations, resolved to "alleviating as much as possible the calamities of war," and subsequent developments of the law of land warfare.[21] The Hague international peace agreements (the 1899 *Convention with Respect to the Laws and Conventions of War* and the 1907 Hague *Convention Respecting the Laws and Customs of War on Land*) incorporated the rules first devised by Dunant and Leiber. States, later, supplemented the Hague Conventions with the Geneva Conventions. The 1925 Geneva Protocol outlawed the first-use of chemical weapons. The Protocol was a response to the employment (first by German and then by British forces) of chemical weapons (mustard gas) during World War I. All the major powers except Japan and the United States ratified the Protocol. The United States finally ratified it in 1975.[22] The 1929 Geneva Conventions (*On the Wounded and the Sick in Armies in the Field and on the Treatment of Prisoners of War*) emphasized protection of noncombatants and prisoners of war. The 1949 Geneva Conventions, supplemented by two protocols in 1977, provided further refinements. Today, the Hague and the Geneva Conventions constitute the core of *jus in bello*.

Late nineteenth-century jurists had high expectations for public international arbitration as an alternative to war. Today's skeptics and pessimists may have difficulty appreciating the idealism and optimism evident at the turn of the last century. At the beginning of the eighteenth century, the philosopher Immanuel Kant's dream of "perpetual peace" seemed, at the outset of the twentieth century, as if it could become a reality.[23] For many, however, the savagery of World War I shattered this optimism for peace. Sadly, today, the Kantian idea of perpetual peace does not even serve as a hope.

6. *Twentieth Century.* It was not until after World War I that it became feasible to refer war criminals to an international court.

> World War I witnessed one of the largest military mobilizations in history, with the Western powers mobilizing more than 40 million soldiers and the Central Powers mobilizing close to 20 million. ... The total cost was estimated at 21 million casualties and 8.5 million combatants dead.[24]

Great Britain, having experienced the brunt of Germany's more spectacular attacks, strongly lobbied through its Prime Minister David Lloyd George to try Germany's wartime leader Kaiser Wilhelm II and others. The Paris Peace Conference (1919) established a Commission on the Responsibility of the Authors of the War and the Enforcement of Penalties. The Commission found numerous violations of the laws of war by Germany and Italy. The Treaty of Versailles (Articles 227–230) included the Commission's recommendations for war crimes trials, but it did not call for any trial for crimes against humanity. The representatives from the United States dissented from the first attempt to impute individual responsibility for crimes against humanity at the Preliminary Paris Peace Conference (1919).[25] In its final form, however, the Treaty included a provision to try the Kaiser before an international tribunal for "a supreme offence against international morality and the sanctity of treaties." Those noble words met with some staunch opposition. The Netherlands, where the Kaiser had fled, refused to extradite him, and the United States further refused to support the trials. The European Allies demanded that Germany surrender 854 persons, but the German government successfully negotiated to reduce the numbers to 45 and won a concession to have them tried in Germany. The resulting Leipzig trials, which began in 1921, turned into a fiasco.

The aftermath of World War I, however, did lead to the establishment of the first permanent international law court. In 1920, the Permanent Court of International Justice (PCIJ) came under the control of the League of Nations. Andrew Carnegie built a home for the already established Permanent Court of Arbitration (PCA) and for the PCIJ in The Hague. Despite the establishment of these structures of peace, the prediction that nations would settle their difference less on the battlefield and more in The Hague proved false. After World War II, the PCIJ was absorbed into the newly formed International Court of Justice (ICJ), which operated under a radically different international organization—the United Nations.

The ICJ issues about three opinions per year. The ICJ consists of fifteen members elected by a complicated procedure. Any state party may appoint a national as a judge to the ICJ for the duration of the case if the state does not already have a national sitting as a judge. Only states may be parties before the ICJ. Theoretically, the ICJ has compulsory jurisdiction over state parties.

However, state parties to a dispute must have first agreed to the court's jurisdiction. Of the 191 state parties to the ICJ, only 65 have agreed to the Court's compulsory jurisdiction. Further, states may issue reservations to the ICJ's rules and procedures. France and the United State have withdrawn their consent to compulsory jurisdiction. The United Kingdom is the only permanent member of the Security Council that has consented to compulsory jurisdiction. Practically speaking, then, the ICJ has only limited jurisdiction. Many ICJ cases deal with boundary disputes between states. Only a few cases have involved the use of force by one state against another. The restrictive access to the ICJ to states represents a devolution, that is, a step backwards, as individuals under the old "law of nations" framework qualified as subjects of international law. The ICJ has jurisdiction only over states and not over individuals.

The treaties beginning with the 1868 St. Petersburg Declaration had addressed only *jus in bellum* conduct within war. Like their predecessors, they did not take on the issue of war itself. Finally, a treaty in 1928 addressed *jus ad bello*. Sixty-three states, including Germany, signed the *Kellogg–Briand Pact* for the Renunciation of War as an Instrument of National Policy. The treaty's signatories verbally renounced war except in cases of self-defense. Forty-four nations, including all the Great Powers except the Soviet Union, accepted the treaty. Most impressively, for the first time, an international treaty outlawed war itself. After World War II, a milder UN Charter (Article 2(4)) prohibited the use of force. The Charter, however, permits states to use force in self-defense and as part of a UN authorized contingent.[26]

Overall, despite the bumps in the road, history shows a progressive evolution of the laws of war from ancient times through the twentieth century. While the development of the laws of war has steadily progressed over the centuries, the institutional structures for adjudicating those laws had to wait until the last half of the twentieth century to take root. After World War II, the international community still did not have legal structures in place for addressing war crimes.

COURTS ON WAR

After six years of fighting, 17 million combatants killed, 27 million wounded, and 20 million captured or missing, World War II ended.[27] The victorious Allies created temporary (*ad hoc*) military tribunals to adjudicate the crimes committed by the Germans and the Japanese. *The London Agreement* (1945) laid the groundwork for the *International Military Tribunals at Nuremberg*. In 1946, the Allies established a similar tribunal for Tokyo. The Nuremberg Tribunal convicted nineteen of the twenty-two indicted defendants and sentenced twelve of them to death. The International Military Tribunal for the Far East. (The Tokyo Tribunal) convicted all twenty-five defendants and sentenced seven to death. On December 23, 1948, the Tribunal executed six military leaders and one civilian, Koki Hirota. In 1948, after the Nuremberg and Tokyo trials, the United Nations passed the *Convention on the Prevention and Punishment of the Crime of Genocide*.

International war crimes tribunals face formidable theoretical as well as political challenges. Before defending international courts, we need to make a case for international law. The very idea of international law has had many detractors. The sharpest critiques of attempts to internationalize law have come from (and continue to come from) legal positivists. The positivist model of law centers on legislatively enacted law. Positivists consider how closely international law fits a certain type of law found in a state, and, generally, they find it wanting. John Austin, an early nineteenth-century English jurist and leading positivist, refused to put international law on the same level as positive, state or national, law. Instead, he categorized it as "positive morality" rather than as law. Austin defined law as a series of commands issued by a sovereign and backed by sanctions. Austin's definition casts doubt on whether there is any such thing as international law.

According to Austin, international law lacks three ingredients needed for it to qualify as law: a sovereign, commands, and sanctions. The concept of sovereignty conveys the idea of a final authority within a system. States have sovereignty; international bodies do not have sovereignty. As evidenced by the reservation system where states can opt out of the ICJ's jurisdiction, the United Nations does not have the final authority over its member states. States do not give their obedience to a superior international body in a comparable way that individuals give their obedience to a sovereign nation-state. To the contrary, the United Nations derives its authority from the states and not the other way around. Further, international law, ultimately, depends on state practice and consent and not on commands of a legislative body. In addition, international organizations owe their existence to nation states. Finally, international law remains largely unenforceable although it may have some moral or political force. Sanctions promulgated by the United Nations depend upon the enforcing power of its member nation states as the United Nations has no policing powers of its own.

Despite the force of these observations, Austin's critique contains common misunderstandings of law. First, Austin and the other skeptics about international law rely heavily on a questionable analogy between national law and international law. International "legislation" differs from state legislation. While the UN Security Council has power to use force granted to it by the UN Charter, the General Assembly does not function like a state legislature. Resolutions from the General Assembly, except those dealing with internal operations of the organization, are not binding. However, resolutions and other examples of "soft law" have considerable impact on nation states. Further, even though international law does not have formal institutions that create law, it does have a number of methods for establishing laws: conventions (treaties), custom (practice among states), general principles (rules and principles common to all legal systems), and subsidiary means (judicial opinions and writings of jurists).

Second, many critics of international law share Austin's view that law requires a physical force behind it. Contrary to Austin's "Gunman Theory" (to appropriate a label used by H. L. A. Hart), states normally comply and seldom disobey international and regional courts. Surprisingly, most nations comply with decisions of the ICJ. Similarly, the European Court of Human Rights does not have a police force to enforce its decisions. Yet, the United Kingdom obeys the court's decisions even when the court does not have "guns" at its disposal.

The establishment of the Nuremberg and Tokyo tribunals faced theoretical objections as well as political obstacles. Important theoretical questions arose concerning international criminal tribunals, particularly given the fragile positive-law base of these tribunals. Legitimate courts that operate within a state apply and interpret laws passed by legislatures. International tribunals do not have analogous legislative bodies. The Nuremberg and Tokyo tribunals were not part of a system where a sovereign issues commands. Perhaps, however, except for the fact that many sovereigns and not a single sovereign created the tribunals, the war crimes tribunals met Austin's recipe for law better than organizations of the United Nations. The tribunals then had easier ways of enforcing their decisions than does the United Nations today. The pre-UN military tribunals had the power of the victorious states behind them. Yet, some critics saw this enforcing advantage as offset by the military character of the tribunals. In short, the military nature of the Nuremberg and Tokyo tribunals gave credence to the charge of "victor's justice."

Finally, critics find fault with war crimes tribunals from the standpoint of due process or procedural fairness. Harvard law professor Lon Fuller refused to classify the Nazi system as a legal system as it had so seriously violated "law's inner morality" by not following the basic principles of fairness. Did the Nuremberg Tribunal also stand justly accused of failing to use the basic principles of fairness that, for example, demand public notice of understandable laws? Did Nuremberg make acts unlawful after the fact? Exactly what positive laws did the Nazi defendants tried at Nuremberg violate? The London Charter that created the Tribunal included the following crimes: crimes against peace, war crimes, and crimes against humanity (see Chapter 3). The critics claimed that these were not crimes at the time of their commission (*nullen crimen et nulla poena sine lege*—no crime and no penalty without a prior law).

The *nullen crimen* argument held little sway in the cases of war crimes charged against the German leaders as Germany had been a party to many of the war crimes conventions before the outbreak of World War II.[28] The *nullen crimen* argument was on firmer ground when it was applied to crimes against peace (aggression). While the Charter of the International Military Tribunals at Nuremberg clearly had designated aggression as a crime, the German government during the Third Reich, obviously, did not sign this treaty. However, the Nazi defense attorneys admitted that, in 1928, Germany had joined sixty-two other nations in signing the General Treaty for the Renunciation of War, commonly known as, the Kellogg–Briand Pact, which prohibited the use of aggressive war as an instrument of national policy. However, the defense noted that while the Kellogg–Briand Pact outlawed aggressive war, it only held states and not individuals accountable. Consequently, the Nuremberg Tribunal had to appeal to the less foundational customary law instead of to the more basic treaty law to interpret the Kellogg–Briand Pact as holding individuals responsible.

The *nullen crimen* attack had its greatest success when applied to crimes against humanity. Admittedly, the 1945 Charter included the first positive international law specification of crimes against humanity. Yet, even here there was a counterargument to "*nullen crimen*."

> The germ of the phrase "crimes against humanity" is to be found in the Martens clause that appears in the rules of land warfare appended to the Fourth Hague Convention of 1907.[29]

As part of the Treaty of Versailles that ended World War I, the British included provisions governing the crimes against humanity committed by the Young Turks against the Armenians. After Turkish nationalists took twenty-nine British subjects prisoners, British efforts to prosecute crimes against humanity dwindled to a standstill. The subsequent Treaty of Lausanne (1923) "contained no clauses on war criminals."[30] Therefore, the concept of crimes against humanity took hold before Nuremberg, but, unfortunately, the Nuremberg Tribunal did not cite it as a precedent (see Appendix B).[31]

Critics launched still another line of attack with their charge that the Tribunal applied the crimes to past acts, thereby making acts illegal that were not illegal when they were committed (*ex post facto*).

> The feeling against a law evolved after the commission of an offense is deeply rooted...The antagonism to ex post facto laws is not based on a lawyer's prejudice encased in a Latin maxim. It rests on the political truth that if a law can be created after an offense, then power is to that extent absolute and arbitrary. To allow retroactive legislation is to disparage the principle of constitutional limitation. It is to abandon what is usually regarded as one of the essential values at the core of our democratic faith.[32]

Robert Jackson, the chief prosecutor at Nuremberg, however, asserted (rather than argued) that nations, nevertheless, have a right to develop, retroactively, newer and stronger international laws.

Even if we admit some of the legal criticisms made against the war crimes tribunals, in the end, the strongest justifications for the Nuremberg and Tokyo tribunals are moral ones. Nuremberg, in particular, did not deserve the label "victor's justice." Rather than merely serving as political show trials, the Nuremberg proceedings established a victory for the "rule of morality," which, in turn, became a victory for "the rule of law." Justice Jackson's plea for the prosecution of the Nazi war criminals rested, ultimately, not on legal but on moral grounds.[33] Morality, rather than simply law, demanded punishment of those responsible for the atrocities that included the slaughter of six million Jews as well as many Roma (Gypsies), homosexuals, and disabled. The Nuremberg trials marked the place where a secular morality gained ascendancy in much the same way that religious morality dominated the medieval period. Placing the burden for justifying the Nuremberg prosecutions on morality rather than on law changes the terms of the debate from "what and whose laws?" to "what and whose morality?"

Nuremberg marked a watershed where the international community laid the foundation stones for a global, universal morality. The precedents set by Nuremberg set out the direction for building a universal ethics. Up to the point of the Nuremberg trials, the recognition of international crimes had developed slowly through history. The undertakings of Nuremberg started the process of codifying the prohibitions against grave injustices. Within a legal framework, the next step was to specify the elements of each crime. The 1948 Genocide Convention initiated the codification process for the crime of genocide. One hundred and twenty-five states have adopted the Convention while sixty other states have signed but not ratified it.[34] Nonetheless, while the Convention has not received universal acclaim, it "has become one of he most widely accepted international instruments relating to human rights."[35]

The military tribunals that operated after World War II further refined the moral rules and continued the process of transforming the moral rules into legal ones. According to one international jurist,

> between 1919 and 1994, there were five ad hoc international investigation commissions, four ad hoc international criminal tribunals, and three internationally mandated or authorized national prosecutions arising out of World War I and World War II.[36]

The two current ad hoc tribunals have further developed these international moral and legal rules. With the establishment of war crimes' tribunals for the former Yugoslavia and for Rwanda by the Security Council in 1992, the judicial mechanisms to address war crimes and genocide changed from ad hoc military tribunals to ad hoc civilian tribunals.

The primary international judicial institution, the International Court of Justice (ICJ), does not have jurisdiction over international crimes committed by individuals on behalf of states. Proposals to establish a permanent international criminal court predate the ICJ. As noted before, the horrors of the 1859 war of France against the Austro-Hungarian Empire led Henri Dunant, a founder of the International Committee of the Red Cross (ICRC), to persuade nations to codify laws of war. Similarly, the devastating 1870 Franco-Prussian War was the stimulus for Gustave Moynier, another founder of the ICRC, to propose the establishment of a permanent international criminal court that would hold individuals responsible for war crimes.[37] It took over one hundred years for the international community to make Moynier's dream a reality.

On July 17, 1998, the world community took a closer step toward creating a global justice structure. Over one hundred nations signed the Rome Statute of the International Criminal Court (ICC). The United States, along with only a handful of other nations, first refused to sign the Rome Treaty. President William Clinton signed the treaty as the last official act of his presidency. President George W. Bush subsequently unsigned the treaty and established unilateral treaties with a number of nations to undermine further the jurisdiction of the ICC. The ICC, unlike the ICJ, has jurisdiction over individuals for genocide, crimes against humanity, and war crimes. In summary, war crimes tribunals have progressed from military to civilian and from ad hoc to permanent status. The establishment of the ICC marks one of the final stages in the construction of an institutional base for the moral/legal rules first adopted at Nuremberg.

CONCLUSION

The moral principles and legal rules that govern war and warfare have evolved slowly over the course of time through a series of successful and progressive stages. The process began with the formulation of principles that later were codified into specific rules and that finally culminated in the establishment of courts. An appreciation of the history of the just war tradition should make the idea of "the laws and ethics of war" less foreign and more palatable. The laws and ethics of genocide emerged through the stages followed within the just war tradition. However, the justification for an international court to hear cases on the crime of genocide does not depend on the viability of the just war tradition. Therefore, those who remain skeptical of convicting anyone under the laws of war should remain open minded about trying cases under the laws of genocide. Still, it would be foolhardy not to take advantage of the gains made by the just war tradition.

Today, the project of trying to codify universal principles of morality, a process that truly began at Nuremberg, faces some exciting challenges. One of the most important goals is to find ways to differentiate among the international crimes. State criminal law systems distinguish and rank criminal wrongs. Defendants, for example, found guilty of premeditated murder face a more severe range of punishments than those convicted of involuntary manslaughter. A criminal code for the ICC, eventually, will have to include analogous distinctions among crimes. The final product will be an international criminal code that embodies a global ethics. Whatever else these laws prohibit and ethics forbids they must give genocide its due. This may seem so obvious that it hardly bears mentioning. Indeed, genocide should present a relatively uncontroversial case for justifying a universal legal and moral prohibition. The international community has the wherewithal to construct a viable, robust system of international criminal law if only it would do the obvious and give genocide its due. The remaining chapters set forth a detailed normative analysis of what the laws governing genocide should look like.

Chapter 2

Genocide: Global Context

GLOBAL CONSTITUTIONAL CONVENTION, AN OVERVIEW

Politics? Who cares? Perhaps, more Americans (who tend to say these things more than others) would care more about politics if they could make a difference by actively participating in the political process. If today's citizens could have played a role in the meetings and conventions that established their nations, they might have experienced effective political action. While today's citizens cannot go back in time, they might otherwise benefit from simply imagining themselves at the constitutional convention. Hypothetical devices help people examine the justifications for the choices made by the founding fathers of a country. Further, the imaginary scenarios challenge them to explore alternative routes that the country's founders failed to take or which they could not have even imagined.

We can challenge our political thinking even more by carrying over the idea of an imaginary constitutional convention to a global scale. Imagine that we can start a new world government from scratch. We get to design the organization of our government. Designing a constitution seems the most logical first step to take. Of course, we must remember the heavy burden that we carry. This constitution will not simply govern a territory with fixed boundaries. Rather, this constitution will govern the entire world. We cannot look out only for our interests. As not everyone can attend the sessions of a constitutional convention, our proposals should reflect the interests of others as well as our own concerns. In fact, some of the absent ones have not even been born yet. We need to realize that our decisions will bind all current citizens as well as many future generations to come. In this chapter, we set out a basic framework for the government design project. First, however, we need to face some strident opponents.

Anti-Global Political Barriers

Any global constitution project must first jump over some hurdles designed to close down the race altogether. This section will attempt to clear the racecourse.

To get a sense of the positions taken against movements to form a world government just listen to how shrill the voices of some American political commentators become whenever someone utters the words "United Nations." Less ideological opponents of a world government simply express their pessimism over the prospects for success. When the naysayers defend their pessimistic outlook, they rattle off a long list of past and present failures made by international bodies such as the United Nations.

The sections that follow use a novel strategy to counter the naysayers. Before countering the pessimists' list of failures with a more progressive reading of developments in international law, we need to think about what types of individuals make up the defenders of international courts. It should come as no surprise that the strongest advocates of global justice are victims of grave injustices. Yet, if we keep this simple but largely unacknowledged observation in mind throughout discussions of even the most technical and abstract issues, then the project will retain its important and noble stature. We can find inspiration in the countless victims of grave injustices who have tried to find justice rather than revenge. Further, by keeping the primary beneficiaries of a system of global justice firmly in view, we can begin to see that the quest for global justice is part of a long, progressive series of developments in international law. The pessimists distort the project by portraying it as an all-encompassing, naïve, utopian vision. With a focus on codifying and interpreting segments of an international criminal code, the chapters that follow take on only a small piece of the overall project. Far from an imaginary delusion, this portion of the global constitutional convention is already taking place.

Realistic Dreams of Justice

The most vocal opponents of the United Nations have recently taken positions of power in the United States. Leaders of many other countries, particularly European nations, however, have had considerable counterbalancing success in international law. Still, the victims of global injustices continue to have the strongest hopes for international justice. Those who need recourse to international courts the most, have the greatest faith in the fragile structures of international justice. Let us think about these contrasting attributes. The most vulnerable, the most needy have the most positive attitude toward the United Nations and its subsidiary parts. The most powerful, those least in need hold the most negative views about international law and justice.

A specific example will illustrate the faith and hope that victims often place in international justice. The film *Cry of the Ghosts* provides a documentary reenactment of how a lawyer and a judge dealt with the aftermath of the 1991–1995 war in Bosnia. In the 1990s, Yugoslavia began to unravel and split into different parts. After two states of Yugoslavia (Slovenia and Croatia) freed themselves from the grips of the federal Yugoslav government, a third state, Bosnia, tried to follow suit. However, Bosnia's quest for independence met far more severe resistance than what either Slovenia or Croatia had experienced. Bosnian Serbs, secretly supported by the Serb-dominated Yugoslavian federal government, launched ruthless attacks against the Bosnian Muslims.

The Bosnian war, then, sets the context for the film. The camera follows a lawyer and the judge as they go through the painful process of making the personal political, of transforming their individual suffering into collective political action. After their horrid ordeals in a concentration camp of Omarska, these former friends could not even talk to each other about their experiences. Eventually, however, they went outside their victim status and began to treat their suffering as part of a collective suffering, as part of what all Bosnian Muslim women endured. They organized other formerly imprisoned women. Collectively, these women of Omarska began to seek some form of justice.

During the film's final sequence, the camera follows the victims-turned-activists as they travel to the Hague in the Netherlands. They made that trip to pursue a case before the Ad Hoc International Wars Crimes Tribunal for the Former Yugoslavia. They wanted justice for those responsible for the crimes committed against Bosnian Muslims during the war. Predictably, the skeptics and pessimists found flaws with the tribunal and defects in the victims' case. Nevertheless, even they would have to applaud the decision these women made to pursue justice rather than to wallow in their personal sorrow or to seek revenge.

These Muslim women and countless others like them are not idealists. Victims of injustices who seek justice through international courts seldom do so naïvely. They fully recognize the limitations and drawbacks not only of these international courts but also of courts in general. Victims of some of the worst crimes imaginable typically have no other choice. They cannot afford to become skeptics or pessimists like those from far richer and enormously more powerful countries can. Despite the inevitable flaws that will arise with any global project, the fact that these efforts would and should serve powerless victims gives a global constitutional convention considerable moral weight. Those who have suffered the most stand to lose the most if we give into the naysayers and abandon the global project.

Progress in International Law

The doubters face another kind of challenge, one that questions their view that little progress and a great deal of backsliding has doomed quests for global justice. The history of the twentieth century seems to support a "gloom and doom" mentality. Many people sincerely believed that they fought World War I "to end all wars." World War II quickly destroyed these overly optimistic hopes. Similarly, after World War II, many believed the determination and resolve contained in the phrase "Never again!" Yet, although under different circumstances and by different means, the atrocities committed under Germany's Third Reich have occurred repeatedly and again—in Cambodia, Bosnia, Rwanda, and elsewhere. The number of mass killings increased greatly during the last part of the twentieth century. The twentieth century may have distinguished itself as the most violent on record.

Yet, despite the ugly record of horrors, there is a more optimistic side of the global coin. The case for optimism relies on the old piece of folk wisdom that prefers to see the glass as half-full rather than as half-empty. It does not take a great deal of knowledge to mock and ridicule the record of the United Nations. However, the international community also has made great strides in international law. We only need to consider how difficult it is to get any group of people, of any size, to agree on anything. Yet, representatives of many radically different nations have managed to agree on some important matters. It boggles the mind to think that so many nations (who have found so many things, past and present, to disagree about) increasingly find themselves in agreement. Most notably, the international community has reached agreement over a number of human rights treaties. The International Covenant on the Rights of the Child, for example, became the fastest adopted human-rights treaty in history. It set a record by gathering signatures from all nations except the United States and Somalia.[1]

We can tell a similar positive story about the development of international courts. We can make a strong case that the international court system has continually strengthened through the different eras—the Permanent Court of International Justice (after WW I); the Nuremberg Tribunal and the International Court of Justice (after WW II); the Ad Hoc Tribunals (in the 1990s); and the newly established International Criminal Court. Even with its flaws, the establishment of a Permanent Court of International Justice (and the still functioning Permanent Court of Arbitration) marked a monumental achievement. Each court built on and learned from its predecessors. The ICJ continued the jurisprudence of the Permanent Court. The Nuremberg Tribunal set the model for all subsequent international war crimes tribunals, particularly for the two Ad Hoc Tribunals established to hear cases arising from the atrocities first in the former Yugoslavia and then in Rwanda. These Ad Hoc Tribunals have produced a rich jurisprudence that, in turn, has provided critical ingredients for the newly established International Criminal Court (ICC).

Given the potential valuable humanitarian contributions of a constitution for a world government, the doubters can only temporarily dampen the fires. Hopefully, we have provided enough resources to overcome the naysayers, to become inspired by those victims of injustice who do believe in global justice, and to see the project as adding further pieces and dimensions to a largely progressive and increasingly successful establishment of a system of global justice.

GLOBAL CONSTITUTION MAKING, PRELIMINARY STEPS

Division of Power

Let us now turn to what should now seem like a plausible project of making a global constitution. Designers of any constitution must first determine how to structure the overall government. A typical design makes a threefold division among executive, legislative, and judiciary. How, then, should these three branches of world government relate to one another? Which, if any, should have the most power? The choice among the executive, legislature, and judiciary roughly mirrors different political philosophies. A strong executive serves inclinations that are authoritarian. Designs with a powerful legislature give greater authority to the people than to leaders. Designs that reserve a powerful role to the judiciary elevate the rule by law over either rule by the elite or rule by the people.

Courts and Laws

Nations that undertake the task of creating a constitution must face these choices. The disintegration of the vast Soviet empire in the 1990s into fragmentary states provided a real laboratory for constitution making. As the record of these efforts in Eastern Europe showed, constitution designers and political leaders tended to undervalue the judiciary. They did little to assure the independent role of the judiciary and put little effort to strengthen its role. Oddly enough, democracy, or at least a particular interpretation of democracy, helps to explain the reasons for a weakened judiciary. Of course, we cannot blame the democracy building efforts for the weak court systems often found in these newly formed states. While the rhetoric of democracy had dominated the political airwaves, it was a particular view of democracy that framed political development then (and now). This view sees democracy primarily in terms of elections. So, if a country holds fair elections, then it qualifies as a democracy. This view leaves little room for the judiciary. In fact, if elections hold the key to democracy, then the judiciary runs against the democratic tide. In some sense, courts are anti-democratic. After all, in most countries, the judiciary is the only branch of government whose officials take pride in not being subject to the whims of the electoral public. Critics peg the judiciary with the troublesome label "counter-majoritarian."

Despite the low esteem given by those who claim to favor democracy, courts have played an important role in the development of democratic states. In fact, the democratic value of courts lies precisely in their counter-majoritarian characteristic. The critics focus on the fact that most judges are not elected. This, according to the critics, violates the basic democratic principle of majority rule. Yet, courts are counter-majoritarian in another, more important sense. Courts, if they fulfill their role of protecting minorities, act as a counterforce to offset a fatal defect of majority rule. Electoral politics condemns the minority to the will of the majority. If courts fulfill their role as protectors of minorities, then they may cure or at least they can lessen the negative consequences of majority rule. These arguments do not provide an airtight case for favoring the judiciary in any constitutional design. Like the previous discussion defending work at the international level, we make these claims to make sure that our projects do not face any impassable barriers.

Let us refine the nature of the project even further. Our hypothetical constitutional convention faces a more manageable challenge than designing the entire governing structure. However, even this project may seem overwhelming. A subcommittee within the convention has the task of codifying an international criminal code.

Historical and Political Context

Like Judge Hercules, a character made famous by the philosopher Ronald Dworkin, we shall charge this subcommittee with creating laws within a legal tradition and according to moral principles. Any attempt to recast or reform international law must do so within the bounds of what others have already done. The war crimes tribunals since Nuremberg have developed their own jurisprudence, one that includes a common law of genocide. Even representatives to the Global Constitutional Convention charged with devising a completely new international criminal code would and should make statutory law in accordance with the developing jurisprudence on genocide. Analogously, the recommendations and interpretations made by our hypothetical subcommittee (and in this book) also must keep within the confines of the past, of what has already been legislated.

In fact, it may seem that any attempts to influence the codification of the laws of genocide come too late. The rapid establishment of the ICC seems to have left little work for political philosophers and theorists as key meetings of something like a Global Constitutional Convention have already taken place without many of us present. The formation of the ICC seems to have left no tasks for lawmakers as the Preparatory Committee already has drafted key provisions of an international criminal code. However, laws, especially international laws, change and evolve. The on-going establishment of a permanent court to try genocide cases gives meaning to the phrase "a living law of genocide."

The laws governing genocide will undergo changes. We might not welcome the changes made by others. Predictably, many interested parties already will have regretted remaining silent while others took the initiative to begin constructing an international criminal code. Fortunately, it is not too late to contribute. Even if you disagree with the interpretations and proposals made here, this book should convince even the ardent skeptic of the value of discussing genocide and justice. After all, the stakes are high. The final product will become part of the foundation of international justice and a global ethics.

Global Ethics

A recommendation for a certain wording or interpretation of the laws of genocide has its basic mooring in philosophy and in ethics. Consider the following questions: What acts constitute genocide? Is "killing" somehow on the same level as "imposing measures to prevent births"? Who are the victims of genocide? Must a genocide victim belong "to a particular national, ethical, racial or religious group" or to any group, including political ones? For genocide, should a prosecutor have to prove that the perpetrator had intent? Do the laws of genocide adequately address the widespread hatred typically associated with genocide?

Although many commentators have raised these questions before, the analysis developed in this book reveals fundamental flaws in the literal wording and the prevailing interpretations of the genocide laws. The drafters of these laws have adopted terms and concepts from a largely individual-oriented criminal law framework. Consider, for example, the prosecution of individuals for genocide in Rwanda (see Chapter 7). The exclusive focus on individual responsibility coupled with the failure to address the role of organizations in the genocide has had disastrous consequences for the entire region of Central Africa.

Normative critiques like the one offered in this work may seem, in the end, largely academic. However, not only is the formation of the ICC an ongoing process, it also has built-in mechanisms for making changes through legislative devices and judicial interpretations.[2] A critique of the laws of genocide is normative in a deeper sense than making recommendations for changes in legal analysis. Depending on the subject, legal critiques often play a vital role in discussions over moral values. In national legal systems, the process of criminalizing behaviors and placing different punishments on them is part of a process of formulating a society's ethical judgments. The development of an international criminal law is also the development of an international ethics. The establishment of laws of genocide within a system of international criminal law provides a new, strong basis for a global ethics.

A legal code is not the same thing as a moral code. However, whatever the differences between law and ethics, there is considerable overlap between the two. Of all the many different type of laws, ranging from contract law to tax law, the one that most readily associates itself with ethics is criminal law. The criminal laws adopted by a society reflect that society's values and vice versa. A society that has laws allowing severe forms of punishment probably provides a glimpse into a society with authoritarian values. The process of codifying an international criminal code provides a unique opportunity to play some role, however minor, in the development of a global ethics.

This project offers a far more plausible approach than most other approaches. The analysis offered here represents a small piece of a far larger strategy. Overall, we shall develop our ethics by telling people what they should not do rather than by preaching what they should do. As we shall see, the focus on prohibitions offers some tactical advantages. By focusing on the "do nots," we shall be in a far better position to find agreement among people than if we exhorted people to "do this" and "do that."

Again, as with all the preliminary claims made in this introductory material, we can only provide a brief account that will open the way for the eventual acceptance of the thesis. We often seem to face barriers of resistance if we try to persuade someone to adopt our particular set of values. Culture poses a formidable barrier to the adoption of the positive values of people from different cultures. People from different cultures raise their children in diverse ways and exhibit a variety of ways of interacting socially. Initially, we have no entirely persuasive reasons for thinking that one culture's ways of doing things are any better than another culture's practices. However, criticisms of one culture from the perspective of another culture have more chances of success if they are formulated as actions that members of the culture should not take. Non-Muslims will have little hopes for success if they voice disagreement about the positive actions Muslims take in their religious conduct and vice versa. Islam has relatively specific requirements that Muslims pay over a sum of money to those in need. We might think that Christianity should have demands that are more exacting on humanitarian giving. Yet, it would undoubtedly be a futile exercise. In contrast, we seem on firmer ground if we demand that a Muslim group stop stoning women to death for adultery and that a Christian group halt its practice of encouraging the killing of doctors and others connected to abortion.

Indeed, the contrast between "thou shall nots" and "thou shalts" becomes most apparent at the extremes. We may command others to carry out actions to demonstrate that they love one another, or we may demand that they stop showing their hatred for one another. It seems reasonable to expect to find more agreement among diverse peoples to join in a campaign to stop hateful acts than it does to persuade them to join a campaign to spread love among people from different cultures. It should now be apparent why we focus on the horrendous harms that go under the label of genocide. If we cannot find widespread global agreement on an ethic that prohibits genocide, then the prospects for the world seem indeed dismal.

However, as these preliminary discussions show, the prospects for carrying out a grand global project are far more realistic than we might have first assumed. To get the process underway, we first had to overcome some preliminary obstacles. In some judicial proceedings, the plaintiff must meet the preliminary thresholds. First, a judge must decide if the case has sufficient evidence to proceed. Second, once the case begins, the plaintiff faces another challenge from the opposing side, namely, a summary judgment. Analogously, we have overcome the initial burden of proof. We have tried to make a *prime facie* case for moving forward on some daunting projects: forming a world government, designing a global constitution, adopting an international criminal code, and constructing a global ethics.

DRAFTING AN INTERNATIONAL CRIMINAL CODE

> It is sad but true that human kind understands itself partly by the crimes it knows itself to be capable of. We must therefore strive to give them their right names.[3]

Humanity knows itself by its reactions to its worst horrors. The twentieth century tested humanity's heart and soul with unprecedented crimes. Rather than trying to make the grand case that we have reached the higher planes of justice as symbolized by the Nuremberg Tribunal, we have opted to take on the far more mundane task of dissecting the crime of genocide, "the horror of horrors."

International criminal law has only relatively recently attempted to specify the elements for the crime of genocide. The treaty that created the Nuremberg Tribunal merely provided general descriptions of the crimes: "the crimes committed by the Nazis . . . could not be neatly encapsulated in a precise definition of requisite acts and mental states" as "the crimes involved [were] composite, large-scale crimes committed by state actors; hence, it [was] necessary to describe the crimes broadly."[4] Similarly, the statutes that created the Ad Hoc War Crimes Tribunals for the Former Yugoslavia and for Rwanda did not spell out the elements of crimes. The International Criminal Tribunal for the Former Yugoslavia (ICTY) and the International Tribunal for Rwanda (ICTR), however, created lists of elements of the crimes under their jurisdiction through case law.

In the preliminary sessions to the 1998 Rome Treaty, the United States insisted on setting out the elements for each crime to restrict the International Criminal Court's judges when they ruled on cases (see Appendices A, B). The Preparatory Committee for the now established ICC met this mandate by drafting a code that specified the elements for genocide and the other crimes under the court's jurisdiction. Unlike all other past temporary war crimes tribunals, the ICC, as a permanent body, has jurisdiction over future crimes. Previous international tribunals had formed after the criminal acts over which they had jurisdiction had been committed. Supposedly, then, the ICC's relatively detailed codification of the crimes will give the public notice as to what sort of behaviors will be considered criminal at the international level. More importantly, as is the case with national criminal systems, ICC prosecutors now know exactly what they need to prove. The subsequent chapters examine the elements of the crime of genocide. To convict someone of genocide a prosecutor must prove a wrongful act (*actus reus*), a wrongful purpose (*mens rea*), and (as we shall argue) a hateful motive. A legal case for the crime of genocide includes two other (partially specified) determinations about the agents, the nature of the victim and the perpetrator. Careful analyses of the three elements (act, intent, motive) and the two agent types (victim, perpetrator) for the crime of genocide will produce important recommendations for changes in international law and provide important steps in the development of global ethics (see Appendix A).

NATIONAL LEGAL SYSTEMS

1. *Crime in National Law*. An analysis of what we know about the elements of the crime of murder makes it easier to understand the analysis of the elements of the crime of genocide set forth in this book. A nation's criminal code specifies the elements of each crime such as murder. The codification, presumably, gives the nation's citizens fair warning as to what society considers criminal behavior. Further, the specifications provide a recipe for what elements prosecutors must prove to obtain a conviction. Although the elements of the crime of murder may seem obvious to a layperson, jurists still debate these elements. Two murder cases will highlight some key points of disagreement. These cases at a national level show the types of problems jurists can expect at the international level when they further codify and begin to interpret the elements for the crime of genocide. The crime of murder within national criminal law makes an obvious choice for us to consider as many view genocide as the most heinous form of murder.

2. *Murder in National Law.* Let us take two cases of multiple murders, one in Canada and the other in the United States, that will serve as excellent ways to begin to appreciate the similarities and differences underlying national and international criminal legal systems.

1. On December 6, 1989, Marc Lépine murdered fourteen female engineering college students at the University of Montreal's École Polytechnique. Yelling, "I hate feminists," he killed nine females in a classroom after asking the males to leave. His suicide note contained a list of nineteen "opportunistic" women, including public figures in Canada.[5]
2. On April 23, 1987, William Cruse randomly murdered six people in a Palm Bay, Florida shopping mall. The jury rejected his insanity plea and found him guilty of first-degree murder. For purposes of this analysis, the most salient feature of the case is the fact that "there was no evidence that Cruse contemplated his attack for any longer than a few moments."[6]

The crimes committed by Lépine and Cruse break down into five component parts, which parallel the elements of genocide: (1) act, (2) intent, (3) motive, (4) victim type, and (5) perpetrator type. Important jurisprudential as well as moral judgments lie at the heart of these two cases. In most national criminal law systems, Lépine probably would receive a more severe punishment than Cruse would receive. However, for now, these murder cases serve primarily as a way to introduce the issues at stake for each element of the similar but different crime of genocide. Indeed, later, we shall focus on the limitations these cases from national criminal legal systems have for serving as models for international law. In the meantime, let us consider the Lépine and Cruse cases.

3. *Elements of the Crime of Murder* (a) *Act.* To convict Lépine and Cruse prosecutors had to prove that each defendant did something criminal (*actus reus*) and that each of the accused committed their respective criminal acts with a criminal mind-set (*mens rea*). An analysis of the criminal acts seems relatively straightforward and noncontroversial. After all, Lépine and Cruse killed many people, and national criminal law treats killing even one person as a serious wrong. National systems simply define the serious acts of murder as the killing of a human being. Still, questions arise even within this seemingly uncontroversial domain. How should a legal system regard killing relative to other crimes? Does the criminal act of killing deserve greater punishments than, let us say, kidnappings?

These and other questions regarding the criminal acts committed by Lépine and Cruse carry over to the international law of genocide. It may seem obvious that the core wrongful act for genocide is killing. However, a description of the "wrongful act" for genocide turns out not to be simple and straightforward. For example, as we shall see in Chapter 3, jurists have taken (unjustifiably as I shall argue) many types of acts other than killing to be acts of genocide in international law.

(b) *Intent.* In criminal law, prosecutors not only must prove that the accused did a criminal act (*actus reus*), but they also must prove that the accused had a "criminal mind." Again, as applied to the Lépine and Cruse cases, the issue of criminal intent or *mens rea* at first seems uncontroversial. Lépine and Cruse deliberately and not accidentally set out to kill many people. However, while each one killed many individuals, the intents behind their acts differed by degrees if not in kind. From the evidence, we can infer that Lépine's acts required more deliberation than Cruse's acts. Whatever intent Cruse had, it was far more short-lived and flimsier than Lépine's intent was as Lépine had carefully planned to kill individuals over a significant length of time. Generally, state criminal codes hold individuals such as Lépine with their well-formed, malign intentions to a higher standard of criminal responsibility than they do those perpetrators such as Cruse who act out of immediate rage and passion.

Is the *mens rea* required for genocide more like Cruse's or Lépine's level of intent? As we shall see in Chapter 4, the *mens rea* for international criminal law differs radically from the *mens rea* of national criminal law.

INTERNATIONAL LEGAL SYSTEMS

1. *Crimes in International Law.* Over the past century, the basics of a system of international criminal law emerged. In the twenty-first century, international criminal law has come of age. Lawyers can confidently appeal to and invoke a body of law globally recognized as international criminal law. With the recent establishment of the ICC, lawyers now can practice in an established, permanent international criminal court. Still, we must admit that international criminal law has not progressed to the point where we have anything comparable in any national criminal system. However, we have enough of a system to explore its parts in some depth and perhaps to affect its development. Should international criminal law simply become a larger version of national criminal law? Alternatively, does international criminal law deal with significantly different crimes?

2. *Elements of the Crime of Genocide* (see Appendix A). (a) *Act.* Oddly, one relatively noncontroversial determination made in national criminal law systems has proved problematic in international law. In most nation states, you probably would not find any great disagreement over the proposition that killing deserves greater punishment than kidnapping. You might expect to find roughly the same comparative judgment in the context of international law. Yet, it is not so obvious there. It may seem beyond dispute that killing is the central wrongful act of the crime of genocide. However, if we look at the way jurists have interpreted the act of genocide, we find that killing is only one of a number of acts that could constitute genocide. We shall take on this issue in Chapter 3.

Another aspect of how to determine the nature of the criminal act for murder and for genocide remains somewhat unresolved even though its resolution seems relatively straightforward. The issue centers on the relevancy of the number of victims. Should the number of victims be a central factor when considering the gravity of the crime and the extent of the punishment? Lépine and Cruse not only killed they also killed many human beings. Should it make any legal or moral difference whether they killed one or many? Should the criminal law have greater punishments for serial killers than for single-victim murderers? Generally, defendants like Lépine and Cruse who kill many individuals in a single incident would receive more severe punishments than those who killed only one individual. We can infer from this that for many national systems numbers count, that is, the number of murder victims makes a legal and moral difference. Citizens seem to agree that the law should impose greater criminal liability for first-degree serial murders than for single murders. Yet, while this seems to be an accurate description of approaches typically adopted nationally, the issue remains unsettled.

The number-of-victims issue arises in a slightly different manner with respect to the crime of genocide. International jurists have voiced disagreements over whether a single killing could constitute genocide. However, even entertaining the possibility of single-victim genocide runs counter to something that lies at the heart of genocide. What makes genocide a particularly abhorrent crime is not only the killing but also the massive number of killings. At the international level, the criminal act of genocide seems to differ from that of "ordinary" single murder in the number of victims. An act of genocide has many victims. In Chapter 3, we shall explore ways in which the number of victims might make a difference in genocide cases.

(b) *Intent*. A consideration of the crime of genocide involves a more preliminary controversy over intent than debates over how to distinguish types or levels of intent for the crime of murder. While national criminal law systems generally accept the intent requirement for certain types of murder, international jurists continue to debate whether to keep the intent element for the crime of genocide. A number of commentators question the need for the intent element. In their view, proof of the first element, the criminal act (*actus reus*), should suffice in obtaining a conviction for genocide. These analysts find the intent requirement unnecessary and unduly restrictive. Accordingly, once prosecutors successfully link a responsible official to the genocide act of killing, they should not have the additional burden of proving intent.

In Chapter 4, we present a case for the opposite position, wherein we argue for retaining the intent element for the crime of genocide. There, however, as the discussion unfolds, we shall find that something deeper lies beneath the "intent or no intent debate." The problem is not with the intent requirement *per se* but with what international legal scholars typically think about intent. In pondering the shape of an international criminal code, jurists rely too heavily on models from national criminal codes. International criminal law needs a different sense of intent than the one that operates in national criminal law systems. Again, the crimes of murder and genocide only superficially appear parallel. Admittedly, in genocide cases, individuals intentionally kill large numbers of people similar to the way Lépine intentionally murdered the female students in the engineering college. If, however, international criminal law focused only on the mind-set of a relatively few individuals, it would miss the underlying dynamic that produces genocide.

The intent involved in genocide does not reside in an individual mind. Instead, genocide intent emerges within collective structures, namely, in the policies of governments and other types of organizations. After we make the case for the intent requirement, we then describe the characteristics of this new sense of organizational or corporate intent. International humanitarian law needs a view of intent that differs fundamentally from the concept of individual intent that underlies national criminal law. In summary, the "act + intent" formula used in national criminal law, then, translates into international criminal law but only with important modifications. The critical ingredients for genocide, then, include acts of mass killing plus corporate intent.

(c) *Motive*. The concept of intent captures a type of mental state whereas the idea of a motive refers to the underlying reason or stimulus for the act. Lépine had a hateful motive, but Cruse (presumably) did not. Descriptions of genocide throughout history often highlight motive. In genocide jurisprudence, the concept of motive serves as shorthand for the deeply embedded hatred that fuels genocide. The venomous nature of genocide lies not only in the mass slaughter of individuals but also in the reprehensible and loathsome hatred that motivated the killings. In Chapter 5, we examine this particularly sinister aspect of genocide in detail.

(d) *Victims*. Earlier, we noted that Lépine had a better-formed intent than Cruse. Now, we can see that this is, in part, because Lépine targeted members of a distinct group. Cruse did not target any specific group.

At the international level, we find perpetrators purposefully directing the massive killings at certain types of victims. Historians and jurists have long recognized that the victims of genocide are not just individual victims. Genocide victims belong to certain types of groups. While analysts struggle with the collective nature of the victims of genocide, they readily recognize that genocide victims are not simply a loose, arbitrary collection of individuals. In fact, the laws of genocide specify the group types for the crime of genocide: perpetrators must direct their killings at members of religious, national, ethnic, or racial groups. Interestingly, Lépine's victim group, namely, women, does not fit any of these categories. By comparing the victim groups of Hitler's Germany and Pol Pot's Cambodia, in Chapter 6, we explain why the genocide laws include the groups that they do, and we propose a more general test to include groups not specifically listed in the laws.

A determination of the victim's status affects the analysis of intent. In a given case, information about a victim's status can significantly alter analyses of a perpetrator's intent. If a perpetrator consciously targeted members of a specific group, then a case of mass murder begins to look more like a case of genocide. Generally, an intent that targets a specific group is better formed than one that does not. If the accused targeted a group itself, this indicates that a certain degree of conscious thought and planning went into carrying out the actions. To single out a group, the perpetrators must have deliberately reflected upon the actions before undertaking them. It takes at least a modicum of thought to identify the group even when the target group's identity is relatively well known (e.g., women). In other cases, it would presumably take even more time and effort to construct the contours of a more specific group (e.g., professional women).

(e) *Perpetrators*. So far, we have assumed that individuals have primary responsibility for the crime of genocide just as they do for the crime of murder. However, with genocide cases, it becomes increasingly difficult to only talk about individual perpetrators in the same way that we talk about individual perpetrators such as Lépine and Cruse in national criminal law. To carry out the purposeful action needed for even partial extermination of a group, to direct the attack at a group *per se*, a number of perpetrators need some form of organization, often in the form of a state. While a single individual could carry out a partial extermination of a group, genocides usually involve the work of organizations, thereby implicating countless individuals. Generally, individuals commit murders, whereas genocide usually takes place with the participation by or collusion of the enormous power of a state. Since the Nuremberg tribunals, the literature contains little examination of the collective nature of the perpetrators of genocide. Motivated by a desire to establish individual responsibility for humanitarian crimes, international jurists have failed to address the organizations to which the perpetrators belonged. In Chapter 7, we show the disastrous humanitarian consequences that result when we overlook the responsibility of criminal organizations. Finally, we shall make proposals outlining ways to move toward a different, restorative sense of justice.

CONCLUSIONS

Armed with a sound understanding of the elements, international criminal law provides a vehicle for the international community to proclaim and to prove its moral revulsion to "the most odious crime." The analyses presented in the following chapters are not merely of academic importance. This study makes recommendations for modifications within the confines of the Genocide Convention, the Rome Statutes, and other existing international laws governing the crime of genocide. This strategy avoids the difficulties encountered by proposing an entirely novel definition of genocide. To have an impact, a new definition of the crime of genocide would require a multilateral treaty, which would be a formidable undertaking. The prospects for statutory change at the international level have become more difficult since the recently adopted definitions for the crimes under the ICC's jurisdiction repeat mistakes from previous treaties. For example, the specifications of the elements of the crimes of genocide for the ICC repeat the mistake of iterating a number of distinct acts, any one of which constitutes genocide. If the crime of genocide can be any one of these harms other than the harm of mass killings, then we have a diluted sense of genocide (see Chapter 3).

The case for a narrow interpretation of genocide runs counter to a growing trend that sees an increasingly broader interpretation of genocide as somehow legally, morally, and politically progressive. The expansive approach reads history as a testament to a continuous pushing out of the boundaries of full citizenship. Accordingly, humanity morally progresses by recognizing more and more types of suffering that warrant moral concern. In the twentieth century, the moral circle has grown to bring women, slaves, and animals into it. Similarly, using this line of reasoning, moral progress will take place by extending the scope of genocide crimes to include not only the prototypical example of the Holocaust but also other types of genocide against other groups, such as cultural genocide against indigenous peoples. This study will attempt to counter the expansionist approach by making a case for a narrow interpretation of the crime of genocide.

The growing jurisprudence from decisions of the Ad Hoc War Crimes Tribunals both hinders and helps the interpretive proposals offered in this study. In many instances, the decisions of the tribunals run contrary to recommendations made throughout this study. Yet, the more acceptable the accumulative jurisprudence of past tribunals becomes, the more receptive it becomes to analyses and recommendations by legal and other scholars. Legal scholarship as expressed in law review articles and books has had an overall positive influence on the development of common law in the United States. The arguments below should help to stimulate a similar body of legal scholarship that has only just begun to develop in international criminal law. International criminal law provides a vehicle for the international community to proclaim and to prove its moral revulsion to "the most odious crime." Minimally, this study should draw attention to the legal resources available for developing a global ethics.

Part II

ELEMENTS OF THE CRIME OF GENOCIDE

Chapter 3

Genocide Act: Mass Killings

Aritcle 6 Genicode

Article 6 (a) Genocide by killing
Elements
1. The perpetrator **killed one or more persons.**

Article 6 (b) Genocide by causing serious bodily or mental harm

Article 6 (c) Genocide by deliberately inflicting conditions of life calculated to bring about physical destruction

Article 6 (d) Genocide by imposing measures intended to prevent births

Article 6 (e) Genocide by forcibly transferring children[1]

—Rome Statute of the International Criminal Court, 1998

Genocide is not war. It is more dangerous than war.[2]

GENOCIDE, ONE CRIME AMONG MANY?

We are told that the American soldier does not know what he is fighting for. Now, at least, he will know what he is fighting against.[3]

—General Dwight D. Eisenhower after liberating the Buchenwald concentration camp

Types of War Crimes

General Dwight D. Eisenhower, Supreme Commander of Allied Expeditionary Forces in World War II, only recognized the full horror of Nazi atrocities when his troops liberated the concentration camps. Eisenhower (known by the nickname "Ike") then launched a publicity campaign to make officials and ordinary citizens more aware of the depth and breadth of (what only later became known as) the Holocaust. At Eisenhower's invitation, members of the American Congress and the British Parliament visited the scenes of massive human destruction at Buchenwald and Dachau. A joint US congressional committee report found it difficult to find words to describe the magnitude of the crime:

> We found the extent, devices, methods and conditions of torture almost beyond the power of words to describe. They reached depths of human degradation beyond belief and constituted no less than *organized crime against civilization and humanity* for which swift, certain and adequate punishment should be meted out to all those who were responsible [italics added].[4]

Eisenhower also helped to bring the evidence of Hitler's plans to exterminate the Jews to the American public. Americans first watched scenes of these mass murders through newsreels procured through Ike's efforts. Since 1945, through the work of Eisenhower and other humanitarians, knowledge of the Holocaust has spread throughout the world. Yet, despite its worldwide recognition, this "crime without a name" never fully achieved its rightful place among the many other horrors and injustices that have occurred before and since. To see what is meant by statements that give prominence to the Holocaust and similar crimes we first need to determine what type of crime the Holocaust was. The nature of the crime now readily identified as genocide begins to come to light when we compare it with other types of crimes of a similar scale.

The Nuremberg Tribunal prosecuted three types of international crimes, which curiously did not explicitly include the crime of genocide.

> *War crimes*: namely, violations of the laws or customs of war. Such violations shall include, but not limited to, murder, ill-treatment or deportation to slave labor or for any other purpose of civilian population of or in occupied territory, murder or ill-treatment of prisoners of war or persons on the seas, killing of hostages, plunder of public or private property, wanton destruction of cities, towns, or villages, or devastation not justified by military necessity.
>
> *Crimes against peace*: namely, planning, preparation, initiation or waging of a war of aggression, or a war in violation of international treaties, agreements or assurances, or participation in a Common Plan or Conspiracy for the accomplishment of any of the foregoing.
>
> *Crimes against humanity*: namely, murder, extermination, enslavement, deportation, and other inhumane acts committed against any civilian population, before or during the war, or persecutions on political, racial, or religious grounds in the execution of or in the connection with any crimes within the jurisdiction of the Tribunal, whether or not in violation of domestic law of the country where perpetrated.

It may seem surprising then that this list does not include (except by indirect reference) the *crime of genocide*. Today, we immediately associate genocide with attempts to annihilate an entire people. Extermination does appear as one of many elements of *crimes against humanity* but only as one example of many other "inhumane acts." Thus, we may conclude that the codification of the Nuremberg crimes gave no particular prominence to genocide. In fact, the crime of genocide had not even been given a legally recognized name at the time of the Nuremberg trials. Among those types of crimes then considered as the gravest ones, genocide, now widely regarded as one of the worst crimes imaginable, was the last to be classified as a separate type. Paradoxically, it seems that, historically, international law recognized the worst of these crimes last.

How do these Nuremberg crimes differ from to one another? The following overly simplified descriptions provide an initial way to distinguish these crimes: First, soldiers commit *war crimes* against other soldiers during wars. Second, nations violate *crimes against peace* against other nations. Third, political as well as military personal inflict *crimes against humanity* on civilian populations. Finally, political/military leaders and their followers commit *genocide* against certain groups. The sections that follow will refine these distinctions to help provide a clear understanding of the war crimes, crimes against peace, crimes against humanity, and, most importantly for our purposes, the crime of genocide.

Differentiating War Crimes

Over the course of the twentieth century, incidents of the four crimes and the attention given to them have varied. At different times, one international crime receives far greater attention than the others do. First, war crimes, then crimes against peace (aggression), and finally, crimes against humanity have each had their turn at the international center stage. This does not mean that any one crime had exclusive and uncontested use of the spotlight. However, we can roughly track periods when one type of crime gained prominence over the others. Before and during both world wars, nations focused on war crimes (see Chapter 1). Among the types of crimes we are considering, those crimes that are committed within the context of combat (war crimes) have the longest history. The criminalization of acts of nations (crimes against peace or aggression) followed this criminalization of acts of the military. After World War II, the crime of aggression (and not genocide) ascended to the top of the list.

This may sound too much like a weekly rating of the top rock songs. Yet, the "hit parade of crimes" has a serious purpose. It undermines some commonly held beliefs. People, for example, think that the Allies fought World War II to halt the spread of genocide and that the Nuremberg Tribunal (1945–1946) tried Nazis leaders primarily for their role in the Holocaust. Contrary to these views, the Allies regarded aggression (crimes against peace) as the worst crime committed by Hitler and his regime during the war. The indictments at Nuremberg also reflected this assessment, which our later analyses will show as mistaken. To varying degrees, the Allies knew about the Nazi genocide, but its leaders never gave this type of mass murder priority. Throughout World War II, the horrors inflicted in the death camps had a secondary importance relative to the unlawful state aggression engaged in by the German state. Only after the Nuremberg trials were underway did these judgments begin to change. Only when the Nuremberg prosecutors presented pictures and other evidence did the "crime without a name" begin to take on a legal life of its own.

Although genocide gained increasing recognition as a horrific crime through the course of the Nuremberg trials, public outcries over genocide atrocities did not completely translate into strong legal recognition of genocide as among the gravest (if not the gravest) of injustices. Nevertheless, the Nuremberg Tribunal made a number of advances with respect to the crime of genocide. The Tribunal (1) made the first explicit use of the word "genocide" in its indictments; (2) indirectly made reference to genocide under the category of "crimes against humanity"; and (3) devoted a section of its findings to the "Persecution of the Jews."

However, each advance became tempered (and, at times, undermined) by other considerations or developments. For example, although the term "genocide" appeared in the indictment of the German war criminals, it did not occur either in the Charter of the International Military Tribunal or in the Tribunal's final opinions. Further, the Tribunal interpreted crimes against humanity (which implicitly included genocide) as a type of war crime. They adopted, in part, the classification "crimes against humanity" to plug a legal loophole. The category "war crimes" covered crimes done within the German state; "crimes against humanity" encompassed those wrongs committed in German occupied territories not captured by the "war crimes" category. Further, the Tribunal did not treat crimes against humanity as a separate, independent category. Instead, the Tribunal viewed crimes against humanity as an accessory crime to war crimes and crimes against peace. As a result, the Tribunal did not regard genocide as a primary and independent crime.

Overall, then, the Nuremberg Tribunal placed its emphasis not on crimes against humanity but rather on crimes against peace, which it found to be "the supreme international crime, differing only from other war crimes in that it contains within itself the accumulated evil of the whole." Crimes against humanity played an even lesser role at the Tokyo trials than it did at the Nuremberg trials. While the Tokyo Tribunal indicted suspects on crimes against humanity, its judgments only addressed war crimes.[5] Thus, we can safely conclude that war crimes and crimes against peace received most of the attention throughout most of the twentieth century.

At the end of the twentieth century, however, a change occurred, a shift away from those types of crimes previously given prominence. Interestingly, crimes against peace, once considered the worst of the international crimes, now have diminished in importance. The Ad Hoc War Crimes Tribunals For The Former Yugoslavia and For Rwanda, established in the 1990s, do not even have jurisdiction over crimes against peace. Further, while the codification of the 1998 Rome Statutes lists crimes against peace (largely at the insistence of the former aggressor states Germany and Japan), the treaty did not specify the elements for the crime against peace and, even more tellingly, made the use of this crime dependent on possible future treaty negotiations for its possible implementation.

The Tribunals for the Former Yugoslavia and for Rwanda (still functioning today) have given increasing priority to crimes against humanity and genocide compared to the attention they previously gave to war crimes and crimes against peace. The International Criminal Tribunal for Rwanda (ICTR) ranked war crimes as "lesser crimes" compared to those "crimes which particularly shock the collective conscience."[6] In 1999, the ICTR, in fact, made history as the first international court to convict someone for genocide in the case of Hutu militia leader George Rutaganda. The International Criminal Court for the Former Yugoslavia (ICTY) increasingly has made nuanced distinctions among the four crimes. The ICTY prosecutor, for example, charged the former Serbian leader Slobodan Milošević with sixty-six "grave crimes." The charges covered three different types of conflicts: the wars in Croatia (1991–1992), Bosnia (1992–1995), and Kosovo (1999). However, the prosecutors only charged Milošević with genocide in the war in Bosnia and with crimes against humanity in the other two conflicts in Croatia and Kosovo.[7] The war in Bosnia involved acts of genocide and crimes directly tied to genocide. According to the prosecution, neither the war in Croatia nor the war in Kosovo involved genocide or crimes tied to genocide.

While legal history reveals differences between genocide and other comparable crimes, political history uncovers distinctions among different kinds of genocide. Although historical trends are notoriously difficult to establish, shifts in the types of genocides that have occurred since World War II do appear. The circumstances under which perpetrators commit genocide have radically altered during that period. From World War II to the present, genocide has gone from a crime committed along with other major types of crimes to a crime increasingly committed independently from those other crimes. The Holocaust took place within the context of a conventional war. In contrast, many of the worst cases of mass killings since World War II, for example in Cambodia in the 1970s, largely happened outside (or prior to) a conventional war context. Cambodia's "killing fields" had little in common with what we think of as typical warfare. At that time, Cambodia's rulers, known as the Khmer Rouge, killed hundreds of thousands of their citizens when no one, including the victims, waged any form of war or revolt against them. Although a more complicated situation than Cambodia, Rwanda's 1994 genocide also exploded outside the context of a conventional war among states. Thus, throughout the twentieth century, genocide has increasingly become recognized as a devastating force in its own right, an independent horror among horrors.

We also can detect shifts in attitudes toward the crime of genocide. The relative weight and importance given to genocide changed dramatically during the twentieth century.[8] The century began with two genocides that remain largely ignored even today—the Hereros (1904) and the Armenians (1915–1916). Slowly, throughout the century, the international community gave higher priority to prosecuting the crime of genocide. This then supports the claim that genocide has only recently begun to take its place of infamy as "the most odious scourge." Thus, the international community has taken some time to admit that genocide is far worse than the crimes typically committed during conventional wars. However, since the September 11, 2001 attacks in the United States, the formerly growing attention given to genocide has begun to diminish in the face of another crime, namely terrorism.

Before the attacks on the Pentagon and the World Trade Center, jurists had classified terrorism along with drug trafficking as "treaty crimes." It proves instructive to examine discussions about terrorism even as recent as the 1990s. In 1998, the nations of the world met at the Rome Conference called to establish an international criminal court. During the discussions, Algeria, India, Israel, Libya, and Russia argued that the new international criminal court should have jurisdiction over the crime of terrorism. Other states, however, opposed this court hearing terrorist cases. Their opposition rested on a comparative judgment that they had made about the seriousness of different crimes. They thought that the crime of terrorism was not serious enough to warrant a place on the same list as war crimes, crimes against peace, and crimes against humanity. In other words, they regarded terrorism as a relatively minor crime. Given the subsequent September 11th terrorist attacks, did these countries drastically underestimate the harmful impact of terrorist acts? Alternatively, did the peculiarities of these attacks lead to an overestimation of the crime of terrorism? Attempts to answer these important questions would take us too far from our main topic. The 1998 discussions among nations, however, nicely illustrate historical shifts over which crime or crimes the international community considers the most serious. Later, we shall see that the developments up to 2001 followed an overall defensible pattern. Perhaps, the 2001 terrorist attacks did not change the world as dramatically as many American analysts and leaders at the time projected. However, as we shall see, 9/11 did have a dramatic affect on international criminal law. Only time will tell if the impact proves reversible.

The 1998 Rome Conference also provides a good illustration of another critical dimension of legal analysis, the central importance of definitions (see Appendices A, B). The jailing and execution of individuals hinge on how jurists fit their acts to the crime as defined by the law. Ironically, at the Rome Conference, the United States and the League of Arab States objected to including terrorism within the court's jurisdiction because they thought that nations could not find a mutually agreeable and legally adequate definition of the crime of terrorism. Now, of course, the US government has no difficulty in readily identifying terrorist acts and terrorists. We shall turn our energies to finding the most defensible definition of another crime, namely the crime of genocide. It seems easier to define genocide than terrorism. Yet, exactly which acts should fit within the reach of the crime of genocide?

GENOCIDE, EVERYWHERE OR NOWHERE?

On the Importance of Defining Crimes

> "Race mixing," drug distribution, methadone programs; and the practice of birth control and abortions among Third World people; sterilization and "Mississippi

appendectomies" (tubal ligations and hysterectomies); medical treatment of Catholics; and the closing of synagogues in the Soviet Union.[9]

The denial of ethnic Hawaiian culture by the American run public school system in Hawaii, government policies letting one race adopt the children of another race, African slavery by whites, South African Apartheid, any murder of women by men, death squad murders in Guatemala, deaths in the Soviet gulag, and, of course, the Jewish Holocaust.[10]

What acts of injustice qualify as genocide? A quick survey of how different writers use the word "genocide" shows little agreement over which acts to include as instances of crimes of genocide. The quotations cited above illustrate the wide range of acts, from the use of birth control to killings by death squads, that analysts think worthy of the label "genocide." This widespread use of the genocide label indicates something about the strong rhetorical force that the word genocide has. Political activists representing many movements grab onto the word genocide to demonstrate the gravity of their particular harm or injustice. They hope that the association of their plight with that of Holocaust and other recognizable genocide victims will provoke a quick and powerful response from the international community. Yet, these loose associations seldom help their causes. Instead, calling whatever one wants genocide only serves to undermine the rhetorical force and moral strength still found in the idea of genocide. If we want to retain whatever power that is still left in the concept of genocide, then we need to reign in the loose talk and settle on a narrow definition of the term.

While the over-extensive use of the genocide label diminishes its impact, the under-use of the label has had more far-reaching and devastating consequences. In 1994, the Clinton administration persistently refused to use the word "genocide" to describe the mass killings in Rwanda. A telling exchange occurred between a Clinton administration spokeswoman and a reporter:

Question: So you say genocide happens when certain acts happen and you say that those acts have happened in Rwanda. So why can't you say that genocide has happened?

Ms. Shelley: Because, Alan, there is reason for the selection of words that we have made, and I have—perhaps I have—I'm not a lawyer. I don't approach this from the international legal and scholarly point of view. We try, as best we can, to accurately reflect a description in particularly addressing that issue. It's—the issue is out there. People have been obviously looking at it.[11]

Later, during the same briefing, a spokesperson for the State Department explicitly refused to use the word "genocide" to describe the situation in Rwanda because "there are obligations which arise in connection with the use of the term." Many commentators contend that if a situation qualifies as genocide, then nations have an obligation to intervene. The United States carefully avoided the "g" word to describe the slaughter of over 800,000 mostly Rwandan Tutsis by Hutu militants. Disagreements over when to use and how to define "genocide" undoubtedly increased the longevity and brutality of the slaughter in Rwanda.[12]

The problems of over-use and under-use of the genocide label provide a strong incentive for wanting to settle on a core area of agreement about what constitutes genocide. We first need to find a description of those acts that most reasonable people would agree to label as acts of genocide, irrespective of whatever other acts they may want to call genocide. Agreement about what acts lie at the core of genocide would improve matters immensely. A precise, core definition of genocide would help policy makers sort out the harms that qualify as genocide from those that do not. By narrowing its scope, the word would retain its rhetorical force. Further, political leaders would have clear guidelines for when to intervene. Armed with a clear sense of genocide, world leaders could make a sensible assessment of when it would be required to take action to stop an on-going genocide. In addition, courts could avoid dealing with an unruly array of genocide claims.

This chapter lays out the case for accepting one type of act as constituting the core of any genocide act. Acts of killing make genocide particularly loathsome relative to most other crimes. Further, it is not only a killing nor a few killings, it is the massive number of killings that spring genocide ahead of other despicable criminal acts. In essence, massive killing is the stereotypic, classic form of genocide. This means that even acts that would otherwise warrant criminal prosecution would not be genocide unless they involved actual (or perhaps imminent) mass killings. By weeding out the many questionable actions that political activists call genocide, a narrow interpretation of what acts constitute genocide runs of the risk of excluding too much. The narrow approach may yield more than we bargain for by excluding some very serious crimes from the genocide category.

A campaign to elevate the status of rape in international law has raised troublesome challenge to an approach that limits the scope of genocide. The movement to push the international community to take the crime of rape more seriously has grown steadily, and, most significantly, it has recently achieved considerable success. Like so many similar movements, some of those who have tried to elevate gender crimes to a higher, more serious level have used the strategy of calling rape genocide. At this stage, let us simply outline the argument against this type of strategy. A limited sense of genocide can enhance rather than diminish the gravity of some crimes. Our envisioned international justice system would regard some criminal acts such as rape as among the most serious because of the connection these acts have to the crime of genocide. Those who accept our proposed narrow interpretation of what constitutes an act of genocide would treat crimes such as rape as having a considerable degree of gravity in those cases where those crimes have a proven connection to mass killing. Within the international criminal code, the recognition of the severity of some crimes, then, would increase because of the connections those acts often have to the core genocide act of massive killings. In summary, a narrow definition of genocide as mass killings would exclude many acts currently classified as genocide acts, but it would also treat other formerly neglected criminal acts (such as some forms of rape) more seriously.

At this stage, many will wonder just how we intend to carry out this project. The prospects for making radical changes in current international treaties are remote, and the probabilities of implementing new treaties are low. A more practical strategy is to keep the analysis and proposals within the bounds of established international law. More specifically, then, we shall make every effort to correct inconsistencies among already accepted international legal frameworks, including the following: the Genocide Convention, the jurisprudence of the tribunals on the Former Yugoslavia and Rwanda, and the statutes governing the new International Criminal Court (ICC). The words contained in these legal documents and judicial opinions are subject to future interpretations. These "doors of interpretation" provide a large enough opening for making radical but feasible and sensible changes in international law. Our proposals about the elements needed to charge someone with the crime of genocide, then, serve as recommendations to jurists, scholars, and politicians about how they should interpret the laws governing genocide.

Definitional Progress

"Genocide" comes from the Greek *genos* meaning "race, nation, or tribe," and from the Latin *caedere* meaning, "to kill." Raphael Lemkin, a Polish Jewish jurist, first coined the term in 1944.[13] Lemkin primarily applied his analysis to Nazis war crimes during World War II. During the formative years of the United Nations, Lemkin led a one-man campaign to make genocide a crime under international law. On December 9, 1948 (one day before the adoption of the Universal Declaration on Human Rights), the UN General Assembly approved the Genocide Convention by a vote of 55 to 0. In 1951, the Genocide Convention entered into force. Over one hundred states have since ratified it.[14] The United States, typically slow to accept international human rights treaties, ratified the Genocide Convention in 1988.[15]

As discussed above, the phrase "crimes against humanity" in Article 6(c) of the London Charter that established the Nuremberg tribunal included acts of genocide,[16] but the Charter's provisions restricted the application of crimes against humanity to situations involving an international war.[17] This meant that international law would not recognize mass killings as genocide if they occurred in the midst of a civil war. Yet, genocide does not always occur in the midst of an international conflict. In recent times, genocide increasingly erupts during civil strife within a nation. A civil war in Rwanda, for example, provided the context for its 1994 genocide. With the adoption of Article I of the Convention on the Prevention and Punishment of the Crime of Genocide (Genocide Convention), the United Nations cured this defect in the London Charter by explicitly recognizing the potential for genocide to occur "in time of peace or in time of war."[18] The drafters of a 1998 Rome Treaty reaffirmed this broader interpretation.

KILLING: THE CENTRAL WRONG OF GENOCIDE

The Case for Killings

Although both national and international criminal law systems require proof of a criminal act, they have different perspectives on the relationship between the act and the actor. National or state prosecutors must prove that a defendant directly committed a criminal act such as murder. In contrast, although international prosecutors must prove that a criminal act such as genocide occurred, they do not have to prove that the accused physically carried out genocide acts. For individual accountability in international law, it would suffice if the accused ordered others to carry out the acts or occupied a position of power and responsibility for acts committed by others. While prosecutors need not show that a responsible official personally engaged in the criminal action, they must show a link between the official and the action.

It is important to distinguish an official who commits acts of genocide and one who fails to prevent genocide. International tribunals do not always clearly separate the commission of a crime from the omission (i.e., the failure to prevent a crime). The ICTR Trial Chamber found Jean Kambanda, Prime Minister of the Interim Government of Rwanda from April 8, 1994 to July 17, 1994, guilty of genocide "by his acts or omissions."[19] The word "omissions" in this context is misleading as the governing statutes only empower prosecuting officials for the commission of genocide acts. As head of the government during the massacres, the tribunal should have charged Kambanda with committing genocide, not for his failure to prevent it.

What acts does international law recognize as acts of genocide? All codifications of the laws of genocide agree that five types of acts meet the requirements of genocide. They further agree that killing is only one of many types of acts that constitute genocide. Article II of the Genocide Convention (1948) lists the following acts of genocide:

(a) Killing members of the group.
(b) Causing serious bodily or mental harm to members of the group.
(c) Deliberately inflicting on the group conditions of life calculated to bring about its physical destruction in whole or in part.
(d) Imposing measures intended to prevent births within the group.
(e) Forcibly transferring children of one group to another group.[20]

Article 6 of the ICC repeats the acts listed in the earlier Genocide Convention (see Appendix A):

(a) Genocide by killing.
(b) Genocide by causing serious bodily or mental harm.
(c) Genocide by deliberately inflicting conditions of life calculated to bring about physical destruction.

(d) Genocide by imposing measures intended to prevent births.

(e) Genocide by forcibly transferring children.

Commentators have taken each of the acts listed in Article 6 as a separate act of genocide. By implication, then, all of the acts represented separately on the list are on par or, at least, on the same footing. "Killing members of the group" and "imposing measures intended to prevent births within the group" would each qualify, independently, as acts of genocide. However, do items (a) through (e) appear in any meaningful order? All of the codifications of the laws of genocide list the act of killing first. The act of killing may come first on these lists for good reasons. Perhaps the lists order the items as a series of gradations of harms beginning with "killing members of the group." We content that this element comes first because it represents the crucial core ingredient of genocide.

Correlatively, the other acts listed in Articles 6(b–e), although listed separately from the act described in Article 6(a), do not constitute distinct, independent categories of genocide acts. Etymology provides an important clue for finding the basics of a genocide act. Given the word's derivation from the Latin *caedere* ("to kill"), whatever else genocide encompasses, it should include the act of killing.[21] Therefore, the other acts (b–e), although listed separately from (a) ("killing"), should not signify distinct, independent categories of acts of genocide.

An interpretation that places killings at the core of the crime of genocide seems contrary to the dominant position taken during the drafting stages of the 1948 Genocide Convention. Let us turn to the drafting stage of this multilateral treaty for insights into how to interpret the law. The debates during the drafting of the Genocide Convention took some steps toward narrowing the acts that would qualify under the heading of genocide. Some national representatives to the Convention tried to add the following separate article on cultural genocide:

> In this Convention genocide also means any deliberate act committed with the intent to destroy the language, religion or culture of a national, racial or religious group on grounds of the national or racial origin or religious belief of its members such as:
>
> 1. Prohibiting the use of language of the group in daily intercourse or in schools or the printing and circulation of publications in the language of the group;
> 2. Destroying or preventing the use of libraries, museums, schools, historical institutions and objects of the group.[22]

A majority of the state representatives rejected this proposal to add cultural genocide to the list of genocide acts. To help forge agreement among the delegates, the drafters decided to limit the acts of genocide to essentially physical acts. According to the majority view, although cultural genocide may lead to physical genocide, the two are quite distinct. Destruction of a culture does not entail destruction of any or all members of that culture. Cultural genocide, as we shall soon see, does not rise to the same magnitude of horror as physical genocide. On a scale of group harms, prohibiting the use of a group's language ranks far below physically harming individuals because of their group identity.

The drafters of the Genocide Convention did not explicitly complete their task. They took the first step in the narrowing process by omitting cultural genocide as a type of genocide act. Yet, even narrowing genocide *per se* to essentially physical acts makes the scope of genocide acts too broad. All of the acts included in the list consist of physical acts.

The drafters, however, further narrowed the range of genocide acts by listing the physical acts in a definite order with the act of killing occurring first. They implicitly accomplished what they had explicitly done by confining genocide acts to physical acts. The Genocide Convention and the Articles of the ICC put the act of killing first on the list of genocide acts. Therefore, these factors support the interpretation that the drafters of the Genocide Convention intended to view genocide as consisting primarily of a certain type of physical act, namely, killing. The other nonlethal physical acts appear on the list because they most often occur in conjunction with genocide killings.

By appealing to political realities and practical difficulties, we could ignore the next challenge to determining how the different types of genocide acts relate to one another. Practical people often remind the idealists among us about the enormous difficulties involved in achieving international consensus. However, the appeals to realism and pragmatism seem out of step with recent accomplishments. If an attendant pessimistic attitude had ruled international treaty making, the ICC would never have become a reality. Let us proceed, then, to determine how the separate listed acts relate to one another.

One strategy for meeting the challenge is to show the unwanted consequences that follow if we adopt the opposite interpretation and treat all acts on the list equally. Each of five listed acts, then, would have the same legal and moral status. Consequently, any given genocide act (killing) would rank no higher legally or no worse morally than any other listed act (imposing measures intended to prevent births). This would lead to the bizarre conclusion that the Nazi sterilization campaign against the "mentally defective" ranks on par with the Holocaust killings. Presumably, no one would find these results acceptable.

Further, treating non-killing acts as acts of genocide has unacceptable implications. The acceptance of acts set forth in Article 6 (a) through (e) as types of genocide undermines a distinction between lethal and nonlethal harms. Items (b) through (e) involve nonlethal forms of harm to individuals because of their group identity. While we should condemn harm to group members, we also should distinguish nonlethal harm to a group from lethal harm to members of a group.[23] Those who kill a member of a group commit a lethal harm. Those who prevent the births of members of a group or any of the other acts listed under (b) through (e) commit nonlethal harms. The acts that fall under items (b) through (e) may have ties to the killings included under item (a). International criminal law should treat the acts listed under (b) through (e) more severely according to whether the acts occur in conjunction with genocide killings. However, it should not construe the nonlethal group harms (b–e) as independent acts of genocide.

"Genocide by killing" stands apart from the other listed acts in another way (see Appendix C). It is difficult to imagine any circumstance that would justify "genocide by killing." In contrast, with some of the other acts, we even can envision scenarios where it might be justifiable to carry them out. For example, the act described under (c) refers to deliberately imposing conditions designed to bring about the physical destruction of a group. The phrase "physical destruction" refers, not to the physical destruction of individual members of a group, but to the physical destruction of the infrastructure needed to support and sustain a group. However, under some circumstances, it may be justified "to destroy, in whole or part, a national, ethnic, racial or religious group, as such" by "(c) deliberately inflicting on the group conditions of life calculated to bring about its physical destruction in whole or in part."

A concrete case illustrates a situation where it may have become justifiable to commit a form of cultural genocide, that is, to destroy a certain group. In the 1990s, Japan had to take action against a terrorist organization, AUM Shinrikyo (AUM or "Supreme Truth"), a doomsday cult.[24] On March 20, 1995, members of AUM released sarin, a deadly nerve gas, in a Tokyo subway, killing twelve and injuring scores of other passengers. Although the Tokyo subway incident was the most spectacular, AUM members had a history of violent acts. In 1989, an AUM member murdered a mother, her fourteen-month-old son, and her husband, a young lawyer who was preparing to sue the cult. Members of Japan's Diet called for the destruction of this doomsday cult. The government withdrew official recognition of AUM as a religion. Many towns refused to allow AUM members to register so that they could not qualify their children for schools or their families for community services.

If we accepted that each listed item could qualify as an act of genocide, then the destruction of a group's culture, such as AUM's, would qualify as genocide. Yet, the AUM case presents a situation where cultural genocide (the destruction of AUM) might be justifiable. The Japanese government decided against applying anti-subversion laws to AUM that would have prohibited AUM from meeting or otherwise operating as an organization.[25] While a complete ban on AUM may not prove justified, we can conceive of rationally and ethically acceptable grounds that would justify eliminating an organization. The AUM case offers a plausible scenario where it may have been justified "to destroy, in whole or part, a national, ethnic, racial or religious group, as such" by "(c) deliberately inflicting on the group conditions of life calculated to bring about its physical destruction in whole or in part."[26] In sharp contrast, genocide, in the sense of intentionally killing group members because of their group affiliation, is not justifiable under any circumstance.[27]

Unfortunately, a scenario that imagines a state under worse conditions than those experienced by Japan may have become a reality with recent terrorist attacks on the United States. Some analysts regard the United States as justified in its efforts to eliminate the terrorist organizations responsible for the attack or to annihilate any terrorist organization. The United States has defensible justifications under international law to take measures to eliminate terrorist organizations that engaged in the killings. Disbanding an organization (perhaps justifiable in the Japan and US cases) does not mean executing its members. Killing members of terrorist organizations because of their perceived membership has no justification. Intentionally killing group members because of their negatively perceived group affiliation is not justifiable under any circumstance.

If we have successfully argued for demanding that the crime of genocide minimally and centrally include acts of killing, we will have accomplished a great deal. Rather than extending the notion of genocide to include cultural genocide and other nonlethal acts, as many have proposed, this narrow definitional interpretation places killing as the core act of genocide.[28] The other nonlethal acts listed in Article II of the Genocide Convention and in the ICC's Articles occur on the list along with the lethal act of killing because they often occur in concert with these killings (see Appendix C). However, even some criminal acts not explicitly listed in items (b–e) would be regarded as more serious when they occurred in concert with genocide killings than if they happened by themselves. Until the recent success of a campaign to have rape considered as a war crime, mass rapes such as the Rape of Nanking did not fall under any of the acts explicitly listed in the Genocide Convention. On a scale of grave harms, mass rapes should fall at least on the same level as forced adoptions and forced sterilization. In the following section, we shall argue against treating rape as genocide while trying to highlight the gravity of mass rapes because of their common tie to genocide killings (see Appendix C). Then, after examining cases of mass rape, we shall show that the act of genocide consists of a certain kind of killing, mass killing.

The Case against Rape as Genocide

1. *The Rape of Nanking*. Japan's military committed numerous atrocities during the capture of the city of Nanking in China, killing over 200,000 and committing rapes against over 20,000 women from the ages of 8 to 70. Foreigners living in Nanking at the time formed the International Committee for the Nanking Safety Zone, which saved 200–300,000 refugees, almost half of the Chinese population in Nanking. John Rabe and Wilhelmina (Minnie) Vautrin, leaders of the Safety Committee, deserve special notice for they saved hundreds of thousands of lives. Rabe, a German businessman who worked for the German industrial giant Siemens, chaired the committee.[29]

It may come as a surprise to learn about Rabe's Nazi party affiliation. According to Rabe, "The Japanese had pistols and bayonets and I . . . had only party symbols and my swastika armband."[30] His Nazi credentials proved valuable for humanitarian purposes. For example, after Rabe informed Hitler of the atrocities committed by the Japanese military, the Japanese limited its previous indiscriminate bombing campaign to military targets. Rabe returned to Germany, bringing a film of the atrocities with him. The Nazi party decorated him, but the Gestapo interrogated him. Siemens sent him off again, this time to Afghanistan. After the war, he returned to Germany only to become a victim of the de-nazification process. A German acquaintance denounced him as a member of the Nazi Party, the National Socialist German Workers Party (NSDAP). A de-nazifying commission of the British sector first rejected but later granted his appeal. The survivors of the Nanking massacre raised money and sent food to Rabe after they learned that his legal ordeal had impoverished him.

Minnie Vautrin, "The Living Goddess of Nanking," who was raised in Secor, Illinois and graduated from the University of Illinois, became President of Ginling College in Nanking. Vautrin saved countless lives (mostly women) in Nanking. However, facing a difficult dilemma, she made a Faustian bargain by granting a Japanese "request" for a few prostitutes from among the many female refugees she protected. She indirectly became part of the Japan's military practice of having *comfort women* accompany the troops as a way to prevent future rapes in Nanking. Sadly, Japan's first Comfort House opened in Nanking in 1938.

The International Military Tribunal for the Far East, Tokyo War Crimes Trials prosecuted twenty-eight military and political leaders, including Hirota Koki, Matsui Iwane, and Akia Muto. Hirota Koki served as Japan's Foreign Minister at the time of the Rape of Nanking. Joseph Grew, the US Ambassador in Tokyo, informed Hirota of the atrocities in Nanking. As Japan's Foreign Minister, Hirota went to Shanghai to investigate reports of the atrocities in Nanking and sent the following message, intercepted by US intelligence, to his contacts in Washington, DC:

> Since return (to) Shanghai a few days ago I investigated reported atrocities committed by Japanese army in Nanking and elsewhere. Verbal accounts (of) reliable eye-witnesses and letters from individuals whose credibility (is) beyond question afford convincing proof (that) Japanese army behaved and (is) continuing (to) behave in (a) fashion reminiscent (of) Attila (and) his Huns. (Not) less than three hundred thousand Chinese civilians slaughtered, many cases in cold blood.[31]

Matsui Iwane, Commander of Central China Expeditionary Force, was not present during the invasion of Nanking by Japan. Akia Muto, Chief of Staff to General Yamashita, was only in Nanking a short period, from December 14–25, 1937. Despite the distant association of these three individuals to the crimes committed in Nanking and elsewhere, the Tribunal sentenced them to death. Hirota, Matsui, and Muto died by hanging on December 23, 1948. Hirota Kiko was the only civilian executed by the Tokyo Tribunal. However, the Tokyo Tribunal did not prosecute Lieutenant General Prince Asaka, a member of Emperor Hirohito's royal family, who had taken actual command of the invasion of Nanking.

If we assume that the Tribunal produced unblemished indictments for the mass killings in the Nanking case, we would still have to conclude that the accused did not commit genocide. While those properly accused of the crimes did commit mass killing, they lacked the requisite intent (see Chapter 4) to eliminate a designated group (see Chapter 6). Although one of the leading authorities on the Rape of

Nanking, the late Iris Chang, sometimes referred to the episode as genocide, she has admitted that "no Japanese equivalent of a 'final solution' for the Chinese people" exists.[32] In other words, a tribunal could not reasonably infer that Japan had instituted a policy to commit genocide against the Chinese people.

However, let us assume that the massive rapes in Nanking would satisfy an intent requirement. It follows, then, that if rape constitutes one of the acts of genocide, then rape would constitute genocide. Should international criminal courts prosecute individuals for rape as a crime of genocide? Law professor Catherine MacKinnon and others have led a fight to incorporate the crime of rape fully into humanitarian law.[33] For MacKinnon, rape is a form of genocide against women. A well-reasoned ICTR case will help to situate the crime of rape alongside the crime of genocide while, contra MacKinnon, not treating it as genocide *per se*.

2. *Rape in Rwanda*. In the *Akayesu* case, the ICTR developed a sophisticated position on the rape-as-genocide issue that other tribunals should follow.[34] From April 1993 until June 1994, former schoolteacher Jean Paul Akayesu served as mayor (*bourgmestre*) of the Tuba commune. Rwanda has four administrative levels from lowest to highest: cells, sectors, communes, and prefectures. When the genocide broke out in April 1994, hundreds of displaced civilians, mostly Tutsis, sought refuge in the commune under Akayesu's authority.[35] Witnesses testified that Akayesu failed to prevent the *Interahamwe* (the militia) from committing the rapes in the compounds under his supervision. Further, they testified that in some cases he aided and abetted the sexual violence. The Trial Chamber found Akayesu guilty of the charges of genocide and rape.

Most importantly, however, a careful reading of the opinion shows that the court did not find the accused guilty of rape as genocide.

> Sexual violence was an integral part of the process of destruction, specifically targeting Tutsi women and specifically contributing to their destruction and to the destruction of the Tutsi group as a whole (731)... Sexual violence was a step in the process of destruction of the Tutsi group—destruction of the spirit, of the will to live, and of life itself (732). ... [I]t appears clearly to the Chamber that the acts of rape and sexual violence, as other acts of serious bodily and mental harm committed against the Tutsi, reflected the determination to make Tutsi women suffer and to mutilate them even before killing them, the intent being to destroy the Tutsi group while inflicting acute suffering on its members in the process (733).

Thus, the court found the rape incidents in question integrally intertwined enough with the primary genocide act of mass killing to qualify as part of the genocide.[36] While rape clearly fits the description of one of the listed acts in the genocide provisions (item (b) "causing serious bodily or mental harm"), rape, according to the Trial Chamber, (only?) becomes a genocide act when it is shown to be an integral part of the primary genocide act of killing. Unlike a court trying the Nanking rape cases, the court in *Akayesu* first had established an independent charge of genocide before making a finding on the rape charges. Presumably, a court trying the Nanking rape cases could not have followed a similar path as it would not have had the primary first element, namely, proof of genocide killings. Although the findings and analysis of the Trial Chamber in *Akayesu* deserve high praise, what it did not establish deserves particular mention. It did not establish grounds for treating rape as an independent genocide act.

MASSIVE KILLING: SHOULD NUMBERS COUNT?

> When someone kills a man, he is put in prison. When someone kills twenty people, he is declared mentally insane. But when someone kills 200,000 people, he is invited to Geneva for peace negotiations.[37]

> After the first death there is no other.[38]

The drafters of the ICC's articles took a different position than those who drafted the 1948 Genocide Convention on whether and how courts should regard the number of victims in genocide cases. In debates over the Genocide Convention, a consensus emerged. Although commentators admitted that it would be difficult to specify a threshold of how many killings constituted genocide, they also generally agreed that genocide required some significantly high number of killings. The 1998 Rome Treaty took a different approach to the issue of victim numbers. The ICC Article 6(a) states that "The perpetrator killed one or more persons. . . ." If courts interpret this phrase literally, the killing of a single individual could suffice for a genocide charge. This interpretation runs counter to a common view that finds part of the particularly horrific nature of genocide to lie in the mass number of deaths it brings.

Genocidal killings become difficult to fathom if not for any other reason than simply because of the enormous number of killings involved. It defies the imagination to consider thousands if not millions of dead victims from genocide. Consider the following death statistics: six million Jews and five million "other victims" in Nazi Germany, two to three million deaths in Cambodia, and nearly one million slaughtered in Rwanda. The punishments handed out for the commissions of these crimes do not reflect the staggering numbers of victims of these crimes. Raphael Lemkin, the one credited with coining the term "genocide," posed a disturbing question that has yet to receive the response it deserves: "Why is the killing of a million a lesser crime than the killing of a single individual?"[39] Philip Gourevitch, a journalist who covered the aftermath of the genocide in Rwanda, offered the following reflections: "When a man kills four people, he isn't charged with one count of killing four, but with four counts of killing one and one and one and one. He doesn't get one bigger sentence, but four compounded sentences, and if there's a death penalty, you can take *his* life just once."[40]

Yet, despite the discrepancies in numbers, the killing of a single individual often receives greater attention and sometimes more severe punishment than the killing of millions of individuals. As an example of a misplaced focus, the media gave more coverage to the killing of two individuals in the O. J. Simpson murder trial than it did to the genocidal slaughter of 800,000 in Rwanda, which took place around the same time. Yet, the genocide in Rwanda should rank as a worse crime than the crimes involved in the Simpson case. To rephrase Lemkin's question, "Why is the killing of nearly a million individuals in Rwanda a lesser crime than the killing of two individuals in the Simpson case?" Admittedly, the question is not entirely fair, but it raises a critical issue. While it may be difficult to prove that two murders are worse than one, the gravity of one million genocidal deaths surely should outweigh any single digit count of victims. The sheer number of deaths should count, legally and morally, for something.

While it proves difficult to defend any particular number threshold, it should be noted that the question of numbers may serve to disqualify some instances of mass killing as genocide. On a number of occasions during Rwanda's civil war (prior to the 1994 genocide), human rights organizations and UN representatives had labeled separate instances of the killings of hundreds as genocide. The lowering of the numerical threshold in this way contributed to the reluctance of the United Nations to call events after April 1994 genocide.[41]

Numbers should make a difference in assessing the gravity of the harms, especially when the victim numbers reach the millions. Yet, obviously, numbers cannot be the only factor, particularly when it comes to the legal finding and to the related moral condemnation of the killings. While genocide usually involves incredibly large numbers of victims, its prosecution does not and should not require them. Under certain circumstances, the killing of a few could conceivably qualify as genocide under current international law. More importantly, a large number of deaths do not and should not automatically qualify as genocide acts. The devastation of nature, the rampage of disease, and the ravages of war sometimes involve larger numbers of victims than genocide. Yet, genocide stands out among these disasters as a peculiarly sinister, purposeful human act that has no reasonable justification or defensible redeeming feature.

In general, it seems reasonable to maintain that the higher the number of killings, the easier it is to make a *prima facie* case for the commission of genocide. There are exceptions to this standard as well. Certain circumstances dictate suspending the "number's game," as critics call this aspect of a comparative analysis. In some cases, the killing of only a few group members might satisfy the *actus reus* requirement for the crime of genocide. For example, the perpetrators might have limited their killings to the leaders and to those in high authority within a persecuted group. The US understanding of its ratification of the Genocide Convention goes against the generally accepted view by requiring that the perpetrators directed their killings against the whole or substantial part of a group. This interpretation would require a high numerical threshold for genocide. The debate over small or large numerical thresholds has potential critical policy implications. With a small numbers threshold, the international community might act too soon. However, with a high numbers threshold, the international community becomes prone to a far greater danger, namely, taking action too late.

The 1998 Rome Treaty, establishing an International Criminal Court, resisted the US understanding and reaffirmed the more defensible idea of a continuum.[42]

CONCLUSION

A judicious application of a careful rendering of genocide's element will do a great deal to retain the force and power of the genocide label. Otherwise, "genocide" will become "too may things to too many people," making it legally and politically useless. International law provides an excellent forum for keeping "genocide" within its limits. While a wide variety of discriminatory acts surround genocide, to meet the *actus reus* requirement the acts must include killings and the killings must be numerous.

Chapter 4

Genocide Mind: Organizational Policies

Article 6 (a) Genocide by killing

Elements

1. The perpetrator killed one or more persons.
2. Such person or persons belonged to a particular national, ethnical, racial or religious group.
3. The perpetrator **intended to destroy**, in whole or in part, that national, ethnical, racial or religious group, as such.
4. The conduct took place in the context of a manifest pattern of similar conduct directed against that group or was conduct that could itself effect such destruction.

—Rome Statute of the International Criminal Court[1]

It is in fact the *mens rea* which gives genocide its specialty and distinguishes it from an ordinary crime and other crimes against international humanitarian law.[2]

People are more likely to escape prosecution in international law for killing a thousand individuals than they would in national (municipal) law for killing one individual. We shall find that the justifications for this odd situation lie within the notion of criminal intent. An analysis of intent also will help us understand another paradox in international law. Individuals who directly carry out mass killings are less likely to face prosecution in an international criminal court than are officials far removed from the actual killings. Resolving these paradoxes, however, depends upon a radical rethinking of the idea of intent in international criminal law. The need for this reassessment becomes apparent if we reflect upon another troubling feature of international criminal law. To appreciate the problem, consider the following hypothetical questions. How would prosecutors have charged Adolf Hitler under the current genocide statute that requires proof of intent? Would they have to prove that Hitler had nearly six million intentional states of mind that led to the killing of nearly six million Jews? Something is wrong here. Obviously, we need to reevaluate how we should interpret intent in international law. As we shall see criminal intent in international law, unlike its counterpart in national law, has little to do with individual minds and a great deal to do with organizational policies.

Before proposing a new sense of intent for international criminal law, we need to show why the International Criminal Court (ICC) should retain any sense of intent. The case for keeping an intent requirement begins with acknowledging the inevitable comparative judgments about the seriousness of crimes in any criminal justice system. No matter how distasteful it might seem, jurists and non-jurists judge some injustices as worse than other wrongs. We might say, for example, that we condemn all killings. However, we do not hesitate to judge the brutal slaying of a child as worse than the compassionate hastening of an elderly cancer patient's death. These, often unexamined, comparative judgments—particularly when seriously made in legal and moral debates—have important consequences for social policy. For many of the reasons set forth throughout our investigation, we regard intentional crimes as worse than non-intentional ones. If we rely on (often without debate) these comparative assessments, then we are more likely to approve of devoting more resources to the prosecution of those accused of committing intentional killings.

For murder convictions, the criminal law requires not only that defendants committed a criminal act but also that they had a "criminal mind." To convict someone of murder under national criminal law prosecutors must prove that the accused intentionally committed the act. To convict someone of genocide under international criminal law should we require prosecutors to meet the same intent standard? Citing the extreme nature of the crime of genocide some international jurists advocate abolishing the intent requirement. For reasons set forth below, this would be a serious mistake. Stripping the element of intent from the crime of genocide would deflate the extreme moral condemnation that the crime of genocide warrants. However, if we keep the intent requirement for genocide, we can only do so if we accept a radically different sense of intent than the one used in national criminal law systems.

The idea of criminal intent should not mirror the sense of intent that is so central to national criminal law. In the latter, a murder conviction requires that the accused individual had intent to commit the crime. Cases of genocide involve more than one individual who commits the crime. It, then, might seem appropriate to require proof of intent for each one of these individuals. Yet, this move would seriously distort the nature of genocide. Genocide is not simply killings carried out by many individuals (see Chapter 3). Genocide is far more insidious than mass killing. It takes far more than the combined intents of a number of individuals to accomplish genocide. Genocide requires considerable organization. Individuals would be incapable of carrying out all of the coordination of resources and other activities needed to commit genocide. Individuals only could do these things if they operated within and through organizations and institutions. Acts of genocide involve institutions and organizations, typically governmental institutions and state organizations. To capture the underlying horror of the crime of genocide international criminal law needs to adopt a more institutionalized sense of intent, which we can label as *corporate intent*. As we shall see, this corporate sense of intent makes more sense when interpreted not as a state of mind but as an organizational policy.

When we interpret criminal intent as organizational policy, we resolve many of the oddities created by appropriating the idea of individual intent from national criminal law into international criminal law. Most importantly, if convictions for acts of genocide require prosecutors to prove individual intent, then prosecutors will have a difficult time separating the little fish from the big ones. A small town café owner who suddenly mutated into a militant Bosnian Serb (Tadić) should not have the same degree of criminal responsibility for the acts, however vicious, that he committed as should the leaders of the militant factions that directly encouraged and guided the commission of them (Karadžić). Otherwise, if prosecutors persistently and fully applied the idea of individual intent in these cases, then they would have to call for harsher punishment of the little fish than for the big fish as it is more difficult to establish individual intent for the big ones than for the little ones. In contrast, if prosecutors sought proof of corporate intent, then they would have to make the big fish the primary targets of their indictments.

Admittedly, the choice of corporate over individual intent also has disadvantages. It would lead to situations where prosecutors might let the little fish escape criminal responsibility entirely. In other words, the individuals closest to the criminal acts, that is, the little fish who actually carried out the horrifying deeds of slaughtering massive numbers of people, would most likely not face prosecution under international law. This dilemma warrants serious attention, which must await our proposals in Chapter 7. At this stage, suffice it to say, that we resolve the problem within the analysis of the appropriate punishments for the crime of genocide.

Given the broad scope of this study, a few confessions about the project's limitations might prove helpful. This study contains a highly select list of cases and incidents. This work is not a comprehensive survey of cases involving international law or of incidents of genocide. The study fits into a genre of normative legal analyses that crowd the literature on national criminal law but that have only slowly made their way into analyses of international criminal law. Further, we address only a piece of a much larger puzzle in this work. Intent is only one of the elements of the crime of genocide. To analyze intent we sometimes need to make claims about the other elements, which we cannot fully examine here.

FOLLOWERS, LEADERS, AND ORGANIZATIONS

> The Hague Tribunal spent much of 1996 and 1997 concerned with the trial of Duško Tadić, a sadistic freelance thug permitted to torture prisoners at Omarska camp, while the commanders and "intellectual authors" of the genocide remained impervious to its warrants for arrests.[3]

A Little Fish: The Tadić Case

Dusan Tadić, a failed art student, owned the Nipon café in Korarac, a town in northwestern Bosnia. He had little interest in Serbian politics, but after Muslims creditors called in his loans, he became a Serb nationalist and banned Muslims from his café. Tadić joined the Bosnian Serb forces after they took over the area. In the process of cleansing Muslims from the area, the Bosnian Serbs put many in detention centers like Omarska, and they killed many other Muslims. The first indictment against Tadić contained vivid descriptions of his barbaric acts.

> 5.1. About late June 1992, a group of Bosnian Serbs from outside the camp, including Dusan TADIC entered the large garage building known as the "hangar" and called prisoners out of their rooms by name. The prisoners were in different rooms and came out separately. The group of Serbs, including Dusan TADIC, severely beat the prisoners with various objects and kicked them on their heads and bodies. After Fikret Harambasic was beaten, two other prisoners, "G" and "H," were called out. A member of the group ordered "G" and "H" to lick Harambasic's buttocks and genitals and then to sexually mutilate Harambasic. "H" covered Harambasic's mouth to silence his screams and "G" bit off one of Harambasic's testicles. Harambasic died from the attack.[4]

Tadić, however, did not command, commit, or participate in these or any other acts in any official capacity. He never officially joined a Bosnian Serb or any other fighting unit. Witnesses described him as a free-lance thug, a little fish in a sea of ruthless sharks.[5]

A Big Fish: The Karadžić Case

Radovan Karadžić, a failed poet from Montenegro, received a medical degree from the University of Sarajevo. He became the team psychiatrist for various soccer teams. When Karadžić married a wealthy Serb psychiatrist, he "moved in with his new wife's family in an apartment building that housed eleven families—one Croat-Hungarian, five Muslim, four Serb, one Croat."[6] During the Bosnian conflict, Karadžić, as shown in the indictment below, held positions of power; unlike Tadić, he controlled a sea of little fish.

> 4. Radovan Karadžić became the first president of the Bosnian Serb administration in Pale on or about 13 May 1992. At the time he assumed this position, his *de jure* powers, as described in the constitution of the Bosnian Serb administration, included, but were not limited to, commanding the army on the Bosnian Serb administration in times of war and peace and having the authority to appoint, promote and discharge officers of the army.
>
> 17. Radovan Karadžić and Ratko Mladic, from April 1992, in the territory of the Republic of Bosnia and Herzegovina, by their acts and omissions, committed genocide.
>
> 18. Bosnian Muslim and Bosnian Croat civilians were persecuted on national, political, and religious grounds throughout the Republic of Bosnia and Herzegovina. Thousands of them were interned in detention facilities where they were subjected

> to widespread acts of physical and psychological abuse and to inhumane conditions. Detention facility personnel who ran and operated the Omarska, Keraterm and Luka detention facilities, among others, including, but not limited to Zeljko Meakic (Omarska)... intended to destroy Bosnian Muslim and Bosnian Croat people as national, ethnic, or religious groups and killed, seriously injured and deliberately inflicted upon them conditions intended to bring about their physical destruction.[7]

Tadić and Karadžić had radically different positions, and yet they stand accused of committing the same crime, namely, subjecting the Bosnian Muslims interned at the Omarska detention facility to abuse. Tadić's trial placed him at Omarska and found him guilty of specific acts while at Omarska. Karadžić probably never came near Omarska during the time Tadić carried out his despicable acts. Tadić, a café owner and traffic policeman, was not even a soldier. Did Tadić and Karadžić both intend to commit criminal acts?

To begin reassessing the idea of criminal intent in international law first we need to distinguish different types of intent (explicit and implicit). Then, we need to refute arguments to abandon the notion of intent in favor of some alternatives (willful killings and strict liability) as well as those arguments for alternative structural analyses.

TYPES OF INTENT

According to the 1948 Genocide Convention, genocide consists of "acts committed with *intent*." Similarly, the Articles of the ICC require that "The perpetrator *intended to* destroy, in whole or in part, that national, ethnical, racial or religious group, as such." The perpetrator must have the requisite special intent (*dolus specialis*), namely, intent to direct acts like mass killings at members of a particular group (see Chapter 6). An insistence on intent as a factor in genocide places genocide within the realm of reason, choice, and reflection. Genocide does not just happen; its occurrence stems from deliberate choices. Until we do some further analysis, let us accept the formulation "someone chooses to commit genocide."

Explicit Intent

The intent behind a chosen act could be explicit or implicit. We shall focus on explicit intent here and examine implicit intent in the next section. An explicit order to conduct mass killings would provide clear evidence of a perpetrator's intent. A recent demand for reparations by an African tribe has brought to light a case of explicit intent. In 1904, the Hereroes rebelled against German colonialism. In response, Lieutenant General von Trotha issued an extermination order (*Vernichtungsbefel*):

> Within the German borders, every Herero, whether armed or unarmed, with or without cattle, will be shot. I shall not accept any more women or children. I shall drive them back to their people—otherwise I shall order shots fired at them.[8]

In what is now the nation of Namibia in southeastern Africa, the Herero population diminished from 80,000 in 1904 to 15,000 in 1911. Later, another tribe, the Nama, also rebelled against the Germans and lost 50 percent of their population. However, the Germans did not issue a written extermination order for the Nama as Trotha did against the Herero.

Inferred Intent

History shows few examples of explicit intent in cases of mass killings. General von Trotha's order to exterminate the Herero provides a rare example of direct, explicit intent. Even the Nazi Fuehrer Adolf Hitler did not leave a "smoking gun." The distinguished historian Raul Hilberg admits, "Hitler himself may never have signed an order to kill the Jews."[9] In the absence of evidence of explicit orders, we must infer intent in the Nazi cases from the proceedings at the Wansee Conference and other acts taken on behalf of the Third Reich. On January 20, 1942, Reinhard Heydrich, Chief of Security Police and Security Services, convened a meeting of high-level officials at a mansion, formerly owned by a wealthy Jewish family, located in the Berlin suburb of Wansee, to discuss "The Final Solution of the Jewish Question in Europe." The leaders and bureaucrats did not draft a series of extermination orders against the Jews. Instead, when they spoke publicly, they used euphemistic codes for genocide—"evacuation of the Jews to the east," "final solution to the question of European Jewry." The euphemisms failed to disguise the regime's true intent.

> However carefully the document for Hitler might have been composed, with elliptical phrasing and with already familiar euphemisms, the tone and language probably would have conveyed the intent of destruction as the result of years of planning and preparation, as the outgrowth of cumulative experience.[10]

Hilberg captures how the intent underlying the act manifested itself through bureaucratic acts.

> In retrospect, it may be possible to view the entire design as a mosaic of small pieces, each commonplace and lusterless by itself. Yet, this progression of everyday activities, these file notes, memoranda, and telegrams, embedded in habit, routine, and tradition, were fashioned into a massive destruction process. Ordinary men were to perform extraordinary tasks. A phalanx of functionaries in public offices and private enterprises was reaching for the ultimate.[11]

In the Nazi case, a plethora of declarations and classifications contained in various documents provided the voluminous paper trail needed to infer intent to commit the crime of genocide. Each act, each bureaucratic maneuver filled in a small fragment of the large mosaic of intent. Heydrich's January 2, 1941 order, for example, classified all of the concentration camps, including a new Auschwitz II.[12] The German railroad even meticulously billed the Security Police for the one-way fare of the deportees for their journeys to the death camps.

THE INTENT REQUIREMENT

Abandoning Intent

1. *Willful Killings.* Analysts ask an important question. Why bother with proving intent in genocide cases? Critics of the intent requirement focus on the fact that history reveals few cases of explicit intent. They correctly note the rarity of cases of explicit intent such as Trotha's order to exterminate the Herero. Further, prosecutors complain that they find it difficult to prove intent. They point out that putting stringent demands on the proof of genocide makes it more unlikely that they can get convictions for the worst of all crimes. These concerns have led to proposals to abandon the intent requirement altogether. However, those who advocate discarding the intent requirement for genocide face two objections. First, the critics unintentionally slip the intent requirement back under a different name into their replacement formulations. Second, their alternative formulations raise more problems than they solve.

Israel Charny, a representative of the first "disguised substitution" group, applies the word "genocide" to,

> ...all situations where masses of human beings are led to their deaths at the willful hands of others for whatever intended and unintended reasons, and through whatever intentional or less intentional programs and means of destruction.[13]

Charny's analysis illustrates the difficulty one has separating the notion of intent from the concept of genocide. Despite Charny's best efforts, the idea of intent sneaks back into his definition of genocide. Charny uses the idea of willful to distinguish types of mass killings. However, the term "willful" simply serves as a disguise for the idea of intent. To counter this problem, Charny might opt to use "willful" in a way that excludes any idea of intent. Suppose that Charny interprets "willful" in a weak sense as "not forced by another" or as "accidental." Then, the genocide category becomes over-inclusive by including too many acts. Consider, for example, someone who non-coercively or accidentally leads a group of individuals to their deaths with the intent of saving them. Unfortunately, under Charny's proposal, the person's acts of leadership would qualify as acts of genocide. To avoid this result Charny must use "willful" to include some aspect of intent. Charny's proposal demonstrates the dangers of making the intent requirement too stringent. Intent, at least in the sense used in international law, does not require an explicit plan to carry out an act. Rather, the intent requirement demands, *inter alia*, that those in positions of responsibility should have foreseen the consequences of the act.

2. *Strict Liability.* We might take a more purist strategy than that taken by Charny and completely replace intent with the idea of strict liability. Strict liability advocates argue that given that genocide acts probably rank as the worst crimes imaginable, then the prosecution of its perpetrators should not be made more difficult by demanding proof of their intent. Whatever the benefits of holding perpetrators strictly liable for genocide, it would radically alter some basic legal distinctions.

The idea of strict liability applies most readily to civil wrongs and not to criminal wrongs like genocide. We might hold individuals and corporations strictly liable for engaging in ultra hazardous activities such as using dynamite in construction. At a Union Carbide pesticide factory in Bhopal, India, one of the worst industrial accidents in history occurred on December 23, 1984.[14] Tons of Methyl Isocyanate (MIC) escaped killing over four thousand and injuring tens of thousands.[15] Was Union Carbide negligent about the plant's safety or was MIC an inherently dangerous chemical that requires strict liability for manufacturers?

Whatever the answer might be, we can agree that the otherwise heavy hand of moral judgment (against, for example, the producers of MIC) remains relatively weak in strict liability cases. Strict liability policies shift the burden for the risks to the producers. A legal judgment against a construction company for causing injuries does not readily reflect moral judgments about the company. In genocide cases, prosecutors take on the dual tasks of establishing the legal *and* moral guilt of the accused. A strict liability regime would preclude carrying out the function of ascribing moral blame.

In contrast to civil law, three aspects of criminal law make it a particularly moral enterprise. First, the state and not an individual has ultimate responsibility for bringing criminal charges. The state indicts individuals, in part, in its capacity as representing the perceived moral judgments of society. Second, criminal law places emphasis on intent because it treats those accused of crimes as autonomous individuals capable of making independent choices; autonomous individuals make moral judgments for which they should be held accountable. Finally, consider the arguments for more severe punishments for criminal wrongs than for civil wrongs. The first step in the argument would be the claim that criminal wrongs are more than purely legal wrongs. As criminal wrongs violate basic moral principles, the criminal law can impose more severe punishment than civil and other types of law. Criminal prosecutions can take away not only the liberties of the accused but also the life of the accused.

A strict liability approach to genocide would seriously undermine these moral underpinnings of a criminal law approach. The actions taken by Unicol on its plant in Bhopal differ categorically from those taken by the Nazis in the concentration camps. A strict liability requirement for genocide would blur the distinction between these acts, and it would undermine the moral foundation of criminal law.

3. *A Case Study, Stalin's Famine*. The Soviet famine provides an excellent test case for the intent requirement as many historians label it as genocide. To determine whether the millions of Ukrainian peasant deaths in 1932 constituted genocide, we need to determine whether the Soviet dictator Joseph Stalin intended to carry out the killings. Malcolm Muggeridge, one of the few foreigners to report the devastating consequences of the famine in Soviet Union in 1932, recounted that,

> ...on one side, millions of starving peasants, their bodies often swollen from lack of food; on the other side, soldier members of OGPU (Stalin's secret police) carrying out the instructions of the dictatorship of the proletariat. They had gone

> over the country like a swarm of locusts and taken away everything edible; they had shot or exiled thousands of peasants, sometimes whole villages.[16]

Estimates of the famine deaths range from 4.5 million to 7.5 million, but everyone agrees that countless innocent people lost their lives. To analyze this case, we need to determine if Stalin (the perpetrator) intentionally inflicted these deaths.

Despite its overwhelming ferocity, *Stalin's October* still does not qualify as genocide. Admittedly, the atrocities resulted from deliberate decisions and not from accident. In Charny's words, Stalin acted willfully. Stalin's acts seem to include an element of intent. Indeed, the following assessment of Stalin's deeds seems plausible:

> The famine has variously been described as "organized", "administrative", "man-made". The man at the center of the causation was Stalin . . . Stalin's "October" was one of our violent century's most monstrous crimes against humanity.[17]

Nevertheless, the *mens rea* involved in the Soviet atrocities is not the same type of intent required for the crime of genocide. Millions of people died *not* because of Stalin's intent to destroy them but because of Stalin's disastrous economic policy of collectivization, including exporting grain and refusing foreign aid during the famine. The Soviets confiscated and exported millions of tons of grain produced by the peasants to earn foreign currency for industrialization. Further, the government refused to accept relief or even to acknowledge that the famine existed. People died because of state blunders, not because Stalin set out to eliminate a group of peasants, the so-called *kulaks* (see Chapter 6).

Stalin may have intentionally caused indiscriminate starvation, but neither he nor his regime intentionally perpetrated genocide. Western scholars increasingly have drawn attention to the horrors of Stalin's regime. Yet, even the most recent scholarly uncovering of Soviet sins fails "to locate a 'master plan' for what would be a vast economic experiment in repression—and—indeed argues that there probably was no such plan."[18] A famine can become a crime of genocide when a regime intentionally attempts to starve members of specific groups. However, a famine, such as this one in the Soviet Union, also can be entirely distinct from genocide. These non-genocide famines do not have the requisite intent (see Appendix C).

While the case of Stalin fails to meet the intent requirement for the crime of genocide, the case gives further insight into the nature of intent. We now see why the accusation that "someone intended to commit genocide" is misleading. The core sense of intent for the crime of genocide is not about a particular individual's mental state. Rather, it is about a state's or some other organization's policies. When we speak of General von Trotha or Stalin, we are not particularly concerned about their intent in the sense of their individual mental states. Both Trotha and Stalin as agents of the state issued orders. The General gave an extermination order; Stalin issued economic orders. Their orders were direct and explicit.

More often, however, mass atrocities occur because of indirect and implicit plans made, not simply by individuals, but within organizational state structures.

Replacing Intent

To show the inadequacies of thinking of criminal intent in terms of an individual's mental state let us consider a second attack on the intent requirement for genocide. Some commentators treat structurally caused genocide as more important than intentionally inflicted genocide. Their focus turns from the individual to the structural elements that gave rise to genocide and other mass atrocities. They want to know what causal factors produced Nazi Germany. Irving Horowitz defines genocide as "a structural and systematic destruction of innocent people by a state apparatus."[19] Violence, on these accounts, is systemic and not a consequence of individual intentional acts. William Eckhardt and Gernot Köhler characterize "structural violence" as "the violence created by social, political, and economic institutions and structures which may lead to as much death and harm to persons as does armed violence."[20]

On this view, structural violence has caused many more deaths than armed violence in the twentieth century.[21] The search for responsible individuals has unjustifiably overshadowed the far more devastating structural causes of violence. It becomes increasingly difficult to locate intentional actors in a bureaucratic world dominated by anonymous forces.[22] A structural analysis indicts an entire system. Tony Barta uses a structural approach to condemn Australian society for taking the lives of more than 20,000 Aboriginals.[23] Barta blames the capitalist system and exonerates individuals for atrocities committed against Australia's indigenous peoples.

The idea of structural violence directs attention to important, devastating, and often ignored non-intentional harms. A focus on structure offers a welcome corrective to analyses that look at social and other problems only in terms of individuals. Those who focus solely on accused individuals have an incomplete and distorted picture of crime. In contrast, a structural approach has clear advantages over an individually oriented perspective. It guides policy makers to poverty and other systemic features that underlie violent acts. Ideally, then, fundamental changes in the system would stem from an initial understanding of the root causes of crime. Presumably, structural approaches to genocide would have similar advantages. Knowledge of the basic causes of genocide would help prevent future ones.

The tasks of establishing individual responsibility and uncovering structural causes do not need to conflict. Even if we understand the root causes of a specific genocide, we still need to determine individual culpability for that genocide. Courts typically address the after effects of an event. When courts sentence and punish individuals, they fulfill this reactive function. Courts begin to perform their duties long after the actions they investigate have transpired. Moreover, courts commonly punish and seldom prevent these and subsequent actions. Even though courts typically do not take the initiative to affect future events, the preventive role for courts deserves further study.

Courts issue orders or injunctions requiring individual and organizations to do something or to stop doing something. California courts, for example, have upheld injunctions that forbid gang members from activities including using cell phones and congregating in groups.[24] In Rwanda, gangs that trained as militia carried out mass killing in 1994. It is certainly worth discussing the effects "gang injunctions" might have on stemming future killings and on chilling freedoms. Some types of courts use preventative devices. Constitutional courts, common in many European countries, may engage in anticipatory judicial review and take other forms of proactive action. Some constitutional courts have the power to overturn legislation in its draft form and to demand that the legislature pass alternative forms of legislation. The Constitutional Court of Hungary prevented its parliament from taking political revenge on former communists through retroactive punishment.[25] The Court also stopped the government from monopolizing the broadcast media by declaring a draft form of a statute unconstitutional. This last example has direct relevance to genocide issues. State control of hate propaganda, for example, helped to pave the way for genocide in Rwanda.

While courts may play a greater systemic role in shaping policy, their central task lies in determining individual guilt. At a basic level, then, the ideas of individual intent still seem in conflict with the idea of structural cause. Criminal intent applies primarily to individual agents, and structural causes, to society. The formation of the ICC offers opportunities to bring the ideas of individual and collective responsibility together in novel ways. In fact, the idea of structure proves critical to making sense of requiring some sense of intent for the crime of genocide. Genocide does not arise from the action of an individual in situations that allow for inferring intent independently before the acts took place.[26] In other words, genocide is not a series of intentional individual acts that add up to a higher level crime than murder. Genocide is not a collection of separate murders. The crime of genocide takes place within the context of organizational structures (see Chapter 7).

CORPORATE INTENT

For international humanitarian crimes, individual intent and collective structure merge in the following way. The intent element for genocide applies to individuals in their capacity within authoritative structures. The placement of intent within an authoritative structure moves the international crime of genocide away from the common understanding of crimes in national/state systems. States commonly sponsor relevant authoritative structures embedded within organizations. The idea of an authoritative structure helps to de-individualize the crime of genocide. In national criminal law, individuals have responsibility for murder in their capacities as individuals with a particular mental state. In international law, individuals should have responsibility for genocide in their capacities as leaders and members of organizations. Legal suits against organizations serve as a good analogue in state criminal systems. A suit against a corporation might include a named individual both in the person's individual capacity and in her or his role within the organization.

For the crime of genocide, the "perpetrator" must have the requisite *mens rea*, but this mental state differs from the mental state required for individual criminal responsibility in state criminal law systems. The *mens rea* for individual responsibility has a relatively direct connection to the criminal act. A national criminal court wants to determine whether the accused thought about the act. The *mens rea* for genocide has a less direct, more mediated connection to the criminal act. An international criminal court should focus on determining not just whether the accused thought about the criminal act but whether the accused planned or knowledgeably acted according to a preconceived plan developed within an (often state sponsored) organization.

The *mens rea* for genocide includes a knowledge test. The defendants must have had the requisite intent in the sense that they had or should have had knowledge of the alleged crime. The jurisprudence on intent for the crime of genocide has taken some odd turns on the knowledge issue. In *Akayesu*, the Tribunal for Rwanda made a questionable distinction between knowledge and intent. Supposedly, on the court's interpretation, individuals could know that their acts contributed to the destruction of a group and yet not have the intent or specific goal of destroying the group. The intent requirement for the crime of genocide goes beyond a determination of an individual's actual or imputed knowledge. Courts should assess the individual's knowledge according to how the individual functioned within an organizational structure. The structure consists of policies formulated according to procedures set forth in an organization. For example, presumptions about an individual's knowledge would vary according to the individual's formal and actual role in the organization.

Earlier we called this different kind of intent that underlies genocides *corporate intent* to distinguish it from individual criminal intent and other forms of intent. An alternative idea of *structural intent* proves inadequate for a number of reasons. The term "structure" in the phrase "structural violence" refers to causal factors found in society. Although the idea of structure meshes well with the emphasis on organizations, it does not adequately convey the necessary sense of agency. In fact, under some interpretations, use of the concept of structural intent would permit the complete abandonment of the ideas of agency and individual responsibility. Similarly, the concept of *collective intent* is too diffuse and does not capture the highly structured forms of organization at work in genocide cases (see Chapter 7).

Scholars should pay closer attention to how to make sense of intent in cases of crimes like genocide. The laws of genocide require intent for a conviction. The intent in question does not reduce to an individual intent or to the intent of a specified number of individuals. A determination of the intents of individual perpetrators, although relevant, does not determine the prosecution of individuals for the crime of genocide. A successful prosecution of an individual for the crime of genocide must prove the individual's complicity in the forming something more akin to a collective intent.

Corporate intent forms roughly in the following way. First consider that what makes a heinous act particularly reprehensible is when it stems from a well-formed but loathsome viewpoint and judgment about groups (see Chapter 5). This perception then begins to gel into an irrational disdain and completely unfounded hatred toward a group. The developing belief-system starts to combine with less spiteful but related past negative judgments about the targeted group. When isolated harmful acts against members of the targeted group begin to recur with increasing frequency, a corporate intent may start to become evident. At first, the perpetrators appear to act independent of an external direction. However, it soon becomes clear that state-sponsored organizations are fomenting, directing, and solidifying the focus and structure of this hate. This, admittedly sketchy and abstract analysis becomes clearer with examples woven into it. To summarize, we propose adopting the idea of corporate intent into international criminal law. The following case studies will demonstrate the advantages of this approach.

CASE STUDIES: THE BALKANS AND CENTRAL AFRICA

The Former Yugoslavia

Section 4 of Article 6(a) of the ICC captures the idea of organizational structure: "The conduct took place in the context of a manifest pattern of similar conduct directed against that group or was conduct that could itself effect such destruction." The key phrase is "manifest pattern," which translates as "plan." The Trial Chamber in *Jelisic* took an interpretive route similar to the one we propose. It admitted that the discussions and actions taken by the drafters of the Genocide Convention made it plausible to hold that proof of the existence of an organization or plan was not a necessary legal ingredient of the crime.[27] The Trial Chamber, however, observed, "that it will be very difficult in practice to provide proof of the genocidal intent of an individual if the crimes committed are not widespread and if the crime charged is not backed by an organization or a system."[28]

On appeal in *Jelisic*, the prosecution argued for interpreting the *mens rea* requirements as proof of the mental state of the accused. According to the prosecution's proposal,

> the accused has the required *mens rea* for genocide if: (i) he consciously desired that the committed acts to result in the destruction of whole or part of the group, as such; or (ii) he knew that his acts were destroying, in whole or part, the group, as such; or (iii) he, acting as an aider or abettor, commits acts knowing that the ongoing genocide which his acts form part of and that the likely consequence of his conduct would be to destroy, in whole or part, the group, as such.[29]

The prosecution in *Jelisic* tried to bring the Trial Chamber's focus on corporate intent back into the realm of individual intent. Fortunately, the Appeals Chamber rejected a reversion to individual intent.[30] Otherwise, if the crime of genocide required only an individual sense of intent, then the ICC would need to consider expanding its reach to include serial killers accused of genocide. Courts with jurisdiction over crimes of genocide, then, would accept cases of "one-man genocide missions." Courts, then, would focus more on the Tadićs of the world than on the Karadžićs.

Serial killers who intentionally carry out their deeds should not stand accused of the crime of genocide. The defendants in the following cases killed many people, but their killings did not involve any organizations. Since 1993, a single individual or a few individuals have murdered over 370 women, mostly prostitutes, in Ciudad Juarez, a Mexican border town.[31] On January 24, 1989, the State of Florida executed Theodore Bundy for the murder of three women.[32] Bundy confessed to murdering another twenty-eight, and authorities suspected that he had killed at least thirty-six more women. On December 6, 1989, the last day of classes before Christmas break, Marc Lépine murdered fourteen women at a Montreal engineering school (see Chapter 2). As horrific as these killings were they still would not qualify as acts of genocide.[33] The border-town killers, Ted Bundy, and Marc Lépine did not carry out their terror at the behest of any organization, particularly ones that promoted a killing plan or policy.

Courts can infer corporate intent if the prosecution cannot prove it directly. While the planners/perpetrators of mass killing seldom exhibit explicit manifestations of their intent through extermination orders as Trotha did, they often say and do things in similar ways to the Nazis that provide evidence of corporate intent. In these cases, a court, then, infers corporate intent from words and deeds that demonstrate "a pattern of purposeful action."[34] As the Ad Hoc Tribunal for the Former Yugoslavia stated,

> intent may be inferred from a certain number of facts, such as the general political doctrine which gave rise to the acts . . . , or the repetition of destructive and discriminatory acts. The intent may also be inferred from the perpetration of acts, which violate, or which the perpetrators themselves consider to violate, the very foundation of the group—acts which are not themselves covered by the list in Article 4(2) but which are committed as part of the same pattern of conduct.[35]

The inference of corporate intent or purposeful action involves historical judgments from a composite of factors, including the thoughts and deeds of individual actors within an authoritative organizational structure. Similar to their Nazi counterparts, the leaders in the Bosnian war—Karadžić, Milošević—did not leave any "smoking guns" in the form of explicit orders. Yet, courts could infer corporate intent from their concealment and complicity within a complex bureaucratic apparatus, their speeches and conferences, and from many other factors and events. The intent needed to prove the crime of genocide is not the mental state of an individual but rather the plans and policies of an authoritative organization, primarily the organization known as a state.[36] The concept of corporate intent clearly directs courts that deal with genocide cases away from "little fish" like Tadić and toward "big fish" like Karadžić and others who operate within and at the top of powerful state organizations.

King Leopold's Congo

A panel investigating the Rwanda genocide faulted scholars for not including the Congo on their list of twentieth-century genocides. The panel charged King Leopold II of Belgium for "the deaths of ten million people—fully half the entire population of the territory."[37] Adam Hochschild, author of *King Leopold's Ghost*, dismissed the genocide charge against King Leopold. Hochschild used the acts of the German commander von Trotha, a contemporary of King Leopold, as a comparison. Unlike the mass deaths in the Congo, the 1904 killings committed by Germany against the Hereroes in German South West Africa (Namibia, today)[38] resulted from an extermination order explicitly issued by General von Trotha.[39] In contrast, King Leopold, wanting to exploit the land's forced labor, never issued an order to eliminate members of any group in the Congo.

Hochschild concludes his analysis too abruptly. He should have anticipated a counter argument that no one explicitly ordered the Final Solution either. Contrary to Hochschild, the acts of King Leopold's regime, then, might not differ from those of the Nazi regime. However, a comparison of the corporate intents of Leopold and Hitler would enable Hochschild to distinguish the two cases (see Appendices C and D). Unlike the Nazis, there is no direct or indirect evidence of a corporate intent emerging within Leopold's regime to exterminate the indigenous population of the Congo.

The cases considered so far have involved the state in some way or another. In truth, King Leopold undertook his exploits in the Congo in his personal capacity and not as the King of Belgium. King Leopold did not turn over his personal control over the Congo Free State to Belgium until 1908. However, King Leopold's wealth, resources, and power intermingled with those of the state. Nevertheless, even if we correctly unveil the corporate intent at work in Leopold's Congo, it still seems difficult to demonstrate a connection between that corporate intent and the many Congolese deaths.

If we ignore complicating exceptional cases such as Leopold's Congo, corporate intent typically refers to the policies and plans of a state agent. Historically, state agents have carried out the worst cases of genocide. Individuals not connected with a state conceivably could carry out crimes of genocide. Mass killings might occur when state authority completely breaks down[40] or when an anti-state revolutionary group takes control of a country. These scenarios seem to challenge the idea of corporate intent as mass killings can occur outside of a governmental structure. However, the idea of corporate intent covers not only governmental structures but also any organizational ones. Genocide committed by non-state agents, then, would still qualify as actionable if the perpetrators acted within the bounds of an authoritative, organizational structure. Groups that form in opposition to (or outside the bounds of) a state generally have to operate within authoritative, organizational structures. Therefore, mass killings committed by non-state actors could still qualify as genocide. If no authority within an organizational structure directed the mass killing, then the acts may not qualify as genocide. The presence or absence of an authoritative organizational plan helps to determine whether an accused has the requisite *mens rea* for the crime of genocide.

The presence of an authoritative structure within an organization sheds light on the nature of violence. Generally, the most lethal and most devastating forms of violence occur because of state direction. The Third Reich directed the Holocaust. Government officials planned, coordinated, and implemented the genocide in Rwanda. Historically, states, the most dangerous form of organization, have been the most active agents of violence. It is difficult to imagine the mass killings on the scale of genocide taking place in the absence of an organization's direction and coordination. Only states, with their legitimated monopolies on violence, possess the power and resources needed to kill vast numbers of people over a sustained period.[41]

Further, the term "genocide" refers to a planned killing and not to a spontaneous form of group killings. Genocide does not spring spontaneously from the inner fears and deep-seated prejudices of individuals. Typically, further investigation into particular cases of reputed genocide uncovers authoritative organizational structures behind some seemingly spontaneous acts. When Western political leaders first looked at Rwanda in 1994, they saw enraged mobs savagely mutilating their neighbors without any direction and under no authority. However, a more careful look has since revealed that organizations, with close ties to the Rwandan government, instigated and carried out the genocide. In future cases, then, we should expect to find the state implicated in genocide.

The concept of corporate intent also underscores a distinction between discriminate and indiscriminate forms of killing. Although instances of genocide might appear highly irrational, they constitute a highly discriminate form of killing. The explicit grounds for those discriminations sometimes hide within bureaucratic structures that include state-sponsored rules, edicts, and proclamations. Acts of genocide do not occur randomly, accidentally, or indiscriminately. Perpetrators identify targeted groups in often-perverse ways, using state mechanisms, including the legal apparatus, to target these groups (see Chapter 6). Then, the killers use state resources, such as the state-sponsored radio in Rwanda, to attack members of a group. Acts of violence committed by individuals like Marc Lépine are horrific, but even the worst case of mass murder in Canadian history pales in comparison to the violence unleashed by states. To understand violence and mass killings, we need to see the links between genocide and the state. Perhaps, indiscriminate mass killings take place without implicating any state or comparable authoritative apparatus. However, once again, let us be wary of describing these acts as instances of purely random killings. As the example from Burundi described below illustrates, we should constantly look for the state directing, sanctioning, and implementing mass killings even when it appears to be absent.

Central Africa

In 1988, the Hutus, constituting a majority of about 85 percent of the population of Burundi, struck out in "blind rage" against all Tutsis, whose members controlled the government.[42] These seemingly spontaneous events led to retributions from the Tutsi-led armed forces. The retaliatory forces selected unarmed Hutus, including babies and children, for execution "simply because they and their parents were Hutu and lived in an area in which members of the Hutu community had attacked and killed Tutsi."[43] Under the analysis proposed here, the Tutsi action, sanctioned by the Burundi government, might qualify as genocide. In turn, the Hutu "spontaneous outburst of rage, triggered by the provocation of a local Tutsi personality and fueled by rumors of an impending massacre of Hutu peasants"[44] would not qualify as genocide *if* the Hutu response did not arise from any directed, organized authoritative structure. While the case is too complicated to examine fully here, it would be important to investigate it more closely to determine whether any non-state organization directed the Hutus to commit the atrocities. It is sobering to acknowledge that in Rwanda the atrocities committed in 1994 also first appeared to be spontaneous acts fueled by rumors. However, closer investigations of the Rwandan case exposed a well-organized incitement of genocide generated through state-supported structures including a hate-propagating radio station (see Chapter 7).

In Rwanda, from April 6 to July 26, 1994, Hutu militants massacred 800,000, mostly Tutsis, children, women, and men. The international community received ample warning signs of genocide. In 1990, President Habyarimana began to support the *Interahamwe*, an armed militia that later carried out systematic massacres of Tutsis. Rwanda's radio stations played instrumental roles in promoting hatred against Tutsis. Previous massacres of Tutsi occurred in October 1990, January 1991, February 1991, March 1992, August 1992, January 1993, March 1993, and February 1994.[45] During this civil war period, some non-governmental organizations (NGOs) labeled these episodic killings of Tutsis as genocide. The NGOs mistakenly equated civilian war deaths with genocide. "The linking of the deaths of only hundreds to the terms apocalypse and genocide throughout the civil war period diminished their impact as warnings" of an impending genocide.[46] Later investigators refused to use the label *genocide* to classify these massacres, but they saw the earlier mass killings as providing clear evidence of a pattern that should have served as warning signs of genocide. An Organization for African Unity investigation panel concluded, "it becomes difficult to avoid seeing a pattern emerging through successive slaughters."[47] The panel further noted that the massacres marked an abrupt change since before the massacres of the early 1990s "the Tutsi had not been singled out for abuse by the government for some 17 years."[48]

Perpetrators seldom explicitly and publicly express their intent to commit genocide. For the Nazis' Holocaust as well as "for the Rwandan genocide, there is no smoking gun."[49] Instead, the intent lies within an intricate network of many seemingly unrelated details. Numerous bureaucratic directives support the presence of corporate intent in Rwanda. The UN Commission of Experts found "overwhelming evidence to prove that the acts of genocide against the Tutsi ethnic group were committed by Hutu elements in a concerted, planned, systematic and methodical way."[50] The report's findings marked the first time since adopting the 1948 Genocide Convention that the United Nations had identified an instance of genocide. The evidence further showed that the government organized the genocide. It takes an incredible mobilization at the state level to carry out the scale of mass killings for over one hundred days in Rwanda.

Yet, the international community refused to recognize the corporate intent behind the genocide in Rwanda. World leaders failed to acknowledge evidence of "a concerted, planned, systematic" attempt to exterminate the Tutsis. On April 29, 1994, UN Secretary-General Boutros-Ghali described the situation as "Hutus killing Tutsis and Tutsis killing Hutus."[51] In May 1994, the United States pressured the United Nations to replace the word "genocide" in a resolution on Rwanda with the phrase "systematic, widespread and flagrant violations of humanitarian law," that is, human rights abuses. On June 10, 1994, the State Department's spokeswoman, Christine Shelly, assessed the on-going atrocities in Rwanda: "Although there have been acts of genocide in Rwanda, all the murders cannot be put in that category."[52] On June 14, 1994, the US Ambassador to Rwanda, David Rawson, described the situation as one of brother against brother, "Cain and Abel all over again."[53] Apologizing for this misguided assessment of the situation in Rwanda, as former president of the United States Bill Clinton and former secretary general of the United Nations Kofi Annan have done, does not address the assumptions political leaders used in formulating the wrongheaded policies. Recognition of the corporate nature of genocide intent would mark a first step in correcting these policies in the future.

CONCLUSION

The closer an accused such as Tadić is to the act, the more the intent begins to resemble the intent for individual criminal responsibility in state law. In *Delalic*, the defense argued that the ICTY had jurisdiction over only "the most heinous atrocities" and not over crimes committed by those without political or military authority.[54] The Trial Chamber found that the tribunal had jurisdiction over the executioners as well as the planners, the little fish and the big fish. Certainly, courts should reject the executioner's defense; they should not dismiss charges against an accused because the accused only committed the heinous act and did not plan the annihilations. Nevertheless, a problem posed by the executioner's defense remains. If tribunals give priority to prosecuting the planners, then many executioners go free. The concept of corporate intent provides a consistent way to begin to encompass little fish like Tadić and big fish like Karadžić within a single, coherent framework. A construction of that framework must await Chapter 7 on organizational responsibility for its completion.

Chapter 5

Genocide Motive: Institutionalized Hatred

> Article 6 (a) Genocide by killing
> Elements
> 1. The perpetrator killed one or more persons.
> 2. Such person or persons belonged to a particular national, ethnical [ethnic], racial or religious group.
> 3. The perpetrator intended to destroy, in whole or in part, that national, ethnical [ethnic], racial or religious group, As such.
> 4. **The conduct took place in the context of a manifest pattern of similar conduct directed against that group** or was conduct that could itself effect such destruction.
>
> —Rome Statute of the International Criminal Court

> On the night of January 22, 1941, the Legionnaires of the Archangel Michael—after singing Orthodox hymns, putting packets of Romanian soil around their necks, drinking each other's blood, and anointing themselves with holy water—abducted 20 men, women, and children from their homes. The Legionnaires packed the victims into trucks and drove them to the municipal slaughterhouse. ... They made the victims, all Jews, strip naked in the freezing dark and get down on all fours on the conveyor ramp. Whining in terror, the Jews were driven through all the automated stages of slaughter. Blood gushing from decapitated and limbless torsos, the Legionnaires thrust each on a hook and stamped it: "fit for human consumption." The trunk of a five-year-old girl they hung upside down, "smeared with blood... like a calf."[1]

Descriptions of any grave injustice sicken the stomach. What could possibly lead individuals to commit heinous acts of barbarity? How could humans hate other humans so much that they commit genocide and other odious acts?

The law generally does not feature the hate element of a crime. The controversy over hate enhancement penalties shows that it takes special efforts to get the law to focus on the hate aspects of a crime. The murderous vendetta against fourteen Canadian women carried out by Marc Lépine, who executed them at the University of Montreal in 1989, was unusual only in the sense that the hateful actions stemmed from a single individual (see Chapter 2). Women have long been the victims of violence engendered by hate against women. Numerous efforts to amend federal hate-crime prevention legislation have failed to add sexual orientation, gender, and disability to the list of hate motives. Narratives of survivors and others, perhaps better than any other form of representation, capture the venomous form of hate at work in murder and genocide. The laws governing violence have not kept pace with the narrative accounts in capturing the hate elements of the crimes. Surprisingly, the hate motive also has not played a prominent role in the development of the laws of genocide.

The concept of motive captures some of the hate aspects of a crime. Two individuals accused of murder may have two different motives. One person may have killed for money while the other one killed for hate. Motive differs from intent in that the former refers to the underlying reason for the act whereas the latter refers to a type of mental state. In general, the criminal law concentrates on intent (and, of course, the act) and does not give central importance to motive. In national criminal law systems, if an individual did the requisite act with the requisite intent, the individual stands guilty of the crime, for example, of murder. Although motive sometimes enters into the determination of guilt, the motive underlying the crime generally receives consideration only at the sentencing phase.[2] A court might consider the motive of bias in a so-called hate crime in determining a convicted murderer's punishment.

The hate element fares slightly better in international criminal law than it does in national law. Courts that have considered genocide and other cases of grave injustices seem to address the motives behind these crimes. We use the phrase "seem to address" because international law (especially the codes and cases on genocide) has not directly embraced and explicitly required the motive element. In this chapter, we shall build a case for the importance of the motive element for the crime of genocide. The despicable and loathsome nature of the motive gives, in part, the crime of genocide its distinctiveness. Absent a focus on motive in genocide cases, courts would inadvertently overlook a crucial feature of the crime of genocide.

However, the idea of motive as applied in national criminal law differs radically from the concept of motive that we propose for international criminal law. Jurists too quickly transfer concepts such as intent and motive from national criminal law into international criminal law without making critical modifications in those concepts (see Chapter 4). It only would distort reality to search for a genocide motive analogous to an individual motive involved in murder. What makes genocide particularly heinous is not that many individuals adopted a hateful attitude or that a demonic leader unleashed hateful fury on the world. Rather, the insidiousness of genocide lies in the fact that a society decayed to a point where hatred bred within its basic structures and institutions. A careful look at a case considered by the Ad Hoc War Crimes Tribunal for the Former Yugoslavia will demonstrate the importance of the motive element in genocide cases and will show that the motive element of genocide consists of institutionalized forms of hatred. Again, before proceeding, we must issue a notice that we offer prescriptions for and not exhaustive descriptions of the motive element.

GENOCIDE AND PERSECUTION: THE *JELISIC* CASE

The indictment before the International Tribunal for the Former Yugoslavia (ICTY) charged Goran Jelisic with the crime of genocide.

> In May 1992, Goran Jelisic, intending to destroy a substantial or significant part of the Bosnian Muslim people as a national, ethnical or religious group, systematically killed Muslim detainees at the Laser Bus Co., the Brcko police station and Luka camp. He introduced himself as the "Serb Adolf," said that he had come to Brcko to kill Muslims, and often informed the Muslim detainees and others of the numbers of Muslims he had killed. In addition to killing countless detainees, whose identities are unknown, Goran Jelisic personally killed the victims. By these actions, Goran Jelisic committed or aided and abetted.

The Ad Hoc War Crimes Tribunal for the Former Yugoslavia found Jelisic not guilty of genocide as he did not have the requisite special intent (or motive?) to exterminate a group. This finding may seem odd given that the court admitted that the prosecution had proved that Jelisic chose his victims because they belonged to a specific group. The court agreed that Jelisic had targeted Muslims. Further, the court accepted the evidence that Jelisic had demonstrated his hatred toward Muslims as a group through his vile words (calling them *balijas* or "Turks") and discriminatory actions (forcing them to sing Serbian songs). Jelisic had even presented himself as the new Hitler. Finally, Jelisic matched threatening words with ultimate deeds by killing countless Muslims. Jelisic's manifest hatred and his killings of Muslims would seem to make Jelisic an ideal candidate for genocide conviction. However, the court found these factors insufficient. It demanded proof of further elements to make the charge of genocide stick. The court noted, in particular, that the prosecution failed to place Jelisic within the chain of command. Jelisic's pretending to have authority (apparent authority) did not give him real authority (particularly, in the sense that his authority did not derive from an organization; see Chapters 3 and 7). Why did the court give so much importance to Jelisic's lack of place in the chain of command?

The court held that inconsistencies in Jelisic's acts demonstrated that Jelisic lacked something called "special intent." This, we submit, is another way of saying that Jelisic lacked the requisite motive. In support of its position, the court cited the fact that although Jelisic had targeted Muslims for slaughter, he also had released some Muslims while singling out some non-Muslims for death. The court granted that Jelisic's actions revealed an intentional plan as the evidence showed that Jelisic intended to kill Muslims. The court ruled that an intentional plan was not enough for a genocide conviction. The accused needed to have a special intent, that is, intent to exterminate a group. To underscore its interpretation, the court drew a distinction between the crimes of genocide and persecution. "Genocide, therefore, differs from the crime of persecution in which the perpetrator chooses his victims because they belong to a specific community but does not necessarily seek to destroy the community as such."[3] However, it is not, as the court seems to think, that Jelisic's individual "killing-plan" did not have the elements of an extermination program. Even if Jelisic did have his own extermination plan, his plan would not have been part of a broader organizational extermination plan. In short, Jelisic still would have lacked the requisite motive for the crime of genocide.

The type of motive involved in genocide cases differs radically from the type of motive found in discussions of murder cases. In genocide cases, courts need to see the motive element (like its counterpart, the intent elements, see Chapter 4) as an aspect of society and its organization and not as part of an individual and his mind. The structural forms of hatred that feed genocide lie deeply embedded in social behavior and government policies. Certainly, Jelisic did not have a pure, unbiased motive for his acts. Nevertheless, his motive did not reach the level of a genocide motive as his motive did not form part of, in this case, a government's policies and plans of hate. Therefore, Jelisic lacked the requisite motive. Jelisic's hatred was not a hatred that was part of a social policy of hatred, a hatred so deep and horrifying that it promoted the annihilation of a group.

The *Jelisic* trial court astutely underscored the distinction between intent and motive.[4] The Appeals Chamber accepted this distinction between intent and motive, but, then, unfortunately, it quickly dismissed the idea of motive on grounds of its inscrutability. The Appeals Chamber reflects the dominant (and, we submit, legally incorrect) position. The Trial Chamber's interpretation fits the original intent of those who codified the law better than the Appeals Chamber's analysis. While the laws of genocide do not mention motives explicitly and international tribunals generally have glossed over the motive element, the drafters of the 1948 Genocide Convention thought that they had included motive. In the first draft by the Ad Hoc Committee, "a Venezuela amendment, eventually adopted, substituted the phrase 'as such' for [a] specific listing of motives."[5] The Genocide Convention delegates agreed that an enumeration of motives in the code would unfairly help defenders who could always claim to have committed their acts for other motives than those listed in the law. The ICC criminal code retained the "as such" language: "The perpetrator intended to destroy, in whole or in part, that national, ethnical, racial or religious group, *as such* (italics added)." Therefore, the courts should return to the original intent of the law's drafters and see motive as an essential element of the crime of genocide. For the crime of genocide, international criminal law clearly needs motive as the third key factor to add to the other two factors of act and intent.

NATURE OF HATRED

Motive provides a link between the intent directed against the group and action inflicted upon the targeted group. It would not be enough to find evidence of the intent and evidence of harmful acts against a group. For a conviction for the crime of genocide, harm to individual group members must come about *because of* an individual's purported group affiliation. Evidence of the killing of group members and evidence of plans about a group will not suffice in isolation from each other. Whether a situation warrants the label genocide depends upon strong evidence that the harms came about primarily because of the group's status.

One explanation for why motive has become an obvious but overlooked additional element is that analyses of genocide presume the presence of a hate motive. For example, the description "an intent to exterminate a group" sounds ominous because a motive-type is readily apparent from the description. In the next chapter (Chapter 6), we shall see how we also presume to know the targeted group types. For anyone with even a rudimentary understanding of Nazi Germany the hate-based motive underlying the Holocaust seems apparent. We assume that those who intentionally try to annihilate whole groups of people have loathsome motives. According to this view, the Nazis carried out their plan for annihilation because of their deep-seated hatred of Jews. Thus, the motive element captures a crucial and often presumed characteristic of genocide. The venomous nature of genocide, on this interpretation, lies not only in the intentional mass slaughter of individuals but also in the reprehensible, hate-based reasons used to initiate, perpetuate, and justify those killings.

When we combine genocide's intentional acts with the reason or motive for the acts, we begin to see another aspect of genocide's distinctiveness. Perpetrators commit genocide for an especially loathsome reason. They engage in mass killings to exterminate part or all of a group. No other crime requires a motive of this magnitude. A peculiar form of hate directs perpetrators toward fulfilling their goals of annihilation. In instances of genocide, individuals become objects of hate because of their group status. Genocide involves mass killing *because of* group hatred. It would be misleading to think of the hate involved in genocide as highly negative perceptions and attitudes that the perpetrators had toward a targeted group. Those who later become perpetrators of genocide sometimes start their journey of hate by first adopting negative opinions about a particular group. However, the hate involved in genocide goes far deeper than this. For one thing, discriminatory attitudes and actions do not always foretell a future genocide (see this chapter, the section on case studies).

Discriminatory attitudes held largely by individuals take on an entirely different form when they become sanctioned, reinforced, and promoted by organizations, particularly by state organizations. Again, let us turn to the case of the 1933 Soviet famine. Here, the Soviet case illustrates differences between individual attitudes and state policies. Some Soviet leaders definitely had highly negative attitudes toward a group of peasants called *kulaks*. Lenin's 1918 highly derogatory proclamation about the *kulaks* clearly gave public vent to the state's animosity toward them. Still, the Soviet state's animosity toward *kulaks*, especially before Stalin's regime, hardly rose to the level of genocidal hatred. First, Soviet leaders expressed a variety of views about the *kulaks*. The moderate Bukharin, for example, recommended alliances with the *kulaks*. Second, before Stalin, the government did not institute any action based on a negative attitude toward them. When governmentally reinforced discriminatory attitudes become governmentally enforced policies—as they eventually did under Stalin, then we have the makings of a genocide motive. While this adds the motive factor to the charge of genocide against Stalin, it does not alter the assessment that the 1933 Soviet famine does not qualify as genocide because Stalin's regime lacked the requisite corporate intent (see Chapter 4).

We need to recognize that genocide forms of hatred go deeper than negative attitudes or animosity. The hatred unleashed in genocide goes far beyond a dislike or disdain for a particular group. A highly negative attitude and discriminatory action toward a group generally implies that the members of the group have human status. Those targeted in genocide often do not even have human status. Perpetrators typically use subhuman labels such as vermin to classify their targets. Perpetrators of genocide view their victims as less than human. Sometimes, the loathing goes, in some sense, beyond hatred. Certain groups sink beneath the human level, and thereby, become hardly worth hating in any traditional sense. According to some interpretations, the Nazis had such a low regard for the Gypsies (Roma) that they saw them as subhumans who were unworthy of their contempt. Jews, of course, did not even register on the human scale for the Nazis.

Therefore, motives underlying the crime of genocide go far beyond individual discriminatory attitudes. In fact, hatred may not be the best word to use as a genocide motive is more like a judgment than an attitude. In genocide cases, a powerful organization makes a collective judgment that a group has no moral worth and sets out to act upon that categorical determination. These organizations further foment and entrench the hatred toward a group a hatred that lies deeply intertwined within the fabric of a society. These organizations amass considerable power, generally as part of the state or in close association with the state. Next, let us see how this institutionalized form of hate takes root.

CASE STUDIES: JEWS, BOSNIANS, ALBANIANS, AND TUTSIS

Groups vulnerable to genocide experience different types of harms and different degrees of harms within each type (See Appendices C and D). Following Raul Hilberg's analysis in his seminal study *The Destruction of the European Jews*, the Nazis' assault on the Jews fell into three distinct phases: *designation*, *discrimination*, and *brutalization*.[6] At each stage, the Nazis embedded hatred toward the Jews deeper and deeper into the structure of German society. Recent cases from the Balkans and Central Africa seem to provide examples of the phases—designation, discrimination, and brutalization. Yet, comparisons of the plight of the Bosnian Muslims, Albanian Kosovars, and Rwandan Tutsis show that the groups do not move through the phases in the same order (see Appendix D). Although the authorities singled out the Albanians and put them through a long period of discrimination, the Albanian Kosovars suffered, contrary to all expectations, relatively little when the war broke out. In contrast, the Bosnian Muslims experienced considerable brutality when their war erupted despite having faced little prior harm either from being classified as Bosnian Muslims or from government policies. Of these groups, only the Rwandan Tutsis traveled a path to brutality in a manner similar to the European Jews.

However, more importantly for this study, the cases examined here demonstrate how the motive element that underlies genocide starts, implants, and grows. Groups devalued by the official classifications solidify their group identities to protect group members from external forces aligning against their interests. "The need for ethnic solidarity arises only when strange, threatening, competitive outsiders must be confronted."[7] The strength and longevity of these defensive postures by vulnerable groups provides a rough measure of how deeply hatred has become institutionalized.

In hindsight, we know that a classification as a Jew by the Nazis meant almost certain death. Official classifications in the former Yugoslavia did not show early signs of similar manifest hatreds. History shows that some official classifications were more negative than other ones. As shown below, Bosnian Muslims had far fewer complaints than did the Albanian Kosovars under each change in their classifications in the former Yugoslavia's constitutions. The Albanians consistently found themselves burdened with a lower political status than their Bosnian counterparts. In sharp contrast, almost every official classification of the groups in Rwanda stemmed from widespread prejudice against the groups.

The different degrees and types of brutality experienced by the groups also give measures of how strong the hate motive has become. Genocide killings arise in part from a hatred that devours the foundation of a society whereas relatively less animosity lies beneath ethnic cleansing (forced removal). Some analysts place the case of Bosnian Muslims in the first genocide category and Albanian Kosovars in the second one. Even if we shy away from this controversial thesis, we can safely say that the attacks on the Bosnian Muslims showed greater animosity than those launched against the Albanian Kosovars. For example, Bosnian Serbs engaged in systematic rapes of Bosnian women to obliterate Muslim offspring from the land. The Albanian Kosovars did not experience the extent and depth of this type of viciousness. Moreover, no matter what we conclude about groups in the Balkans, no one would deny the almost unprecedented hostilities that the Hutus perpetrated on the Tutsis in Rwanda. The point of all these unpleasant and sometimes bizarre comparisons (summarized in Appendix D) is to use them to make the case that international criminal law should incorporate a motive element in its future prosecutions of genocide.

Phase 1, Group Designations

1. *European Jews*. The development of anti-Semitism in Nazi Germany sped through Hilberg's three stages. Hilberg described the overall "inherent pattern"

of this Nazi "machinery of destruction": "no group can be killed without a concentration or seizure of the victims, and no victims can be segregated before the perpetrator knows who belongs to the group."[8] The first phase of embedding hatred occurs in the process of officially defining or designating a group. The destructive paths paved by the state bricks of hatred begin with a seemingly innocuous road sign found at the highway's entrance. "When in the early days of 1933 the first civil servant wrote the first definition of 'non-Aryan' into a civil service ordinance, the fate of European Jewry was sealed."[9] If the history of anti-Semitism provides a model, then the signs of officially sanctioned animosities toward a group occur when the state denies (discrimination phase) social goods (employment, education) to those it previously classified as a lesser group (designation phase). The institutionalization of hatred under the Third Reich began when the Nazis began classifying individuals as Jews.

Group identities often solidify defensively when hatred begins to take shape as an official policy. Many individuals recount that they felt little or no identity with a group before the group became a target of hostility. Powerful groups like the Nazis who attack other groups find ways to identify those group members as Jews or whatever even if their criteria for identification make little sense (see Chapter 6). The Nazis classified some individuals as Jews who had no past self-identification as Jews; they refused to identify other individuals as Jews even if they had a history of self-identification as Jews; and they failed even to consider the possibility that some individuals who did not fit their criteria might have been practicing, religious Jews. Some Holocaust survivors later admitted that they had little or no self-conscious identity as Jews until the Nazis implemented their bizarre classification scheme.

2. *Bosnian Muslims*. Constitutional law helped to mold group identities throughout the relatively brief history of the former Yugoslavia. The 1946 Constitution used a three-tiered classification system of group types. Federal Yugoslavia had three types of citizens: "nations" or *narodi* (Serb, Croat, Slovene, Macedonian, Montenegrin, and Muslim), "nationalities" or *narodnosti* (those with "national homes" outside Yugoslavia such as the Albanians), and "other nationalities and ethnic minorities" (Jews, Yugoslavs). The 1946 Constitution recognized Serbs, Croats, Slovenes, Montenegrins, and Macedonians as nations, but it did not recognize Bosnian Muslims as a nation or nationality. Bosnian Muslims did not attain formal recognition as a *narodnosti* or nationality until passage of the 1963 Constitution. The 1974 Constitution reflected an improvement in their status by designating them as a *narodi* or nation, that is, Muslims who had a national home in the republic of Bosnia-Herzegovina. Therefore, it was not until 1974 that Bosnia-Herzegovina became one of the country's six republics. Yet, despite these identity setbacks, the history of the former Yugoslavia reveals little evidence of official sanctioning of any latent hostilities against Bosnian Muslims that might have existed in its society.

3. *Albanian Kosovars*. The case of the Albanian Kosovars differs in important ways from that of the Bosnian Muslims. A history of constitutional design again

sets the overall context, and geography sets the stage. Two regions—Vojvodina and Kosovo—border the Republic of Serbia. The 1946 Constitution designated the Vojvodina region, with its majority Hungarian population, as an Autonomous Province. The Constitution reserved a clearly lower designation (Autonomous Region, in contrast to an Autonomous Province) for Kosovo. Kosovo, unlike Vojvodina with its higher status, did not have an independent legislature or a supreme court. The 1963 Constitution upgraded Kosovo to the same status as Vojvodina but with a twist; the new constitution decreased the powers of all the autonomous provinces including Kosovo and Vojvodina. Thus, Kosovo finally achieved a higher status but at the cost of fewer powers. With the 1974 Constitution, Kosovo became a full constitutive member of the Yugoslav Federation as one of eight federal units. However, unlike the Muslims of Bosnia who by that time had attained nation status (*narodi*), the Albanian Kosovars remained in the lower category, a nationality (*narodnosti*). Albanians remained second-class citizens (a nationality) "despite their numerical superiority over less numerous Slav nations of Yugoslavia, which did have their own republic within the federation."[10] In summary, we see hostilities toward the Albanians becoming much more entrenched through official classifications than any animosity toward the Bosnians.

4. *Rwandan Tutsis*. One does not have to search far through the classification schemes of the colonialists in Rwanda to find evidence of harsh judgments about Hutus and Tutsis. The Germans had a far more favorable impression of the Tutsis than they did of the Hutus. Rwanda's Belgian rulers, who inherited Rwanda after Germany's defeat in World War I, at first, also favored the Tutsis. Then, in 1962, just before the granting of independence to Rwanda, Belgium, in response to the increasing militant demands from the Tutsis, reversed their policies and helped the Hutus attain power. Official identity cards, first introduced by Belgium in 1926, became a badge of inferiority for Tutsis when the Hutus took power after independence.[11] The Rwandan case shows how quickly a positive group designation can turn into a negative one.

Phase 2, Group Discrimination

1. *European Jews*. Throughout the 1930s, the Nazis introduced legislation that clearly discriminated against Jews. First, in 1933, Nazi laws excluded Jews from receiving retirement funds for their public service. They also prohibited Jews from entering the legal profession and limited the number of Jews attending universities. The 1935 Nuremberg laws prohibited marital and extramarital relations between Jews and Germans and forbade Jews to work as pharmacists. The 1938 laws excluded Jews from practicing law or medicine. The expulsion decrees of 1939–1941 marked a new phase of policies of hate. The deportation orders that followed represented a short prelude to death camps. Each new law further embedded hatred toward Jews into official policy.

2. *Bosnian Muslims*. Bosnian Muslims experienced comparatively little discrimination before the brutalization against them erupted. Despite portrayals to the contrary, "Bosnian Islamic identity has historically been moderate. . . ."[12] Although incidents of prejudice against Bosnian Muslims as Slavs who had converted to Islam under Ottoman rule occurred, the discrimination remained relatively mild and isolated. Most importantly, the discrimination did not take on institutionalized forms nor did it become legally sanctioned. As a group, Bosnian Muslims bypassed much of the discrimination phase and moved quickly through the designation to the brutalization phase. For the most part, the various classifications of Bosnian Muslims by Yugoslavian officials show little evidence of deep-seated hatred toward Bosnians being put into official policy. Circumstances changed abruptly in the 1990s. Only as the Yugoslavia state began to implode did the label *Bosnian Muslim* became a badge that signaled potential horror to those stuck with the label. The dynamics of group formation followed a different trajectory for the Albanian Kosovars.

3. *Albanian Kosovars*. The Albanian Kosovars, unlike the Bosnian Muslims, can point to a period of severe discrimination from roughly the 1980s through the 1990s. In reaction to a series of Albanian riots throughout the 1980s, neighboring Serbia increased its repression of the Albanians. Elections, boycotted by the Albanians, became part of this repression. In one farcical election, a political figure known as "Arkan" became a representative of a Kosovo constituency in Serbia's assembly. After the election, Arkan proposed that the government should treat the 1.5 million Albanians, whom he claimed had emigrated from Albania to Kosovo, as tourists with temporary visas.[13] Later, authorities singled out Arkan and his paramilitary organization as being responsible for some of the more horrifying atrocities committed against Bosnian Muslims.

Serbia's repressive actions led the Albanian Kosovars to form an underground government and society—a clear manifestation of a defensive group formation. Over 18,000 Albanian teachers taught 335,000 students in an unofficial education system that included fully functioning law and medical schools. Thus, having in some sense solidified their identity earlier than the Bosnian Muslims, the Albanians under the nonviolent leadership of Ibrahim Rugova established an underground parallel state. The US State Department and Amnesty International documented the severe and widespread human rights abuses carried out against Albanians during this period. By 1996, the severity of the discrimination against Albanians in Kosovo reached apartheid levels. It is difficult to defend the legitimacy of any state that keeps a majority of its population so oppressed that they become noncitizens. The severe apartheid policies forced on the Albanian Kosovars were worse than any policies directed at the Bosnian Muslims over the same period.

4. *Rwandan Tutsis*. Rwandan independence ushered in varying waves of discrimination against the Tutsi minority under two Hutu-led regimes. The system put into place in the First Republic (1961–1975) under Gregoire Kayibanda (president until a 1973 coup) functioned as an apartheid system placing quotas

on Tutsis in education and government jobs. Unlike the reactions to apartheid in South Africa, international protests against apartheid in Rwanda, similar to those in Kosovo, remained largely muted. Rwanda's experiment with apartheid in the First Republic ended with massive slaughters of Tutsis. During the First Republic, Rwanda also lost over one half of its Tutsi population to refugee flight to Uganda and other neighboring countries. President Kayibanda's army chief of staff, General Juvenal Habyarimana, seized power and ended the First Republic's anti-Tutsi pogroms.

Habyarimana, president of the Second Republic, abandoned the First Republic's discriminatory policy of "national Hutuism," but discrimination against Rwandan Tutsis living abroad increased. In 1986, Uganda changed its citizenship requirements from ancestry to residence. The Tutsi Diaspora group in Uganda formed the bulk of the Rwandan Patriotic Front (RPF), the force that later invaded Rwanda (and ended the genocide). The Ugandan government, for internal political reasons, reversed its liberal citizenship policy and made members of the RPF refugees in Uganda. Rwandan Tutsis no longer had a safe legal home in Uganda. Habyarimana responded by explicitly granting citizenship to indigenous resident Tutsis but not to those Tutsis who had fled to Uganda from, especially, Rwanda. The Tutsi guerrilla fighters found themselves between the Rwandan devil and the Ugandan deep sea. According to one historian, the 1990 RPF invasion of Rwanda represented an attempt of Diaspora Rwandans to escape the closing scissors of a postcolonial citizenship crisis in both Uganda and Rwanda.[14] The 1993 internationally brokered Arusha Accords, designed to end the civil war brought about by a 1990 RPF invasion, required the repatriation of Tutsi refugees back to Rwanda from Uganda and other neighboring countries. Thus, we find that the Tutsis suffered relatively less discrimination at the beginning of the Second Republic than they did at the end of the First one.

Phase 3, Group Brutalization

1. *European Jews*. Some scholars have underplayed the motive element even in the case of a clear-cut genocide such as the Holocaust. In an article published in a premier philosophy journal, Margalit and Motzkin proclaimed that *only* World War II Germans "both systematically humiliated and systematically killed."[15] They hedge their bets with the admission that this combination is "exceedingly rare and *maybe* unique" (Italics, mine). The authors say little about extermination; instead, they concentrate on humiliation. Contrary to the implications of their analysis, however, humiliation does not occupy the same moral plateau as extermination. Whatever the moral condemnation humiliation warrants, it pales in comparison to the moral condemnation demanded by acts of extermination. The concept of humiliation does not come close to capturing the venomous and despicable hatred that the Nazis had for Jews. Killings motivated by hatred, not humiliation, lie at the heart of genocide. The awkward legal phrase "extermination,... as such" and not the term "humiliation," better captures the

Holocaust's morally important features, including the horrifying brutality and the despicable institutionalized hatred.

2. *Bosnian Muslims*. Within the Balkans, in the 1990s, the Bosnian Muslims experienced considerable horrors. Srebrenica, a city in Bosnia-Herzegovina, came to symbolize the tragedy of ethnic conflict when Bosnian Serb forces massacred some 7,000 Bosnian Muslims under the helpless eyes of UN soldiers from The Netherlands.[16] The Bosnian Muslims had little military hardware to protect themselves. According to one estimate, "the Muslims had two tanks, twenty-four artillery pieces, and no planes, whereas the Serbs had more than 300 tanks, 400 artillery pieces, and at least sixty planes."[17] Instead of protecting the more vulnerable Bosnian Muslims, the United Nations, through its initial support of the Bosnian Serbs, chose the wrong side in the conflict. This raises a disturbing possibility. Perhaps, the United Nation's refusal to see that brutalization was disproportionately committed against Bosnian Muslims stemmed from prejudiced attitudes that became entrenched in United Nation's operations procedures.

However we assess the role of humanitarian intervention in the Bosnian conflict, Bosnia's contemporary history clearly demonstrates that hatred can explode suddenly with little warning. This hatred can become particularly vicious when it becomes entrenched within warring military organizations. The government of the former Yugoslavia did not give official recognition to animosities that may have existed among its populace. Only when the country imploded did serious forms of hatred toward Bosnian Muslims emerge in the midst of widespread brutalization, including forced removals, rapes, and extermination campaigns.

3. *Albanian Kosovars*. The experiences of the Bosnian Muslims and the Albanian Kosovars also differed radically during their respective brutalization phases. The Bosnian Muslims speak the same language as the Serbs who mobilized hatred against them. The more impoverished Albanian Kosovars speak a different language than their Serbian nemesis. Given that the Albanians differed more from the other recognized groups in the former Yugoslavia than they did from each other and that Albanians probably experienced more discrimination in the former Yugoslavia, one might have predicted that greater hatred would have been unleashed against the Albanians. Yet, while the comparisons remain debatable, Bosnians suffered more severe harms than the Albanians did. Bosnian Muslims probably received more brutal treatment than Albanian Kosovars during their respective recent conflicts with the Serbs. The death tolls for Bosnians, for example, numbered in the one-hundred thousands and that of Albanians in the tens of thousands.

4. *Rwandan Tutsis*. The severity of the final brutalization phase in Rwanda clearly distinguishes it from the brutalization carried out in Bosnia and Kosovo. The extent and gravity of the harms perpetrated against Bosnian Muslims and Albanian Kosovars pale in comparison to those inflicted on the Rwandan Tutsis. "More people were killed, injured, and displaced in three and half months in Rwanda than in the whole of the Bosnian campaign."[18]

Historically, the Rwandan case comes the closest to matching the order of the phases and the severity of harms within each phase as the horrors experienced by Jews under the Nazi regime (see Appendix D). The solidification of Tutsi as a defensive identity occurred earlier in the last part of the twentieth century than did the full formation of Bosnian Muslim and Albanian Kosovar identity. However, the case of the Tutsis in Rwanda also breaks rank with that of the Jews in Nazi Germany. The plight of the Jews became continuously and increasingly serious through the designation, discrimination, and brutalization phases. The plight of the Tutsis did not follow the same, continuously downhill descent into the hells of brutalization. The Tutsis fared better under Rwanda's Second Republic than they did under the apartheid policies of the First Republic. Further, brutalization occurred soon after outside policy makers imposed a quota system for Tutsis in Rwanda. Well-intentioned policies, especially when they solidify ethnic categories, often have adverse affects. The results of the Arusha Accords now haunt its promoters. In any event, severe group brutalization does not always follow from increasingly severe group discrimination. Brutalization may erupt after discrimination seems to have abated. The Rwandan case illustrates one clear lesson. Patterns of severe group brutalization demand swift and immediate humanitarian intervention to stop them. Sovereign immunity does not apply, legally or morally, as a defense to genocide. A conceptual cleansing of our understanding of genocide should clear the road of any remnants that impair the effective implementation of an international moral mandate to stop it. The cases also illustrate the importance of recognizing the formative stages and end-point of an overlooked crucial element of the crime of genocide—motive.

CONCLUSION

Of the five elements of the crime of genocide (act, intent, motive, victim type, and perpetrator), jurists pay the least attention to motive. Yet, a motive of hate lies at the very essence of genocide. Genocide is the consummate hate crime. This hate element is not something peripheral to the act of genocide. Hate makes genocide the horrendous crime that it is. It might somehow even make sense to treat hate as a peripheral item in murder cases. Penalty enhancement statutes, for example, tack on considerations of the hate aspect of a crime of murder after a court has made a ruling on the "real" issue, that is, the murder itself. A court can conduct a trial of a person accused of murder without the slightest mention of a hate motive underlying the crime. This would and should be unthinkable in cases of genocide. No one would even think of accusing someone for killing millions of Jews or thousands of Tutsis without examining the hatred that motivated these crimes. It is critical for jurists to bring the hate element that nurtures and sustains genocide to the center of the international legal stage.

Chapter 6

Genocide Victims: Perpetrator Defined

> Article 6 (a) Genocide by killing
>
> Elements
>
> 1. The perpetrator killed one or more persons.
> 2. **Such person or persons belonged to a particular national, ethnical ethnic, racial or religious group**.
> 3. The perpetrator intended to destroy, in whole or in part, that national, ethnical, racial or religious group as such.
> 4. The conduct took place in the context of a manifest pattern of similar conduct directed against that wrong or was conduct that could itself effect such destruction.
>
> —Rome Statute of the International Criminal Court

VICTIM TYPES: ISSUES AND SOLUTIONS

The Nazis obliterated millions of individual lives *and* attempted to annihilate entire groups. It may sound strange to describe the death of individuals in the same sentence as the death of groups as if harm to individuals and harm to groups stood on equal footing. Talking about groups in the same way that we talk about individuals indicates more than an odd way of speaking. The placement of individuals and groups on the same descriptive level brings a peculiar feature of the crime of genocide to the surface. Most people would readily admit that genocide involves more than killing massive numbers of individuals. Yet, few would recognize that one of those crucial additional factors is that genocide involves attacks on groups. Insisting that the laws governing genocide should include a careful analysis of groups may seem like a purely academic indulgence. One may wonder what more there needs to be for something to count as genocide beyond the fact that countless individuals lost their lives. Legally speaking, however, the element of mass killings does not differentiate genocide from other international crimes. After all, an act of mass killings fits "crimes against humanity" as well. Along with intent, the group characteristics of the victims truly mark the crime of genocide as distinct from other lethal international crimes. No other international war crime singles out groups as victims.

The concept of genocide has the notion of groups built into it. The word "genocide" comes from the Greek *genos* meaning "race, nation, or tribe." Racial, national, and tribal groups serve as examples of the type of groups that perpetrators have targeted throughout history. Genocide consists of an act committed against these types of groups. The individuals killed in genocide belong to certain group types. To understand the nature of genocide, we need to know what it means for victims "to belong to a group." In particular, we need to understand what it means for victims of genocide "to be members of a certain group type."

Before taking on these challenges, let us integrate the conclusions from the previous chapters with the discussions in this chapter so far. Genocide involves the killings of massive numbers of individuals (see Chapter 3). Perpetrators kill according to explicit or implicit policy directives from organizations (see Chapter 4) and because of hatreds deeply embedded in the fabric of those organizations and in the wider society (see Chapter 5). Victims of genocide possess a special quality of having ties to a group. Genocide, then, consists of mass killing of members of a group because of their group identity. Hence, to qualify as genocide the perpetrators must direct their killings not just at any kind of group but against members of certain kinds of groups.

To see why it is that not just any group will do as targets of genocide consider the following. All wars, for example, would fall under the heading of genocide if "the enemy" qualified as a relevant targeted group for the crime of genocide. This would mean that when the United States attacked its enemy Iraq in Gulf Wars I and II, it could stand accused of the crime of genocide as it clearly targeted a group, namely, "the Iraqi enemy." To retain its rhetorical force jurists should restrict the scope of genocide. The problem before us in this chapter is to find the best way to restrict the reach of targeted groups within the laws of genocide.

Those who have codified the laws of genocide have chosen to restrict the targeted groups by designating a set number of group types. The drafters gave certain group types a special status. The 1948 Genocide Convention specified four group types: religious, national, ethnic, and racial groups. When the drafters limited the groups to these four types, they created an expectation that all future groups would have to resemble these groups. Jurists have come to regard the group types first designated in the Genocide Convention not merely as models but as an exhaustive list of those group types covered by the law. According to the dominant way of thinking on these matters, if members of a candidate group do not fall into one of the categories specifically designated by the laws, then the laws of genocide do not apply to them. Thus, as political groups did not make the original list, the targeting of communists or any other political group would not qualify as genocide targeting.

The case for a narrow range of group types gains support from a key source, namely, the initial debates over the drafting of the Genocide Convention itself. The Convention drafters explicitly rejected proposals to include other group types (specifically, linguistic, political, and economic groups). In practical policy terms, many individuals, some organizations, and a few governments have expressed their dismay that the laws of genocide do not apply readily to injustices such as the massacres of political groups in the killing fields of Cambodia. As Cambodia has become a particularly troublesome case, we shall later devote considerable attention to it (see this chapter, the section on case studies).

How, then, should international law interpret this group element? Attempts to answer this question face the following complication. Genocide does not involve the targeting of just any group. Only certain groups find themselves within the scope of the laws of genocide. This leaves an even more perplexing question. How can the law defend protecting only certain types of groups, namely (as specified by the laws of genocide) "national, ethnical, racial or religious groups"? Despite the abstract nature of the discussions about the elements of the crime of genocide and the hair-splitting distinctions theorists make in these types of debates, a legal analysis of groups quickly lands in the thicket of historical and political disputes. In this chapter, for example, we shall find ourselves having to propose solutions to seemingly intractable disputes over how to assess the mass slaughters that took place in Cambodia from 1975 to 1979. The challenge is to find the proper instruments that will dull weapons (at least the intellectual ones) used to fight over past issues and sharpen the legal tools needed to confront future challenges.

A description of the targeted group is a critical element of the crime of genocide. Not every targeted group qualifies as a genocide group. If we could write a new law on genocide, what conditions would we place on the victim element of the crime? More realistically, if we could propose new interpretations of the existing laws on genocide, how would we read the phrase "Such person or persons belonging to a particular national, ethnical [ethnic], racial or religious group"? The legislative writing or the judicial interpretation of the victim element may look easy, but we need to make some difficult choices. First, we must face the skeptic who wants to do away with requiring any kind of group identity for the crime of genocide. Why should we need to identify the groups involved in mass killings? A killing is a killing regardless of whether the victims belong to any group. Second, we need to choose between a proposal that lists the specific groups targeted for genocide in the past and one that simply includes the classifications of these specific groups. Did the Nazis simply target Jews, or did they target Jews as a racial group? Third, we need to decide how to relate the designated groups to each other and to other groups not designated in the law. Why did the drafters of the original genocide law specify national, ethnic, racial, and religious groups? Did they mean to make this an exhaustive list closed to any future additions?

Identifiable Versus Non-Identifiable Groups

Perhaps, the group identification requirement for the crime of genocide is overly restrictive. Israel Charny dismisses the requirement that genocide involve an identifiable group by pointing out that,

> mass killings, on an enormous scale, can fail to qualify as genocide under the present [UN] definition if the victims are either a heterogeneous group or native citizens of a country that is destroying them. How absurd, and ugly.[1]

According to Charny, under the United Nations' definition of genocide, "planned killing of even millions of one's political opponents would not constitute genocide if one were careful that they were all of different faiths or different ethnic backgrounds."[2] Thus, Charny questions why mass killers must target groups to qualify as perpetrators of genocide. In his view, mass killings of any individual, whether or not they belong to groups, should suffice. Like Charny, we oppose adopting an exhaustive list of group types. However, we adamantly disagree with Charny's proposal to jettison or to set aside the requirement that genocide involve an identifiable group type. What makes genocide a particularly heinous crime is the *genos* element, that is, the targeting of groups. Crimes-against-humanity, another international war crime, also includes the criminal act of mass killings just as the crime of genocide does (see Chapter 3). Genocide, in contrast, signifies something distinct and, in many ways, worse than mass killings. In a case of genocide, the accused set out to eliminate a group by killing its members. Within international law, genocide, therefore, represents the analogue to the worst kind of murder in national (municipal) criminal law, namely, premeditated murder.

Types of Groups Versus Specific Groups

After we have chosen to retain the idea that the laws of genocide should include reference to identifiable groups, we then have to decide whether the law should identify those groups specifically or generally. If we opt for the specific approach, we would list those groups (e.g., Namibian Hereroes, Turkish Armenians, European Jews, and Rwandan Tutsis) that already have been victims of genocide. Presumably, then, the law would focus on protecting these specific vulnerable groups. Let us assume that we could agree on a list of specific groups previously victimized by the crime of genocide. The shortcoming of any specific list lies in the high probability that other, non-listed specific groups will become future victims. To remedy the problem of overly specifying the list of particular targeted groups, the law might retain the list of past victim-groups but treat this as an incomplete sampling. However, this sample-list interpretation leaves open the important issue. We would still need to determine the similarity between the presently listed groups and other non-listed future groups so that we could choose among future candidates. In short, we cannot avoid grappling with the problem of designating types of groups and the further challenge of how these types relate to each other and to other groups that we leave off the list.

Designated Group Types

Once we have rejected proposals that would radically alter the current law, we must face the problems created by the current law's reference to only four types of groups (national, ethnic, racial, and religious groups). First, we need to decide how many of these type-labels a group must have to qualify under the provision. Does the fact that a group qualifies under a number of the categories have any bearing on the legal case? Second, we need to find a way to handle those types of groups not specified in the law. Do perpetrators automatically escape prosecution for genocide if they target political or some other group that is not designated in the law? Third, we need to face the challenge of weighing the four classifications against one another. Do the group types recognized in the law tell us anything important about the crime of genocide? Is the targeting of some groups (racial ones) worse than the targeting of other ones (religious ones)?

1. *Relations among Designated Group Types*. Does a group increase its chances of qualifying as a genocide victim group if it falls under more than one of the four classifications recognized in the law? In past genocide cases, groups often fell under a number of different types. The Nazis, for example, classified the Jews according to their religion as well as their race. The Armenians who became victims of the Young Turks in 1915 fit under both the religious and the ethnic categories; and the Hutus attackers thought of their Tutsi victims as part of a despised ethnic and racial group.

If past cases of genocide involved groups classified under various combinations of national, ethnic, race, and religious categories, then it seems reasonable for the law to reflect history. The law should recognize the multi-group dimension of genocide just as memorials and museums have increasingly come to do. The multiple group nature of the Nazi genocide has only recently received considerable public acknowledgment. After a great deal of political wrangling, the Holocaust Museum in Washington, DC accepted exhibits about "other victims" of the Holocaust. For example, visitors to the museum may select from identity cards that feature not only Jews but also Polish prisoners, Jehovah's Witnesses, homosexuals, Gypsies, and euthanasia victims.[3]

However, while groups targeted in genocide typically overlap a number of types (say, religion and race), perpetrators generally focus their wrath on a single feature of the group (race in the case of the Jews by the Nazis). In fact, the idea of a single-category group serves as the paradigm for genocide. When we think of genocide, we generally imagine mass killings directed at members who fit under a single category. The Holocaust, marked by the loss of nearly six million people from one group (the Jews), has become the typical case, the model, and the exemplar of genocide. The Nazis were obsessed with the complete elimination of one (and only one?) racial group, the Jews. Historians now generally agree that the Nazis even sacrificed winning World War II by diverting scarce resources from fighting the war to the mission of annihilating the Jews. There are good reasons, as we shall see, for the law to reflect the importance of a single classification for genocide victim groups. As we shall see it was the racial and not the religious classification of Jews that proved to be the truly sinister grouping.

Before we leave this discussion about the number of victim categories, we should note an oddity about these group types that has proved to be more than an intellectual curiosity. Indeed, a perpetrator group may target members of its own group type. These, admittedly rare, situations involve a group turning on itself. Members of one part of a group attack members of another part of the same group.

A subset of a group, in effect, tries to annihilate the remaining part of the group. In these circumstances, victim group and perpetrator group overlap. Later, we will examine an actual case of a so-called *auto genocide* that took place in Cambodia.

2. *Relation of Designated Group Types to Other Group Types*. After we have accepted the four designated group types, we then need to find ways to relate these to each other and to other types. Drafters of the recently adopted laws governing the International Criminal Court (ICC) accepted the Genocide Convention's language almost verbatim. Now, only certain types of groups fall under the protected reach of the international laws of genocide. The controversy, however, continues over whether to add more types of groups (especially, political groups) to the list of categories already mentioned in the law. We could simply accept the present four categories and treat them as making up a complete and exhaustive list. Alternatively, we could accede to the demands and tack on additional group types (linguistic, social, economic, and political). The first approach makes the law too inflexible, and the second one, too flexible. With the exclusive method, we would automatically have to reject any different type of mass killing. With the inclusive method, we would have to accept almost any form of mass killing as genocide. If we use either device, then we will fail to ask the most fundamental question. Is there anything about the four types that are included in the law that captures something important about the crime of genocide?

Can we find a feature common to the accepted categories to use to assess future candidates? If so, then new candidate groups would qualify if they shared these common characteristics. Unfortunately, analysts cannot reach a consensus about the underlying assumptions that tie the accepted designated group types together. The drafters of the Genocide Convention uncritically granted some questionable claims about the underlying nature of the designated categories. For example, they assumed that the laws of genocide would cover only permanent and stable groups.[4] Thus, the drafters construed the Convention's purpose as protecting groups that already existed, that is, those that already had a long history. In other words, the drafters thought that the Convention should protect only clearly recognizable and fully formed groups. One distinguished legal expert on minority rights claims that the right for these groups to continue to exist is a prerequisite for other rights.[5] Yet, despite the benefits of having minority groups around for long periods of time, neither the past stability nor the continual existence of a group should influence the determination whether it is a type of group covered by the laws of genocide. A group does not need stability or to have a long history for perpetrators to target it for annihilation.

Why, then, does the genocide law include religious, national, ethnic, and racial groups? Perhaps, the types listed in the law simply reflect the fact that past perpetrators of genocide primarily have targeted these group types. This obvious observation helps to uncover another well-known but critical factor. Perpetrators of genocide not only targeted the types of groups listed in the law but they also determined the composition of these groups. The Nazis devised their own racial criteria for who qualified as a Jew. The important point is not that past perpetrators of genocide classified individuals according to their religious, national, ethnic, or racial affiliation. Rather, the critical factor is that perpetrators defined the targeted groups. To accommodate this *perpetrator perspective*, we need to change the way we commonly think about victim groups. The laws of genocide make more sense when we determine the nature of the targeted groups from the point of view of those who set out to harm groups. Adoption of the perpetrator's perspective lends credibility to the choice of categories, and it permits sufficient flexibility to include previously non-designated or new future group types.

The failure to apply the international laws of genocide to Cambodia in a timely fashion dramatizes the powerful grip that a dominant perception of genocide and hatred has on policy thinking and law making. Admittedly, group hatred, on a global scale, typically has involved quite distinct groups with long histories. However, targeted groups also can have a transient, ephemeral existence. Some victim groups quickly coalesce and rapidly dissolve. Further, some of the most pernicious forms of hatred arise among groups similar to one another (e.g., Bosnian Muslims and Bosnian Serbs). Oftentimes (and paradoxically), the more similar the characteristics of a victim's group are to those of a perpetrator's group, the more severe the animosity and hatred.[6] Finally, group hatred can even develop within a group. Recent history has provided a curious example of ethnic Khmers turning on themselves (see this chapter, the section on case studies). The constantly changing characteristics of group formation argue against assuming and insisting on the prior stability of vulnerable groups.

To clarify the difference between focuses on a group's continual existence and harms inflicted upon a group consider the following. Some individuals may not acknowledge that they even belong to a group before they experience discrimination as a member of that group. Suddenly, they find themselves attacked because of their perceived group affiliation. Some individuals did not consider themselves Jewish until the Nazis attacked them as Jews. If we emphasize the continual existence of a group, then we run the danger of overlooking cases where a group has little identifiable existence apart from actions taken against the group. Further, on the group-stability thesis, the perpetrators of genocide would have to threaten the existence of an already defined group. According to this interpretation, a readily identifiable group must have had a life of its own before any discriminatory and otherwise harmful acts took place. However, for legal purposes, a group's identity has more to do with the thoughts and deeds of those determined to harm the group than it does with the prior status of a group. As the examples from the Nazi court cases illustrate (see Chapter 7), perpetrators inconsistently, if not irrationally, establish group membership criteria. Nazi stereotypes led the judiciary to classify as Jewish individuals people whose beliefs and practices had little to do with Jews and Judaism. In turn, the Nazi stereotype of how a Jew looked led to legal decisions that refused to label practicing Jews as Jewish.

Efforts to find consistent and rational ways to determine grounds for group membership independent of the perpetrator's means of identification often obscure the immediate harms inflicted upon members of a group. The primary focus should fall on group harm rather than on (but not to the exclusion of) group identity. The group-identity approach focuses on efforts groups make to establish their identity outside of the context of harms directed against them. We should interpret the genocide law's lists of victim types as a list of typical victims and not as a limited and exclusive list.

We cannot predict which type of group will find itself threatened in the twenty-first century. We do not know whether "national, ethnic, racial, or religious groups" (the 1948 Convention's list) or "linguistic, political, and economic groups" (the critics' list) will become objects of attack. Nevertheless, this does not leave the future completely indeterminate. We know a few things about the future. We know, for example, that we cannot guarantee that any future group will readily fit under any of the group types currently considered. Further, nobody knows whether some way of grouping people other than in racial categories will become the most lethal excuse for killing massive numbers of people. These tidbits of common sense should deal a fatal blow to those who want to retain the designated list as an exclusive one or who want to extend the designated list by finding some common positive features of the designated groups themselves.[7]

Commentators have shown how confusion over group identity has infected the International Criminal Tribunal for Rwanda (ICTR). In an earlier *Akayesu* judgment, the Trial Chamber stated:

> The Chamber notes that the Tutsi population does not have its own language or a distinct culture from the rest of the Rwandan population. However, the Chamber finds that there are a number of objective indicators of the group as a group with a distinct identity. Every Rwandan citizen was required before 1994 to carry an identity card which included an entry for ethnic group, the ethnic group being Hutu, Tutsi, or Twa.[8]

However, as Eltringham astutely observed, the court later in that same opinion, "declares that what really defines Tutsi is that they constitute a 'permanent and stable' group, one which is determined by birth."[9] Eltringham found that the ICTR made some progress on the issue of group identity when, in the later *Kayishema* judgment, the ICTR stated that:

> An ethnic group is one whose members share a common language and culture; or, a group which distinguishes itself, as such (self-identification); or, a group identified as such by others, including perpetrators of the crimes (identified by others).[10]

In summary, then, the ICTR refined its analysis of groups by including a perpetuator-determined sense of group identity, but it fell short by treating the perpetuator-centered view as only one of a number of possible ways to establish group identity.

In analyzing genocide, courts should concentrate on the negative claims about a group from the point of view of perpetrators who are intent on harming members of that group. Among theorists, Chalk and Johanassohn come closest to this "negative/external" approach when they define genocide as "a form of one-sided mass killing in which the state or other authority intends to destroy a group *as that group and membership in it are defined by the perpetrator* (italics added)."[11] The last part of the definition (italicized above) provides an excellent starting point for establishing a sound analysis of groups.[12] Chalk and Johanassohn, in a sense, leave the problem of how to define a particular group to the perpetrators of the harms.

The jurisprudence on genocide is moving toward adopting perpetuator-based definitions of groups. In the *Jelisic* case, the Ad Hoc Tribunal for the Former Yugoslavia (ICTY) adopted this perpetrator perspective.

> Although the objective determination of a religious group remains possible, to attempt to define a national, ethnical, or racial group today using objective and scientifically irreproachable criteria would be perilous exercise whose result would not necessarily correspond to the perception of the persons concerned by such categorization. Therefore, it is more appropriate to evaluate the status of a national, ethnical or racial group from the point of view of those who wish to single that group out from the rest of the community. The Trial Chamber consequently elects to evaluate membership in a national, ethnical or racial group using a subjective criterion.[13]

While the court called the standard it adopted "subjective," it clearly meant subjective from a perpetrator's and not from a targeted group's perspective. When considering cases of genocide, courts first should turn to the perpetrators (not to group members or theorists) for the most useful definitions of groups.

3. *Differentiation among Designated Group Types*. We need to allow for the possibility of making comparative judgments about various categories of groups. Through this study, we shall find that not all group types rank equally on a scale of vulnerability to serious harms. While the group types listed in the genocide laws ("national, ethnical, racial or religious groups") do not seem to appear in any particular order, it will clarify issues (and, in many cases, resolve disputes) if we arrange them on a scale according to how susceptible a group type is to harm from others. We propose the following reordering of the sequence of group types ranging from the least to the most vulnerable group: religious, national, ethnic, and racial groups. "Vulnerability" in this context means, "group susceptibility to annihilation or extermination."

To appreciate that groups within different categories tend to have different vulnerabilities let us consider examples from opposite ends of the spectrum. Is there any prima facie difference between cases where perpetrators stigmatize a group as racial and ones where they treat a group as political? The Nazis targeted both Jews (a racial group) and communists (a political group). Jews suffered far more than did the communists. This difference was not accidental. The racialization of Jewish identity made Jews far more vulnerable to harm than groups that the Nazis placed under other categories. Once an identity takes on racial characteristics, those so stigmatized can do nothing about it. Racialized Jews are born Jews; communist parents do not necessarily have communist children.

This does not mean that genocide could never include a political group. The laws of genocide should not exclude political and other non-listed group types. It would make a difference, for example, whether the targeted group was an organized or an unorganized political group. The latter are more vulnerable than the former because they have fewer means of defending themselves. A relationship generally exists between how organized a group is and how well a group can protect itself. Generally, unorganized groups are more likely than organized groups to become objects of harm. Organizations, by their nature, provide group members some degree of protection from harmful identification and treatment by perpetrators. Group leaders might respond, collectively and effectively, to early mistreatment of members by outsiders. Obviously, however, organizations and their leaders do not always provide sufficient protection.

Whether the killing of members of an organized political group because of their political affiliation qualifies as genocide depends on the details of a particular case. For example, whether the massive killings of over 500,000 people associated with the Indonesian Communist Party (PKI) from 1965 to 1966 qualified as genocide would depend on a number of factors. With respect to the group element of the crime of genocide, we would need to ask the following questions. First, did the PKI, an organized political party since 1920, determine its own membership or did the Indonesian government cast its net wide to include those loosely associated with the PKI (including friends, relatives, and family)? Second, what harms did those labeled as party members receive? Third, how confining was the party label? Could PKI members readily change their party affiliation?

Overall, then, we should allow for expansion of the list of victim types by (1) adopting the perpetrator's definition of a targeted group; (2) assessing the magnitude and depth of the harm experienced by members of the group; and (3) judging where among the designated group types to place this new group type on the vulnerability scale. We are now ready to apply this method to cases that would otherwise prove problematic.

CASE STUDIES: HITLER'S GERMANY, POL POT'S CAMBODIA

Historical comparisons demonstrate the importance and relevance of the abstract distinctions made so far. The Nazi and Khmer Rouge regimes targeted many groups.[14] Hitler's megalomaniacal exploits should need little introduction. The lesser-known Pol Pot and the Democratic Kampuchea (DK, the official name of the Khmer Rouge State from 1975 to 1979) regime went to extraordinary lengths to recapture for the Khmer people the lands and glory accumulated and lost under the ancient kingdom of Angkor. The chairman of the United Nations Human Rights Sub-commission called the massacres in Cambodia "the most serious [human rights violations] to have occurred anywhere since Nazism."[15] Given the enormity of the Nazi and Khmer Rouge atrocities, these two blights on recent history make ideal subjects for a comparative study. An analysis of similarities and differences between Hitler's and Pol Pot's victim groups will produce some unsettling results.

One difference between the Nazi and Khmer regimes arises immediately. While few jurists would question calling Nazi acts genocide, the same does not hold true for the deeds of the Khmer Rouge. The mass killings carried out by Pol Pot's Khmer Rouge have perplexed scholars, jurists, and politicians who continue to argue heatedly over whether the Cambodia case qualifies as genocide. Investigators of Cambodia's killing fields disagree about the categories of victims and their relative degrees of victimization. The Cambodian case, then, proves more difficult to assess than the Nazi case. Unlike the Nazis, for example, the Khmers did not clearly target one group for total extermination. Did harms and killings experienced by members of various groups occur because of Khmer policy directed at those groups or did the regime strike out in all sorts of unpredictable ways and target many different types of people? As a first step to answering this question, consider the following difference between Nazi and Khmer policies. While the Nazis had relatively clear-cut categories for classifying their victim types, the Khmer Rouge had a comparatively messy and vague classification scheme. Let us, then, see how well both the Nazi and the Khmer Rouge's policies and practices fit the current and the proposed legal classificatory schemes for victim groups.

Designated Groups

The four group types (religious, national, ethnic, and racial) codified into the laws of genocide shall frame the analysis. This may sound like an overly formal approach to a cognitively messy and emotionally loaded subject. However, important rationales underlie the use of this schematic. The law uses particular group types for good reasons. History bears witness to how often certain group types have become victims of serious harm. The following discussion examines the legally designated group types in an order that begins with the least vulnerable type (religion) and ends with the most vulnerable one (race). Within each category, we match a group targeted by the Nazis with a comparable one victimized by the Khmer Rouge. These comparisons will suggest the most fruitful ways to use the types of group designations found in the genocide law.

1. *Religious Groups*. History contains a long list of groups persecuted because of their religion. Sometimes, discrimination against a religion has turned into mass killings of the religion's members. A relatively unknown religious genocide occurred in Japan. In 1587, Japan's rulers banned Christianity, practiced by some 300,000 devotees. In 1614, a national campaign to suppress Christianity began. From 1637 to 1638, the discrimination campaign culminated in the massacre of some 40,000 Christians.

Fortunately, in modern times, religious genocide has become a rarity. History records relatively few examples such as the case of Japan where perpetrators specifically target a religious group for extermination. This should come as no surprise. The nature of religious identity makes the targeting of religious groups for annihilation relatively unlikely as belief and practice lie at the heart of religious identity in a way that they do not for the other listed group types, particularly ethnicity and race. This means that, overall, religious identity has a more malleable character than ethnicity or race. Ethnicity and race become intractable when perceived as embedded in biology. In contrast, it is difficult to imagine someone arguing that a person's religious identity has biological roots. Even though people might find religion at the heart of their identity, individuals can change and modify their religious identity. Racial identity does not have the same permeable quality that religious identity has. The relatively transparent and malleable nature of religious identity makes it more difficult for perpetrators to target religious groups for mass killing and annihilation. This does not mean that religious groups will never find themselves the object of genocide or that members of religious groups will not suffer horrible harms. As we shall see, however, while the Hitler and Pol Pot regimes clearly attacked Jehovah's Witnesses and the Buddhist monks respectively, the evidence does not show convincingly that their regimes tried to exterminate these religious groups.

(a) *Jehovah's Witnesses*. Jehovah's Witness began in the United States during the 1870s and quickly spread to countries abroad, including Germany. Some scholars find the suffering of Jehovah's Witnesses under the Nazis comparable to the horrors experienced by the Jews.[16] The Nazis tolerated some religious identifications and practices, but the Jehovah Witnesses openly defied the Nazis. Proclaiming their sole allegiance to God, Jehovah Witnesses refused to take oaths of allegiance to Hitler's Third Reich.[17] Incensed by this disloyalty, the Nazis aimed their killing machine at Jehovah's Witnesses. However, the evidence shows that the Nazis did not target Jehovah's Witnesses for annihilation in the same way that they targeted Jews.[18] The Nazis targeted Jehovah's Witnesses for what they believed and practiced, not (as they did for Jews) for what the Nazis perceived the Jehovah's Witnesses to be. The Nazis, for example, sent the children of Jehovah's Witnesses to school for re-education. In contrast, they sent Jewish children to death camps.

(b) *Cambodian Buddhists*. Countless Buddhist monks met their demise at the hands of the Khmer Rouge. As evidence of Pol Pot's intent to eradicate Buddhists, Ben Kiernan cites a government document that proclaimed that "[t] he foundation pillars of Buddhism . . . have disintegrated. In the future they will dissolve further."[19] *The United Nations Group of Experts for Cambodia Report* (1999) cited the following as evidence that the Khmer Rouge targeted Buddhists:

> Khmer Rouge's intensely hostile statements towards religion, and the monk hood in particular; the Khmer Rouge's policies to eradicate the physical and ritualistic aspects of the Buddhist religion; the disrobing of monks and abolition of monk hood; the number of victims; and the executions of Buddhist leaders and recalcitrant monks.[20]

However, the following considerations raise questions about the charge that the Khmer Rouge committed genocide against the Buddhists. Many Americans think of the United States as a Christian country. Yet, Christianity does not infect all aspects of American life to the same extent that Buddhism infuses Cambodian life.

To be American is not to be Christian, but "To be Cambodian is to be Buddhist." Buddhism became so ingrained in Cambodian society that it constituted a way of life for Cambodians. Any attempt to diminish or eradicate Buddhism would seem to have cataclysmic consequences as it would have to transform the fundamental pillars of Cambodian society. The Khmer Rouge regime was not the first to attack Buddhism. Lon Nol, Pol Pot's predecessor and opponent, also had initiated a campaign against Buddhists. When the Khmer Rouge followed suit and sought to eradicate Buddhism, they, in effect, would have had to demolish every vestige of Cambodian culture, which they did not do.

The Nazis and the Khmer Rouge seem to have adopted fundamentally different national policies. The Nazis prohibited the religious practices of Jehovah's Witnesses, but they did not try to annihilate the religion entirely. In contrast, the Khmer Rouge tried to eliminate Buddh*ism*, but it remains unclear whether the regime attempted to eliminate Buddh*ists*. The distinction between doctrine (*ism*) and proponents of the doctrine (*ists*) proves important. Apparently, the Khmer Rouge killed only those Buddhist monks who refused to defrock. If the regime had engaged in a wholesale attack against Buddhists, it seems that they would not have allowed Buddhists to renounce their faith. Further, Khmer policy prohibited the practices of any reactionary religion, which also included Catholics, whose main cathedral in Phnom Penh they dismantled stone by stone.[21] Yet, evidence of a state forbidding a religious practice or even killing those who refuse to abandon the practices does not provide a definitive case for a charge of genocide. The ruthless forces of genocide would not distinguish religious believers from religious practitioners.

A number of more general claims emerge from this analysis of religious groups. Future regimes probably will continue to forbid religious practices, and some regimes will eliminate some religious practitioners. However, it seems unlikely that regimes will seek to exterminate (in whole or in part) religious groups *per se* as they can strip people of a considerable portion of their religious identity without targeting the religious practitioners for annihilation through mass killings. This helps to explain a reluctance to count Jehovah's Witnesses and Cambodian Buddhists as genocide victim groups. A pattern now begins to emerge. Many of the Democratic Kampuchea's victim groups do not fit smoothly under the headings of targeted groups explicitly recognized within the laws of genocide. The absence of clearly targeted groups makes it difficult to understand exactly what went on during the Khmer Rouge's reign. However, by the end of our discussion, we shall be in a position to offer some explanations.

2. *National Groups*. While religious groups are readily identifiable (primarily through the claims, habits and deeds of their members), international humanitarian law has not clearly defined national groups. For the sake of clarity, the law should distinguish national from ethnic groups as the two are often confused. Although national groups sometimes overlap with ethnic groups, they remain distinct categories. Unlike a purely ethnic group, a national group has ties to a nation other than the one in which they live.[22] In the context of war, the fate of a national group

often depends upon the relationship between the group's host state and its affiliated nation state. A national group often becomes a targeted group because of its ties to another state and not (entirely?) because of its distinct ethnicity.

The way a nation targets a group proves important when deciding whether genocide laws should apply. A nation may target national groups with ties to its war enemies. A nation may understandably restrict an alien national group's movement during a war. The debate over the justifications for the internment of Japanese Americans during World War II continues to this day. Even those who condemn the US government's actions understand the government's rationale for moving thousands of people of Japanese descent from their homes to internment camps. Further, even those opposed to the death penalty might treat a nation's execution of proven spies from a national group as falling in the realm of rational moral action. In sharp contrast, however, most jurists and moralists would agree that when a country similarly targets an entire national group for annihilation primarily or solely because of the group's identity, then that country has acted immorally.

It makes a difference whether a group qualifies as a purely ethnic or as a national one. A purely ethnic group does not have ties to a potential enemy state. Overall, it would be more difficult for a state to defend attacks launched against an ethnic group than a national one. In the case of an ethnic group, a state cannot avail itself of the excuse that a national group's ties to another country pose threats to a state's security. A state can rationalize and perhaps even justify taking actions against a national group in the context of an external war. It is difficult to see what plausible grounds a state could offer for targeting an ethnic group or, even more so (as we shall see in the next section) a racial group.

(a) *Poles, Jewish and Non-Jewish.* The Poles, a national group, lost a higher percentage of its citizens to Nazi brutality than any other country. According to some scholars, if World War II had continued, Hitler would have targeted Poles as the next group after the Jews slated for elimination.[23] Of course, this academic judgment rests on a counter-factual that asks us to imagine a different past than the one that occurred. Factually speaking, the Nazis did not have a chance to set their sights on exterminating the Poles. More importantly, the target status of the Poles becomes suspect given that the Nazis had mobilized to target not the Poles *per se* but a particular group found among Poles. The Nazis treated Jewish Poles differently than other Poles. Non-Jewish killings by the Nazis, for example, took about 10 percent of the Poland's population whereas Jewish losses almost obliterated the entire Jewish population of Poland.[24] Quite plausibly, then, the Nazis had targeted non-Jewish Poles primarily as wartime enemies and Jewish Poles as Jews, that is, for what the Nazis perceived Jews to be, that is, for their group identity. This shows that not all targeted groups stand on an equal footing. The Nazi action against Polish Jews probably had little or nothing to do with them being part of the same national group as the Poles. The Nazi attack on Polish Jews occurred because of the target group's Jewishness not because of its Polish affiliation.

The laws of war strongly condemn attacks on noncombatant enemies (see Chapter 1). However, this prohibition is neither universal nor clear-cut. Humanitarian law and international ethics leave room for exceptions to prohibiting the targeting of national groups. Some analysts, for example, have defended the dropping of nuclear weapons on Japanese civilians during World War II.[25] Advisedly, we must approach these issues with great care. The recognition of exceptions to the condemnation of targeting national groups does not mean an acceptance of the Nazis targeting them. However, once we acknowledge the complexities of the concept of a national group, an odd but important question remains. Can a national group also be a genocide group?

(b) *Vietnamese Cambodians*. The Vietnamese Cambodians, who also made up a significant portion of Cambodia's Catholic population, numbered over 400,000 before 1975. In contrast, "it was not possible to find a Vietnamese resident who had survived the Pol Pot years there" after 1979.[26] These figures may be somewhat misleading if, as speculated, over 300,000 Vietnamese fled Cambodia in 1975. Still, no one disputes that a large number of the Vietnamese Cambodians lost their lives during Pol Pot's reign.

Similar to the case of the Poles in Nazi-controlled Europe, the case of the Vietnamese in Cambodia raises the question whether the Khmer Rouge targeted them as a national "genocide group" or as a national "enemy group." These labels make a difference. If the Khmer Rouge attempted to exterminate the Vietnamese as a national group, we would have the makings of a serious charge of genocide. An acknowledgment of the gravity of attempts to exterminate a *national group* as a crime of genocide should not detract from a recognition of the seriousness of killing members of an *enemy group*. Still, the cases differ legally as well as morally. Certainly, international law and global ethics should condemn states that kill citizens whose nationality ties them to an enemy state. However, law and morality might permit some negative treatment of a state's enemy group. A state might make a defensible case for restricting movement of enemy groups during wartime. Yet, it seems clearly beyond good moral sense to try to justify extending the negative treatment of an enemy group to a point where it sanctions killing its members simply because of their group affiliation. It is difficult to imagine circumstances that would morally permit even placing restriction on a national group merely because of the group's national identity.

At first glance, it might seem plausible to label the Vietnamese Cambodians as an enemy group. From 1975 to 1977, Cambodia and Vietnam engaged in a border warfare that culminated in Vietnam's full-fledged attack on Cambodia. Vietnam's 1979 victorious invasion ended the mass killings in Cambodia. Given a state of war between Cambodia and Vietnam, perhaps, the Khmer Rouge did target the Vietnamese Cambodians as an enemy group even though they went beyond any reasonable moral bounds by killing Vietnamese Cambodians. The Group of Experts in considering charging the Khmer Rouge leaders with crimes against humanity rejected any appeal to armed conflict as an excuse for these mass killings.

> Were that nexus [to armed conflict] still required as of 1975, the vast majority of the Khmer Rouge's atrocities would not be crimes against humanity; historians have not

> linked the bulk of the atrocities of the Khmer Rouge to the armed conflicts in which it engaged (with Viet Nam or domestic rebels such as those in the eastern zone), except to point out that the Khmer Rouge leadership's concept of self-reliance included an overall hatred of foreign and Vietnamese elements that they manifested in numerous ways, including killing many people accused of being agents of Viet Nam.[27]

While the bulk of the atrocities probably had little to do with the actual war with Vietnam, the Khmer Rouge, in their twisted logic, may have perceived the connection. The link lends support to the hypothesis that the Khmer Rouge targeted its Vietnamese citizens because they were members of a national group with ties to its enemy Vietnam. A connection, actual or perceived, between attacks on Vietnamese Cambodians with Cambodia's war with Vietnam, does not entirely remove them from the list of targeted groups associated with the crime of genocide. A pattern of discrimination against Vietnamese Cambodians persists to this day. As the infliction of these harms has continued long after the cessation of the fighting between the Cambodians and the Vietnamese, the continuing discrimination gives credence to the claim that Pol Pot targeted the Vietnamese not only because of their presumed ties to Vietnam but also because of their ethnicity.

In any event, the current vulnerability of groups like the Vietnamese Cambodians underscores the importance for international law to recognize the harms experienced by a group. A bright and continuous international spotlight on a group's past plight might make it less likely that members of the group will continue to experience severe forms of discrimination.

Although attacks against groups often occur during wars, the previous discussion should not leave the impression that war excuses killing or harming members of any group. In fact, war often serves as a convenient cover for a state to turn on a specific group. States use war as an excuse to harm groups, especially, as discussed in the next section, ethnic groups. In summary, even though the Khmer Rouge may have targeted the Vietnamese Cambodians as wartime enemies, this does not exonerate the regime's harmful action against them.

3. *Ethnic Groups*. Ethnicity, in general, is a more deeply entrenched group type than religion or nationality. Overall, members of religious or national groups seem better able to renounce, escape, or change their identity during times of crisis than members of ethnic groups do. While a number of ethnic groups in Cambodia would qualify as candidates, the Khmer group itself proves to be the most challenging one.

(a) *The Slavs*. What ethnic groups did the Nazis target? Interestingly, it proves difficult to find viable candidates. Perhaps, the Slavs come the closest to qualifying as an ethnic group targeted by the Nazis. Hitler certainly disliked the Slavs, and the Nazis regarded them as an inferior race. To support the victimization claim of Slavs, some scholars have collected data to document the severe losses experienced by some Slavic groups during World War II. Millions of Slavic Ukrainians perished and millions more found themselves in slave labor camps.[28] Other scholars have sought to deflate the Ukrainian case by citing other data. They note, for example, the high incidence of collaboration among Ukrainians with the Nazis in carrying out the extermination programs against the Jews.[29]

The actions of some members of a target group should not be a crucial factor in determining whether that group qualifies as a genocide victim group. Members of a victim group may collaborate with (or, as we shall soon see, even come from the same ethnic group as) the attackers. The case for Jews as a victim group is not undermined in the least by the fact that some Jews cooperated with the Nazis in the ghettoes and the death camps. Instead, the telling issue is whether the attackers targeted a group as such. If we view the case of the Slavs from the perspective of the Nazis, we find little evidence that the Nazis targeted the Slavs for extermination.

(b) *Eastern Khmers.* Can one group commit genocide against its own members? Does it make any sense for a group to try to eliminate itself "in whole" (or even "in part")? Does *auto genocide* exist? Let us answer these general questions about the so-called "zero groups" in the context of the Cambodian case. At first, analysts applied the term "auto genocide" to the entire range of killings under the Khmer Rouge. The fact that Cambodians killed Cambodians made the case particularly troublesome. Later, this sense of auto genocide was used to refer not to Cambodians killing Cambodians but to Khmers committing genocide against fellow Khmers. The Khmer Rouge's reign of terror provides a candidate case for the highly unusual situation of a group turning on itself. Khmers from the Khmer Rouge political party performed mass executions against fellow ethnic Khmers from the regional Eastern Zone of Cambodia that borders Vietnam. The non-Eastern Khmers (the Khmer Rouge) distinguished themselves from their eastern ethnic kin by forcing the latter to wear blue scarves.[30] Should the laws of genocide cover this seemingly bizarre form of auto genocide? Fortunately, the genocide laws do not require any expanding to include this case as the Eastern Khmers also would qualify as a national group.[31] Further, the law does not need to adopt an even more bizarre notion of group suicide to apply genocide laws to cases of auto genocide as the genocide laws do not require that perpetrators try to eliminate the entire group. Auto genocide does not entail group suicide. Thus, a targeted genocide group could be a subset of a larger group.

However, it remains an open question whether the killing of the Eastern Khmers qualifies as genocide. The answer may turn, in part, on whether the Eastern Khmers had become an *enemy group*. In the previous section, we asked whether the Khmer Rouge targeted the Vietnamese Cambodians as a *national, external enemy group*. Here, we can ask a similar question about the Eastern Khmers. Did the Khmer Rouge target the Eastern Khmers as a *national, internal enemy group*? Were the killings connected to accusations of treason or other purges? Vickery offers evidence that the attacks against the Eastern Khmers had ideological and not ethnic roots. The strength of Vickery's claim may stem from an inability to see how part of a group can turn on its own kind to the point of genocide. While the current laws of genocide can apply to auto genocide, it remains debatable if they apply to the case of the Eastern Khmers.

4. *Racial Groups*. If a regime begins to unleash serious discriminatory acts against groups because of their racial identity, alarms should ring loudly to warn that discrimination harms could turn into genocide brutalization. Among those group types singled out in the laws of genocide, racial groups have a special status. The purported biological elements of race mark it as distinct from religious, national, and ethnic classifications. Individuals supposedly inherit their racial groupings through their bloodlines. Admittedly, people are born into religious, national, and ethnic groups. However, according to an all-too-common way of thinking about group types, only race has inherited biological markers. Race, allegedly, grows "in the blood" in a way that religion and ethnicity do not.

Given how deeply entwined race can become in the social fabric of a nation, those who prosecute crimes of genocide should carefully examine the studies, policies, and actions of the accused regime to determine how well developed the state's race classifications are. As the examples below demonstrate, the Nazis had highly sophisticated racial classifications; the Khmer Rogue did not. However, even in some instances where the Nazis used race classifications to carry out mass killings, we still do not have a sure case of genocide. We need to separate two closely linked questions. An affirmative answer to the question "Did the perpetrators target racial groups for harm?" makes an affirmative answer to the question "Did the perpetrators target racial groups for annihilation?" likely but not certain. The case of the Nazi treatment of the Gypsies (also discussed below) illustrates the distinction.

Where do we find parallel race classifications in Cambodia? The Chinese Cambodians might seem like a good candidate group. On the surface, they seem to fit into three of the four victim types: nationality, ethnicity, and race. It makes a huge difference which of these group types becomes the primary category for the Chinese Cambodians. Race, as noted above, strictly sets groups apart from one another. When regimes fully develop a pseudo-scientific basis for race classifications, they erect effectively insuperable barriers among groups, thereby, creating conditions ripe for genocide. Members of a group classified according to race have little chance of escape, and they have a good chance of serving as a scapegoat for the ills of a dominant group. Therefore, it is important to determine if the Khmer Rouge viewed the Chinese as a separate race. The evidence suggests (as we shall see) that the Khmer Rouge perceived the Chinese more in ethnic than in racial terms. If the regime saw the Chinese as a distinct ethnic group, it remains doubtful that it targeted them for elimination in the same way the Nazis targeted the Roma.

(a) *Jews and Gypsies*. Race classification systems are notorious for inconsistently applying criteria for group membership. Many applications of these criteria used to determine racial identity produce illogical or even bizarre results. The applications of irrational race classification systems had horrifying consequences in Nazi Germany.

Hilberg traced the difficulties the Nazis first faced in promulgating precise definitions of "Jew." The Nazis divided non-Aryans into Jews and *Mischlinges*. They further differentiated *Mischlinges* into Second Degree, those with one Jewish grandparent, and First Degree (half Jews), those with two Jewish grandparents but not belonging to a Jewish religion. In one court case, the petitioner, a half-Jew who had married a half-Jew, had attended a synagogue with her father and had designated her religion as "Jewish" on an employment application to a Jewish community organization. The Reich Administrative Court interpreted "belonging to a Jewish religion" as an attitude. The court further noted that her father had undoubtedly dragged her as an unwilling child to the synagogue and that her self-identification as Jewish on a job application stemmed from economic need. Yet, in another case, the Nazi court classified a petitioner with four German grandparents as a Jew because he felt bound to Jewry despite his Aryan blood. These classifications determined which marriages to permit and which ones to prohibit. Second Degree *Mischlinges* could marry Germans, but they could not marry Jews. First Degree *Mischlinges* could not marry Second Degree *Mischlinges* or Germans, except by special permission, but they could marry other First *Mischlinges* and Jews. Further, Hitler decreed that, regardless of race, men (but not women!) could be punished for the serious crime of *Rassenschande* (race defilement), that is, having extramarital intercourse with a Jew.

As illustrated by the inconsistent judicial classifications made in the early stages of Nazi rule, the relatively detailed distinctions that accompany discriminatory harms may become blurred as the genocide engines ignite and accelerate. The road to genocide sometimes begins with an externally imposed definition of a group—ethnic or racial. Classifications of groups, even those applied with good intentions, intertwine with evaluations of groups. Although classifications of groups seem relatively innocuous, group designations often reflect hostilities toward certain groups. The animosities underlying these classifications may appear tame, but they have the potential to grow into far worse forms of hatred (see Chapter 5). Designation can serve as a precursor of genocide.

A number of contemporary scholars draw parallels between how the Nazis dealt with the Jews and how they treated the Roma or Gypsies (see Appendix C).[32] The Nazis handled the Gypsies with brute force. In Nazi Germany, when it came to humiliation and killings, Gypsies often found themselves one fateful step behind Jews. The Citizenship Law of 1943 clearly stated, "Jews and Gypsies cannot become German citizens."

> [I]n January or February 1940, 250 Gypsy children from Brno in the concentration camp at Buchenwald were used as guinea pigs for testing Zyklon B cyanide gas crystals, a lethal insecticide that from 1941 onward was used for the mass murders at Auschwitz-Birkeneau.[33]

Mass murders of Gypsies began at Auschwitz in 1943. Nazi Germany lost about two-thirds of its Gypsy population in concentration camps; Nazi-occupied Europe lost about 20 percent of its Gypsy population.

Over time, the Nazis developed racial classifications for Gypsies. However, the formation of a group into a racial one does not always follow a straightforward trajectory. It takes considerable effort for future perpetuators and their present cohorts to construct racial classifications. The process takes roughly the following steps. First, the state employs scientists to substantiate and legitimate racial groups. The Nazis had two agencies engaged in research on whether the Gypsies had Jewish origins. Second, the politicians enact policies and pass laws that use the "scientific" race designations. The 1935 Nuremberg laws, which first legally defined Jews, officially identified Gypsies as non-Aryan. The 1938 Decree for Combating the Gypsy Plague, however, marked a change in Nazi policy from one that treated the Gypsy problem as behavioral to one that perceived Gypsies as a racial group.[34] Yet, even with the scientific data and legal enactments in place, the potential perpetrators still have a long way to go. In fact, we still would not have a genocide case in a situation where perpetrators killed large numbers of members of a pre-designated racial group. A racial designation and mass killings do not prove the existence of a policy to exterminate a targeted group.

Some scholars, while readily agreeing that the Nazis harmed Gypsies, claim that the Nazis generally considered Gypsies only a minor irritant compared to the "evil vermin" represented by the Jews. They argue that merely because Gypsies shared racial classification and brutal treatment with Jews does not mean that the Nazis committed genocide against the Gypsies. According to their views, Jews alone "occupied the precise place at which humiliation and extermination intersected."[35] To support their position, these scholars point out that "no plan ever emerged to annihilate all Gypsies analogous to the 'Final Solution' of the Jewish Question."[36] While some Nazi leaders demanded the extermination of the Gypsies, a different and influential racial assessment of Gypsies dampened rather than augmented the calls for Gypsy annihilation. Heinrich Himmler, who by 1936 controlled Hitler's entire repressive police and security forces, promoted the view that Gypsies had Aryan origins. Data from research institutes, some directly under Himmler's control, bolstered the idea of racially pure Gypsies.

Despite the similarities, a critical asymmetry between racial designations for Jews and Gypsies emerged. The Nazis marked pure Jews for extermination, but some classifications of "part Jews" (*Mischlinges*), especially early in the Nazi period, gave individuals a degree of protection. In contrast, while the Nazis exempted some pure Gypsies from deportation, they treated mixed Gypsies (*Mischlinges*) harshly. Even some of these "good Gypsy *Mischlinges*" had possibilities of becoming part of the racially pure group. Further, when the Nazis sent Gypsies to Auschwitz, they permitted them, unlike any other targeted group, to live together in family camps. One scholar, Lewy, claims that as late as the 1990s German prosecutions of war criminals found no Final Solution for Gypsies from the evidence.[37] However, another scholar, Greenville raises a disturbing rhetorical question: "If persecution [of Gypsies] was not based on racial theory, why murder [their] children?"[38] Perhaps, we can safely conclude that the Gypsies became a quasi-racial group targeted for annihilation, in part.

(b) *Chinese Cambodians*. The Chinese suffered enormously under the Khmer Rouge. For example, as a group, they experienced a disproportionate number of deaths. During the reign of the Khmer Rouge, the Chinese population of Cambodia decreased from 430,000 to 215,000. The Khmer Rouge killed about one half of the total Chinese population. Did the Khmer Rouge target the Chinese Cambodians as members of a national, ethnic, or racial group? The Chinese Cambodians seem to qualify as both a national and as an ethnic group. As a national group, the Chinese Cambodians probably were less vulnerable to harm than the Vietnamese Cambodians were as the former posed less of a threat to the regime than the Vietnamese did. This difference stems from the fact that the Khmer Rouge at least made a pretense of keeping friendly relations with China whereas Vietnam clearly remained Cambodia's enemy throughout the reign of the Khmer Rouge.

Scholars disagree about whether the Khmer Rouge systematically targeted the Chinese as an ethnic group. International jurists Ratner and Abrams, for example, find support for the claim that "the Khmer Rouge targeted the ethnic Chinese as an ethnic group... [in] reports that their mistreatment continued well after the Khmer Rouge had confiscated their property and had forced them to live as Khmer peasants."[39] In contrast, Vickery denies that Pol Pot directed mass killings against the Chinese as such. Instead, Vickery sees the atrocities arising from a peasant revolution.[40] In other words, the largely urban Chinese Cambodians simply had landed at the wrong end of a revolution that glorified the peasantry. Vickery may be correct in discounting the killing of Chinese as genocide. Neither disproportionate killings nor discriminatory acts against a group suffice to warrant a charge of genocide. Perpetrators of genocide must define and target the group for partial or total annihilation. Again, as in the case of looking at the Chinese as a national group, we need more information to decide. However, from the available evidence, it seems unlikely that the Khmer Rouge targeted the Chinese Cambodians for extermination as an ethnic group.

For purposes of this discussion, the more interesting issue is whether the Chinese Cambodians constituted a racial group-type. If the Khmer Rouge targeted the Chinese as a racial group, this would support a genocide charge. While the Nazis clearly developed racial categories for Jews and Gypsies, the Khmer Rogue did not construct similar racial divides for the Chinese or for any other groups. Scholars agree that the idea of *racial superiority* of the Kampuchean people formed the foundation of the Khmer Rogue's ideology. They disagree, however, over whether the idea of *racial inferiority* further motivated the mass killings.[41] Within Khmer Rouge thinking, however, it seems that the Chinese, Vietnamese, Thais, and Chams represented separate groups but not distinct races.[42]

Race has qualities such as immutability that set it apart from other group types. Race represents something more fundamental and less changeable than religion, nationality, ethnicity, or class. Admittedly, individuals seem to "pass on" their religion, nationality, and their ethnicity to their offspring. There is a sense in which current generations receive these traits or "group-identity markers" from past generations and passed them on to future generations. Therefore, in a way, individuals inherit group types. However, the biological language here is largely metaphorical. Further, it is important to keep in mind that classifications such as religion, nationality, and ethnicity have permeable boundaries. Under certain circumstances, individuals can escape religious, national, and ethnic designations. People may have opportunities to change their religion, nationality, or their ethnic status. However, a racial label, as something supposedly "deeply biological," permits little or no room for escape or change. When left to grow and solidify, race becomes an inescapable and intractable group type. When perpetrators take the fateful plunge and build their ideology around race, these actions signal something sinister in the making.

Fortunately, racial distinctions did not fester long enough during Pol Pot's reign to take over the Khmer Rouge's ideology of hate. To deny, retrospectively, that the Khmer Rouge fully used its version of the Nazi race card on the Chinese is not to deny the Chinese their status as victims. Certainly, the Chinese experienced terrible suffering under the Khmer Rouge. The question is not whether the Chinese Cambodians were victims but rather whether they were victims of a certain type.[43] However, before we accept the proposition that the suffering inflicted upon the Chinese Cambodians did not rise to a level that warrants a charge of genocide, let us consider whether they were targeted not as one group-type but as multiple ones.

Compound Designated Groups

Let us return to the issue of multiple group types, which we addressed previously but largely in the abstract. Groups seem to become especially vulnerable when one of their recognized group identities overlaps with one or more of the other designated group-types. The Democratic Kampuchea's (the DK) treatment of the Muslim Chams illustrates how multiple identities can increase a group's vulnerability to harm. The Muslim Chams became vulnerable on two fronts, religious and ethnic. Ethnicity is a more firmly entrenched group type than religion. Ethnicity is something that people seem to be born into, something that they cannot easily discard. Ethnicity, in general, seems more difficult to change because of its (largely unsubstantiated) connection to physical characteristics. Italians supposedly have defining physical features; Catholics do not. We do not need to agree with all or any of these interpretations of the nature of ethnicity to appreciate their force and widespread acceptance. For one thing, these interpretations help make sense of why Muslim Chams seem to have experienced greater harms than the Buddhists. Cambodian Buddhists only had one thing that made them vulnerable—their religion; the Muslim Chams, had two. Therefore, we must slightly modify our previous claim. While single group types, especially racial ones, prove the most important, multiple types can also help us explain other comparative vulnerabilities. In the end, however, we shall find that even the Muslim Chams do not clearly qualify as a targeted genocide group. First, however, we need to give long overdue attention to a clearly targeted, compound group—the Jews.

1. *Racial and Religious Groups*. (a) *Jews*. Primo Levi, in his last book written before he committed suicide, provided one of the more telling accounts of the Holocaust:

> The human ashes coming from the crematoria, tons daily, were easily recognized as such, because they often contained teeth or vertebrae. Nevertheless, they were employed for several purposes: as fill for swamp lands, as thermal insulation between the walls of wooden buildings, and as phosphate fertilizer; and especially notable, they were used instead of gravel to cover the paths of the SS village located near the camp, whether out of pure callousness or because, due to their origins, they were regarded as material to be trampled on, I couldn't say.[44]

The Holocaust pushed civilization's moral categories to the limit or perhaps beyond the limit.[45] The Nazis stretched the previously unthinkable idea of *total destruction* into a now imaginable form by ordering the destruction of every aspect of Jewish identity—including the grinding up of the bones of dead Jews. Nazi barbarity surpassed those of serial killers such as Jeffrey Dahmers, who ate the hearts of his victims. The repulsive acts of serial killers may show, in a perverted sense, more respect for their victims than the Nazis' acts of complete annihilation. As the philosopher Emil Fackenheim notes, graves characterize civilization, and the Final Solution had no burials for Jews. The Nazis extended "annihilation of the living" to "annihilation of the dead." As repulsive as this conjecture might be, if the Nazis had eaten their victims' hearts as Dahmers had done, they might have shown that they had some respect, however perverted, for their victims.

The Nazis pushed the limits of malevolent imagination and the bounds of deplorable morality. They directed their terror primarily at one target. "The Nazis terror was a selective terror, and Jews were the terror's most important targets."[46] The Jews fit into a number of group types. They were a religious group and, arguably, an ethnic group. They were not a national one since before the founding of the state of Israel in 1948, European Jews had no nation outside their country of residence. Yet, the Nazis actually paid little attention to Jews as a religious, ethnic group or, even if they could have, as a national group. The Nazis regarded the Jews as a separate race. The Nazis directed the bulk of their hateful venom at the Jews as a race. The racialization of groups makes members of that group particularly susceptible to the worst nightmares of genocide.

2. *Religious and Ethnic Groups*. (a) *Muslim Chams*. There is certainly evidence that the Khmer Rouge tried to destroy the cultural practices that helped to define Muslim Chams. The Khmer Rouge banned the Cham's Islamic schools, prohibited their religious practices, and forbid them to speak their native language. Commentators take these actions as ample proof that the regime intended to destroy the Chams.[47] However, we must distinguish attempts to destroy the cultural aspects of group identity and plans to obliterate the group through the mass killings of its members. If "planned mass killings of members of a group because of their group identity" are central to the crime of genocide, then, as we have seen in the case of AUM, attacks on the cultural practices of a group are insufficient (see Chapter 3).

While the Khmer Rouge killed enough Chams to qualify as genocide, they do not seem to have targeted them for extermination.[48] Vickery, for example, searches for an alternative explanation for why the Khmer Rouge killed disproportionately large numbers of Chams in other regions.[49] He hypothesizes that the Khmer Rouge targeted Chams not because of their religion or ethnicity but because of their class. In the next section, we shall turn to a discussion of class and other groups not specifically mentioned in the genocide laws. Let us first, however, summarize the argument so far.

The analysis undertaken in this chapter should have erased negative reactions generated by comparing Hitler and Pol Pot. Further, the analysis should have sufficiently demonstrated some important comparative legal and moral judgments that we can make about these ruthless leaders and their regimes. First, Pol Pot was not Hitler; the Khmer Rouge regime was not the Nazi regime. The group types targeted by the Nazis more clearly meet the criterion for genocide victim groups types than the groups harmed by the Khmer Rouge. Second, among the groups targeted by the Nazis, the Jews, as a racial group, have the dubious distinction of being the one group unequivocally targeted for annihilation. The Khmer Rouge did not target any groups in any way comparable to the Nazi onslaught against the Jews. Each stage of the analysis taken throughout the book builds portions of a legal and moral framework for dealing with genocide cases. The conceptual framework constructed at this point should help to clarify the issues and perhaps to resolve some of the scholarly disputes over the German and the Cambodian cases. More importantly, each stage of the analysis establishes aspects of an analytically sound and morally defensible legal framework for dealing with future genocide cases.

Some important theses have emerged. First, the choice of a limited number of group-types mentioned in the genocide laws makes sense. Throughout history, religion, nationality, ethnicity, and race have been the characteristics around which hate and terror consistently and persistently have mobilized. Hate against others has massed its ugly forces along the battle lines of religion, nationality, ethnicity, and race. Second, the analysis has shown why it makes sense to list these group markers in a hierarchical order of vulnerability with religious and national groups at one end and ethnicity and race at the other end. Finally, we still need to resolve the issue whether the list of group-types designated in the genocide laws is exhaustive. As we shall see in the following section, this problem calls for a new strategy of legal interpretation. Instead of adding new group-types, jurists should accept a more general sense of victim groups as defined externally by perpetrators.

Non-Designated Groups

1. *Political Groups*. The challenge of reconciling the idea of designated with non-designated groups forces us to provide a general solution to the problem of how to determine which groups qualify as genocide victim groups. Although we

have seen that jurists have had good reasons for listing four types of groups, those who want to expand the list also have a good case. The expansionists argue that even if we assume that the designated list includes all past genocide groups, we have no reason to presume that future cases will fit into the assigned categories. Some future demagogue might try to eliminate a completely new group such as those perceived to hold certain philosophical beliefs. To prepare for these contingencies we need to appeal to a more general way of determining genocide victim groups. While those who want to add new groups rightly criticize those who take the list of groups as exhaustive, their proposal to add political and other types to the list is inefficient and implausible. Their strategy presupposes that the added types will exhaust future possibilities, and as we have seen, we have no way of telling how future perpetrators will perceive of groups they hate. A more efficient and sounder strategy lies in utilizing the ways perpetrators have defined and characterized the groups they targeted. A strategy that takes a *perpetrator perspective* on defining and determining victim groups enables us to draw some important distinctions between cases involving Stalin's famine victims, Hitler's political opposition, and Pol Pot's enemies. Most importantly, the analysis provides a critical insight into the Cambodian massacres.

(a) *Stalin's and Hitler's Enemies* (see Appendix C). Before returning to the comparison of cases from Germany and Cambodia, we need to complete an analysis of a case we have intermittently highlighted throughout the book. The case from the 1933 Soviet famine, which took the lives of millions of Soviet citizens, will also help us understand the Cambodian case. We have already shown in Chapter 4 that the case does not qualify as genocide as Stalin and his regime lacked the requisite intent. Here, we add another reason for rejecting it as a case of genocide. Stalin's targeted group does not meet the criterion of a genocide victim group. For the sake of argument, let us assume that Stalin's regime had the requisite intent for a charge of genocide. Then, we need to ask whether Stalin intentionally inflicted starvation on any one readily identifiable group. In this case, the following three groups contend for victim status: a national minority (the Ukrainians), a class (the *kulaks* or rich peasants), and a socio-economic group (the peasants, in general).

The argument for treating the Ukrainians as Stalin's genocide victims hinges on the disproportionate number of deaths suffered by the Ukrainians during the famine. Yet, the conclusion that supposedly follows from this observation runs counter to Soviet programs that successfully promoted Ukrainian national culture from 1927 to 1933. Further, the fact that Ukrainian people died in disproportionate numbers from the famine does not qualify the killing of Ukrainians as genocide as other groups in the North Caucuses and Lower Volga shared the suffering and the generic label the *enemies of collectivization*. Overall, the case that Stalin's regime negatively defined the Ukrainians and that it aimed to destroy them remains weak.

Perhaps, the idea of class fits the Soviet famine case better than the category of national minority. Letgers, a proponent of using the notion of class, laments that the UN definition of genocide excludes categories based on class such as the *kulaks*:

> If an allegedly socialist society, whose primary form of classification is that of class, either targets or invents a class with extermination in prospect, that program must count as genocide for the contemporary world in all its variety.[50]

The idea of a class as a genocide victim category has its share of problems. First, Letgers and other analysts need to provide a more precise definition of the general term "class" and the specific term "kulaks." Otherwise, it remains unclear whether to understand *kulaks* as the more prosperous peasants or as the village moneylenders and mortgagors. Many villages did not have *kulaks*, if that term meant peasants who employed hired hands. In some villages, peasants slightly better off than others peasants carried the label *kulaks*. Moreover, even if we ignore definitional problems, we still need to explain why the famine extended beyond the *kulaks* to many average-income farmers and to poor peasants. As this case illustrates, adding class to the list of victim group types in the genocide laws would not help.

Finally, consider that the target group might cut across national and class lines to encompass peasants (*muzhiks*) in general. The writings of Marx and Lenin provide evidence of a disdain for the peasantry (see Chapter 5). However, historians have not shown that Stalin and his regime held any deep-seated animosity toward the peasants. While Stalin wanted to discipline the peasants, he did not want to exterminate them. Thus, Stalin's regime lacked two ingredients needed to call the Soviet famine genocide, namely, corporate intent and, as we now see, an appropriate victim group-type.

The actions that Stalin took against political dissidents have closer parallels to the policies that Pol Pot implemented than do his policies directed at peasants. Perhaps, Stalin's treatment of political dissidents would warrant a charge of genocide. Instead of pursing the case of the Soviet Gulag, however, let us return to a comparison of Hitler and Pol Pot.

Hitler's political opponents, primarily members of the communist party (*Kommunistische Partei Deutschlands*, the KDP), suffered greatly under the Third Reich, especially during its early years. In 1933, under an emergency decree, the Nazis arrested over 25,000 political dissidents and sent them to Dachau, the only concentration camp located in Germany. However, little of any organized political opposition survived into the later, most brutal phases of the Third Reich's extermination campaigns. Organized political groups, then, did not stand out among Hitler's most loathsome, targeted groups.

As we shall see, a consideration of unorganized political opposition under the Nazi regime sheds light on the Cambodian case. During the Third Reich, contrary to popular beliefs, ordinary unorganized German citizens expressed little opposition to the Nazis.[51] When ordinary citizens did speak out, they received relatively mild punishments, if any. Although the *Heimtücke* laws proscribed malicious attacks on the Nazi party and its leadership, a vast majority of the cases that fell under this law ended in dismissals or mild punishments.[52]

(b) *Pol Pot's Enemies.* In sharp contrast to the situation in the Third Reich, Cambodian citizens with political views different from those of the Khmer Rouge became the regime's primary targets. To underscore how the Khmer Rouge targeted even those they imagined to harbor contrary political views let us return to the controversy over whether Pol Pot's targeted groups fit under ethnic/racial or political/class classifications. Some historians find that ethnic hatred and racial persecution were at the heart of the Khmer Rouge's madness while other historians think that a Marxist sense of class set the foundations for the atrocities. David Chandler claims that the Khmer Rouge regime largely "discriminated against the enemies of the revolution rather than against specific ethnic or religious groups."[53] Chandler thinks that using the word "genocide" to describe the killings in Cambodia invites "egregious" comparisons to Hitler.[54] Kiernan, a fellow historian and Chandler's one-time book collaborator, sharply disagrees and argues that "Khmer conceptions of race overshadowed those of class."[55]

Indeed, the polemical stakes seem high. A resolution of the Chandler/Kiernan debate might determine whether Pol Pot had become the next Hitler. The choice of victim categories also has important legal implications. The genocide laws include ethnicity and race, but they do not include political groups or classes. Further, a resolution of the issue has important political repercussions as for over a decade various interest groups have tried to bring the leaders of Democratic Kampuchea to justice. The *United States Cambodian Genocide Act* (1994) and the *United Nations Group of Experts for Cambodia Report* (1999) demanded trials for Khmer Rouge leaders. Although the United Nations withdrew its support of the trials in 2002, it seems likely that trials will soon take place.

The policies and actions of the Khmer Rouge blurred the regular legal categories. Further, it seems that Pol Pot had an even fuzzier idea of class than Stalin did of the *kulaks*. Yet, the Khmer Rouge clearly did target a group type not found on the legal list. A key to understanding the Cambodian killings lies in recognizing that the Khmer Rouge targeted a specific group, namely, its *political enemies*. The fact that its leaders and soldiers used bizarre ways to determine whether an individual belonged to this group does not undermine the viability of it as a legal category. In fact, recognizing the odd contours of the Khmer Rouge victim type provides a key to making sense of the Cambodian massacres. The Khmer Rouge did not set out to eliminate impure races or despised ethnicities from their land. Rather, they became obsessed with the elimination of any political impurity, of any individual who belonged to *the enemy*.

Testimonies from survivors help to open windows into the perpetrators' mind-set. "Having been a soldier, a student, a civil servant, a petty bourgeois vendor, an admirer of the monarchy, or having been related to someone with such characteristics" could qualify individuals for membership in *the enemy group*.[56] Witnesses cited a variety of reasons why the Khmer Rouge first labeled people as *the enemy* and then proceeded to kill them. Grounds for killing included traveling from one village to another without permission and unauthorized possession of foraged food.[57]

The following case pointedly illustrates the strange state of the perpetrator's mind-set in classifying individuals as *political enemies*.

> Cadres ordered farmers to 'walk on the right' side of the plough rig behind the oxen, but instead the unwary peasants followed their traditional practice of walking on the left side. As a result, they were accused of being the enemy and killed immediately in front of all the people who plowed there.[58]

Oddly enough, these examples help to make sense of why the Khmer Rouge appeared to target groups such as Buddhists, Vietnamese, Eastern Khmers, and Muslim Chams. According to a number of analysts, the Chinese Cambodians, for example, "were not murdered as such, but [were targeted] as traders and capitalists in the greatest need of reformation."[59] The Khmer Rouge targeted the Chinese Cambodians, like the other groups, primarily as *enemies of the regime*.

The Cambodian case demonstrates the power of using the perpetuator's mind-set as the basis for determining which victim groups merit the dubious distinction of being covered under the crime of genocide. Perpetrators define the legally relevant, genocide victim-types. Ruthless dictators kill massive numbers of people. Their victims often do not fit into any typical genocide victim categories. The victims of the Khmer Rouge, for example, did not belong to any religion, nationality, ethnicity, or race. What tied together the diverse victims is that they made the mistake of being perceived as political enemies of their rulers.

CONCLUSION

In many ways, this chapter and previous ones demonstrate that international legal practice often outdistances academic thinking about law, justice, and ethics. There are good reasons for retaining the categories of groups as designated in the genocide laws. Throughout history, roughly the same groups appear on the horrifying list of victims. Racial groups have received the most and worst harms over time. Jews, of course, have had a long, tragic history as targets. The horrors directed against blacks also have a long history. Recent events have witnessed a resurgence of harms directed against ethnic (national, tribal) groups whose victimization has deep historical roots. Finally, religious persecutions and killings have a well-known history. The characteristics of race, ethnicity, nationality, and religion mark off boundaries of hated groups. The boundaries are seldom real and mostly imagined—which makes their targeting even more devastating and problematic. What makes these dynamics particularly despicable is that these group designators have little or (more likely) nothing to do with what people did and only with what they are perceived to be. Nothing individuals have done or will do, for example, marks them off as a separate race.

As we have seen, these markers do not exhaust the contours of hate. The laws on genocide should be based on past cases, but they also should apply to future ones.

Future mass killers may find novel ways of classifying a group of people for extermination. A future victim group such as a political group may not meet the "national, ethnical, racial, and religious" designations as specified in the current laws of genocide. Future perpetrators may target a political group. As we have seen, to meet this contingency, some critics have proposed to expand the list of designated group-types to include political, social, linguistic, and other group types. However, for the genocide laws to handle the unexpected groupings that perpetrators can conjure, prosecutors and judges need to employ criteria for genocide victim groups based on how perpetrators came to categorize their objects of hate. Paradoxically, genocide may have more to do with perpetrators than with victims. This leaves one final but crucial task, to determine the nature of the perpetrators.

Chapter 7

Genocide Perpetrators: Organized Barbarity

> Article 6 (a) Genocide by killing.
>
> Elements
>
> 1. **The perpetrator** killed one or more persons.
> 2. Such person or persons belonged to a particular national, ethnical [ethnic], racial or religious group.
> 3. The perpetrator intended to destroy, in whole or in part, that national, ethnical, racial or religious group as such.
> 4. **The conduct took place in the context of a manifest pattern of similar conduct directed against that wrong** or was conduct could itself effect such destruction.
>
> —Rome Statute of the International Criminal Court

Despite the overwhelming impact that organizations have on violence, current legal and ethical approaches underplay the organizational features and focus almost exclusively on the individual aspects of violent crimes. An examination of debates within the Nuremberg Tribunal uncovers persuasive arguments for holding organizations criminally liable, banning them, and requiring restitution from (and not retribution against) their members. The adoption of a restorative justice model has important policy implications. It leads to a recommendation that the newly established permanent war crimes tribunal, the International Criminal Court (ICC), should have jurisdiction over criminal organizations. This expansion would go beyond the jurisdictional scope allotted to the two currently operating ad hoc war crimes tribunals, the International Criminal Tribunal for the Former Yugoslavia (ICTY) and the International Criminal Court for Rwanda (ICTR), which have jurisdiction only over natural persons and not over organizations. In fact, the Security Council rejected France's proposal to include jurisdiction over groups in the ICTY Statute.

Although an expansion of the ICC's jurisdiction to criminal organizations represents a departure for the practices of the ICTY and the ICTR, it revitalizes an important judicial approach adopted (and then largely abandoned) at the

Nuremberg trials. The issue of the liability of organizations in international law presents far more than interesting academic questions. The failure to hold organizations criminally responsible in international criminal law has far reaching effects throughout the world. The 1994 Rwanda genocide and its tragic aftermath, which sadly continue through the present, amply demonstrate the disastrous consequences that follow when international criminal law does not hold criminal organizations accountable for grave injustices. In some sense, this analysis represents a shrill cry that begs the world to pay considerably more attention to the mass graves of unknown human beings, especially those in Central Africa.

ORGANIZED VIOLENCE

Textbooks on teaching methods recommend beginning the lessons on unfamiliar subjects with ones on subjects the students already know. It seems quite natural, then, to use the more familiar and more established national criminal law as the starting point to learn about the less familiar international criminal law. Later, however, we shall see how this seemingly innocent strategy actually leads us astray. Perhaps, we should not always do what the textbooks tell us to do. At this point, however, let us turn to some examples of criminal actions that vividly illustrate the critical role that organizations play in spreading violence.

Criminals do not always act alone. Rather, in some cases, followers within a group carry out violent acts in the name of their leader or group. When these group members successfully inflict violence on others, the leaders of religious cults and hate organizations and not their captured followers receive most of the media attention. In 1995, members of Aum Shinrikyo (AUM or "Supreme Truth"), a doomsday cult in Japan, released sarin, a deadly nerve gas, in a Tokyo subway, that killed twelve and injured hundreds.[1] Yet, Shoko Asahara, AUM's self-appointed guru, and not his accused followers received most of the media attention. Should the heavy media attention given to AUM's leader compared to the accused followers find a parallel in the efforts of criminal prosecutors? Do these cult leaders deserve more severe punishment than their soldiers who carry out the evil deed do?

Prosecutors may have some choice of indicting one or more of the following for the crime. The first category of criminals, that is, those that actually commit the crime, seems uncontroversial. Under limited circumstances, prosecutors may also charge group leaders. According to the criminal conspiracy principles of most national legal systems, leaders such as Asahara may have criminal liability for the criminal acts of their followers. Some leaders may even receive greater punishments than their followers may. The follower Ikuo Hayashi, a former heart surgeon, received a life sentence for his role in the Tokyo subway attack while, in 1994, a Tokyo district court sentenced the leader Asahara to death. Finally, and even less likely, prosecutors may pursue certain organizations. In 1999, the Japanese parliament passed laws to increase the regulation of AUM and similar organizations, but it refused to heed public demands to ban AUM.

Disturbing cases involving leaders and followers also have occurred in the United States. Richard Butler leads the Aryan Nation, a white supremacist organization based in Idaho. In 1998, Jesse Warfield and John Yeager, Aryan Nation guards, assaulted Victoria Keenan and her teenage son Jason as they drove along a public road near the compound. The Southern Poverty Law Center brought a civil action on behalf of Keenan and her son. In a verdict likely to bankrupt one of the nation's most notorious white supremacist organizations, an Idaho jury on September 7, 2000, returned a $6.3 million civil judgment against the Aryan Nation, its founder Richard Butler, and the security guards. In this case, the leader, some followers, and the organization each had some form of civil liability.

In the heartland of the United States, Matt Hale directed the World Church of the Creator in East Peoria, Illinois. Hale graduated from Southern Illinois University Law School and played violin in a professional orchestra. On the Fourth of July 1999, Benjamin Smith, a Hale disciple, went on an ethnic and racially motivated shooting spree throughout Illinois and Indiana. Smith killed two and wounded nine non-whites before he committed suicide. Hale denied giving any orders to Smith.[2]

In each of these incidents, the followers and not the leaders committed the crimes. The leaders—Asahara, Butler, and Hale—did not commit the actual crimes. Nevertheless, should we hold them in some way responsible? Commentators have largely focused on this question of leadership responsibility. Here, we want to focus on slightly different questions. Where do so-called "hate organizations" fit into the scheme of criminal liability? Should the law ban organizations that foster hate and violence? What responsibility, if any, do members of these organizations have? These questions help to redirect the legal and moral inquiry. Instead of looking at the relationship between leaders and followers, we turn the spotlight on the organizations within which the leaders and followers acted.

Hate groups or criminal organizations do not simply provide incidental background features for criminal activity. Hate organizations, directly and indirectly, sanction harmful action against individuals singled out for their (perceived or actual) identification as members of status groups. Analyses of hate crimes sometimes address the responsibility of these organizations, but these concerns often become swamped by efforts to ascribe responsibility to individual criminal wrongdoers in the organization and their leaders. While hate organizations receive their share of publicity, they seldom shoulder the primary legal and moral responsibility for hate crimes. What, if any, legal and moral responsibility should organizations have for hate crimes?

Let us consider these questions in contexts that are more specific. Do Aum Shinrikyo, the Church of the Aryan Nation, and the World Church of the Creator have anything in common with more notorious hate organizations such as the Nazis' *Sturmabteilung* (SA) and the *Schutzstaffel* (SS) or with more recent militant hate organizations such as Arkan's Tigers (Yugoslavia) and the *Intèrahamwe* (Rwanda)? Are the growing numbers of hate organizations nascent forms of more lethal ones whose impact goes far beyond national borders? Should states dismantle hate organizations in their early stages?

Questions about the criminal responsibility of an organization conflict with deeply embedded notions of criminal responsibility. It makes sense to ascribe criminal responsibility to an individual leader and to those followers who committed the crimes. In contrast, the idea of an organization's responsibility runs counter to the dominant way of thinking about criminal law. Powerful individualistic intuitions underlie the prevailing conceptions of criminality. Yet, notions of criminal responsibility rooted in ideas of individual guilt do not provide good models for devising a sound legal and moral approach to genocide.

To appreciate how firmly entrenched the idea of individual responsibility is ask people to imagine a violent act. They will most likely "see" or associate violence with an individual or a few individuals. Yet, many instances of violence do not fit completely into a frame that pictures only individuals. The most devastating occurrences of violence have organizational features. Self-professed racists with only loose connections to hate organizations can do considerable harm. However, when hate-mongers act under the authority of an organization, the harms that they can inflict grow exponentially. Violence, in its most horrendous manifestations, emanates not only from individual acts but also from organizations.

Yet, even this seemingly innocuous description is misleading because it suggests that organizations make up just another additional feature of violence. Organizational features, however, are not merely add-on ones. Organizations do not operate on the periphery of violence. Rather, the organizational aspects typically provide the conditions needed for the violence to happen in the first place and for the extent and severity of the violence to increase. The more serious incidents of violence occur not because of increasing numbers of perpetrators (the many actors in an organization versus a single wrongdoer) but because of the increased organizational capacity of the perpetrators. The potential harms from the deeds of an unorganized mob pale in comparison to those conducted by organized groups. Compared to unorganized crowds, organized militias have a greater capacity to sustain and increase the commission of violent acts. Despite the overwhelming impact of organizations on violence, current legal and ethical approaches underplay the organizational features and focus almost exclusively on the individual aspects.

To underscore the strong ties between organizations and violence let us turn to some mental images and word associations. When asked to picture hate, individuals often imagine an irrational individual or an emotionally inflamed group of individuals. Contrary to common associations, when severe incidences of hate occur, they most often have a planned, organizational character. Hate needs organizations to thrive and to grow into its most insidious forms. Genocide, mass killing, and other grave injustices require organization. The sheer magnitude of "crimes against humanity" precludes, for all practical purposes, solitary individual actions. To achieve a level of large-scale atrocities the violent acts must move beyond a few followers carrying out the wishes of a leader. The scale of many horrors necessitates the coordination of large numbers of individuals.

Scenarios that imagine a lone individual releasing a deadly poison in the water supply of the people that the individual hates leave out details that would begin to raise questions about an individual's ability to perform an act like this. How, for example, did the individual learn about the intricacies of the water supply system? How did the individual take precautions to contain the poison so that it affected only members of the targeted group? Despite the critical role that organizations play in the execution of grave injustices, the responses to them often stay focused on individual criminal guilt. It is important to keep in mind that our claims apply to particular kinds of grave injustice, namely, those stemming from hatred of a group. While the public might berate the demonic character of dictators by calling for severe punishments of political leaders responsible for atrocities or demanding that key figures in the undertaking of a grave injustice of this type be brought to justice, common practice leaves the organizations that breed the harms largely untouched.

Scholars and jurists have not confronted fully the problem of reconciling the organized character of violence with the individualized approach to responsibility. Criminal justice systems, national and international, primarily accuse and punish individuals. Admittedly, debates within these legal systems do not ignore organizations altogether. For example, in the United States and elsewhere, the issue of whether to extend the core concept of individual criminal responsibility to organizations, such as corporations, has received considerable attention. However, discussions about criminal law typically address organizational responsibility as an extension of individual responsibility.[3]

In international law, in contrast to national (municipal) legal systems, organizations receive even less attention. This trend becomes especially worrisome considering that international criminal systems typically deal with the most widespread and severe crimes. War crimes that involve military organizations, for example, surely qualify as exemplars of organized violence. Questions about organizational responsibility would seem most appropriate in cases where international law is applied to genocide, crimes against humanity, and war crimes. Yet, the history of war crimes tribunals reveals that the idea of individual criminal responsibility has held sway over all other types of responsibility. In addition, war crimes tribunals have largely ignored organizations because of a common perception that events at Nuremberg definitively decided the issue. After Nuremberg, it seems that organizations no longer had criminal responsibility in international humanitarian law. Since Nuremberg, war crimes tribunals seldom have entertained alternative ideas to individual criminal guilt. The ICTY and ICTR do not have jurisdiction over organizations. Similarly, the statutes governing the formation of an International Criminal Court (ICC) do not include procedures for declaring organizations criminal. Further, the issue of whether to hold organized militias criminally responsible for war crimes has not arisen in current debates over the ICC.

International jurists should work to reverse the current trend. They should lobby for a more widespread adoption of standards for the criminal responsibility of organizations. The concept of *individual guilt*, whatever its role in national criminal law, should not serve as the foundation for building a system of international justice. A global legal system needs to incorporate a certain sense of collective guilt into its laws. International tribunals need the flexibility to take action against criminal organizations that play a prominent role in carrying out grave injustices.

To make the case for organizational responsibility we begin with an analysis of the reasons why the Nuremberg Tribunal began by indicting Nazi organizations. This historical analysis, undertaken in the next section, paves the way for an affirmative response to the question "Should the jurisdiction of war crimes' tribunals extend beyond natural persons to criminal organizations?" An examination of the debates within the Nuremberg Tribunal uncovers persuasive arguments for holding organizations criminally liable. While the organization approach to liability for war crimes ultimately lost at Nuremberg, speculations about what the results would have been if the organization strategy had succeeded bear considerable fruit. What effects would the Nuremberg judgments have had if the Tribunal had held Nazi organizations fully (but not exclusively) responsible for war crimes? The exercise in "what ifs" further reveals a more fundamental debate between competing theories of justice. As we shall see, the debate about organizational responsibility at Nuremberg did not turn on considerations of legal strategy. Instead, the controversy hinged on a more fundamental issue, namely, the choice between retributive and restorative approaches to punishment.

A closer look at Nuremberg demonstrates that by adopting a retributive instead of a restorative punishment model, jurists have learned the wrong lessons from Nuremberg. The choice between retributive and restorative approaches has monumental policy implications. The 1994 Rwandan genocide and its aftermath provide a critical testing ground for the competing models. A restorative model provides an optimistic and enlightening perspective on the Rwandan case.

To avoid embracing the organization responsibility position too quickly, a cautionary note is in order. The history of states declaring organizations criminal should make one skeptical of any attempt to ascribe responsibility to organizations. History paints a disturbing picture of how governments have dealt with organizations they deem criminal. States often adopted a "nip-the-hate-groups-in-the-bud" strategy. The British India Act (1836), for example, included provisions to sentence all members of an organization called "the Thugs" to a life of hard labor.[4] In the United States, New York (1802) became the first state to adopt criminal syndicalism laws. Thirty-two other states followed New York's lead after World War I. Syndicalism laws banned radical organizations (social anarchists), unions (International Workers of the World), and other organizations that promoted illicit means to effect political change. The Soviets, French, and Germans had similar laws. Later, the Smith Act (1940) made the Communist Party of the United States illegal. Finally, we must add Germany to the list of countries that prosecuted organizations. On May 30, 1924, the German courts declared the entire Nazi Party a criminal organization.[5]

These examples seem to support moves to ban hate organizations before they become too strong. Imagine how different our world might be if the Weimar Republic had succeeded in banning the Nazi party. Yet, the Nazi case demonstrates just the opposite. Official attacks on the Nazi party strengthened it. Our brief excursion into history's underside should serve as a stark reminder of how the label "criminal organization" has stifled and repressed political dissent. The lure of the Nazi banning case rests on looking at it retrospectively, that is, after we knew about the atrocities connected to its name. The case for prior restraint (in this case, banning the Nazi party) depends on our ability to predict what the organization will in fact do. Given the unreliability of predictions of individual violent behavior, the art of atrocity forecasting for organizations proves even more unreliable. A determination of whether the model developed here falls victim to similar government excesses must await the full construction of the model, but we shall make every effort to heed these historical warnings throughout this study.

In the interim, consider the following preliminary response to the history lesson. Constant vigilance is required when it comes to legislative attempts to place *prior restraints* on organizations. Any attempt to deal with organizations that preach and instill hatred should attempt to find the *least restrictive* political means of regulation. The proposals defended in this study do not condone prior restraints in any form. Within the context of our restorative justice model, courts would take action only after the harms instigated by the organization have reached a stage of perpetuating actual (and not just threatened) widespread and grievous harm. This does not mean that with a restorative justice approach we, thereby, promote passivity in the face of increasingly heinous deeds committed by hate organizations. The reactive nature of restorative justice does not signal any incompatibility with morally and legally justified efforts to prevent injustices. Restorative justice practices are perfectly compatible with strong humanitarian interventionist programs. In fact, a restorative model goes hand-in-hand with prevention programs. The model's role in preventing the spread of hatred and violence will become more evident when we apply it to the complex events surrounding Rwanda. Through that case study, we shall uncover flaws in the current policies in Central Africa. As we shall see, the current individualist guilt and retributive punishment strategies have failed (by largely ignoring organizations) to stem the tide of violence by not dismantling the organizational structures responsible for it. The reasons for the failure of some current international policies lie in policy makers learning the wrong lessons from Nuremberg.

LESSONS FROM NUREMBERG

Before the end of World War II, Churchill, Stalin, and many of Roosevelt's advisors (including Treasury Secretary Henry Morgenthau) favored summary executions of Nazi leaders. Immediately after the war, the victorious military forces adopted a wide array of punishments for captured Nazis, but no one championed these methods as models of fairness and justness. As the war operations wound down, some prominent proponents of an improved system of military justice became influential. Rafael Lemkin, a Polish jurist, who almost single-handedly assured the passage of the *International Convention on the Prevention and Punishment of Genocide* (1949) (hereafter, the Genocide Convention), also had an important influence on the establishment of a war crimes tribunal. In *Axis Rule in Occupied Europe* (1944), Lemkin emphasized the criminally conspiratorial character of Nazi organizations.[6]

Within the Roosevelt administration, Lieutenant Colonel Murray C. Bernays used Lemkin's criminal conspiracy theory as part of his case in favor of a war crimes tribunal. Bernays, with a background in corporate securities-fraud conspiracy cases, argued that a conviction of organizations "should serve as *prima facie* evidence of the guilt of any of its members."[7] Bernays saw the indictment of organizations as a way to spread responsibility for Nazi atrocities beyond a few leaders. Through his lobbying and the efforts of others, especially Secretary of War, Henry Stimson, the idea of organizational responsibility began to play a key role in the establishment of a military war crimes tribunal.

The plan to indict organizations molded the shape of the tribunal that ultimately emerged. During negotiations over the London Agreement, which set forth the Charter of the International Military Tribunal, Robert H. Jackson (Associate Justice of the US Supreme Court and later the Tribunal's chief prosecutor) made Bernays's proposal to indict Nazi organizations the cornerstone of the US position. Jackson argued that the case against the defendants should focus on, "the Nazi master plan, not with individual barbarities and perversions which occurred independently of any central plan."[8] General I. T. Nititchenko (Vice President of the Supreme Court of the Soviet Union and later member of the Tribunal) rejected making charges against named organizations on grounds that their guilt had already been established.[9] Jackson's arguments to include organizations in the criminal indictments prevailed over Nitichenko's skepticism. Under Edit 10, the London Charter authorized the International Military Tribunal to declare organizations criminal and to make membership in criminal organizations a punishable offense.

The Nuremberg Tribunal indicted six organizations: the *Reichskabinett*, the General Staff and High Command, the Leadership Corps of the Party, the SA (*Sturmabteilung*), the SS (the *Schutzstaffel*, which ran the concentration camps), the Gestapo, and the SD (*Sicherheitsdienst*, a part of SS that carried out intelligence, clandestine, and liquidation operations). The German people paid close attention to news about indictments of Nazi organizations. The Tribunal's Edict 10 on criminal organizations awakened an indifferent German public. By setting forth initiatives against potential criminal organizations, it potentially affected, by some estimates, seven million German citizens. "Potentially, half the families in Germany had members who would be touched by Edict 10."[10] The SA had 4.5 million German members; the SS, "hundreds of thousands" of members; and the Leadership Corps, some 700,000 members.[11] Robert Kempner, head of the Defense Rebuttal Section, after surveying German public opinion, wrote to

Jackson, "If [only] the leaders are found guilty then the onus of guilt is removed from those who merely did their bidding."[12] German citizens did not know how far the Tribunal's arm would reach into German society. The United States alone, at that time, held some 200,000 potential German war criminals.[13]

Many books and textbooks reprint Jackson's eloquent opening speech to the Tribunal. Jackson's arguments about organizations seldom receive the attention they deserve. The following excerpt from Jackson's presentations before the Tribunal shows how seriously he took the indictment of organizations:

> These organizations penetrated the whole of German life. The country was divided into little Nazi principalities of about fifty households each. A thousand little Führers dictated; a thousand imitation Goerings strutted; a thousand Schirachs incited the youth; a thousand Saukels worked slaves; a thousand Streichers and Rosenbergs stirred up hate; a thousand Kaltenbrunners and Franks butchered and killed; a thousand Schachts and Funks administered and supported and financed this movement.
>
> They served primarily to exploit mob psychology and to manipulate the mob. These organizations indoctrinated and practiced violence and terrorism. They provided the systematized, aggressive, and disciplined execution throughout Germany and the occupied countries of the plan for crimes which we have proven. It seems beyond controversy that to punish a few top leaders but to leave this web of organized bodies in the midst of postwar society would be to foster the nucleus of a new Nazidom. These organizations are the carriers from this generation to the next of the infection of aggressive and ruthless war. The next war and the next pogroms will be hatched in the nest of these organizations as surely as we leave their membership with its prestige and influence undiminished by condemnation and punishment.[14]

The responses to Jackson's arguments included the following: attacking the idea of collective guilt; invoking pleas of involuntary membership or of unknowing minds; claiming that an individual's actions against the organization exonerated that person; and asserting a *tuo quo que* ("you too") argument, which claimed that members of Allied organization committed the same or similar "crimes" as the Nazis did. The defense collected 96,000 declarations from SS men who denied knowledge of any atrocities.[15] Hans Lateness, counsel for the German General Staff and High Command, argued (and the American *Army and Navy Journal* agreed) that the indictments constituted an attack on the military profession.[16] This, the first of the counter-arguments, became politically decisive in molding the final structure of the Nuremberg Tribunal and its legacy.

Although indictments of organizations marked the centerpiece of the prosecution's case and seven Tribunal judges sympathized with this position, the eighth judge, Francis Biddle, completely undermined the case against organizations. For Biddle, it only made sense to speak of individual guilt; it did not make sense to talk about collective guilt in any form. Biddle saw no reason to alter the paradigmatic sense of criminal responsibility used in national criminal justice systems. The idea of criminal liability presumed an intended action. From this widely shared premise, Biddle inferred the obvious, namely, that only individuals performed actions and only individuals had minds to form intentions (see Chapter 4). As Biddle then pointed out, organizations could not perform actions, and they did not have minds.

In response to Biddle's persistent pleadings, the other judges waffled. They agreed with the prosecution that organizations were criminal if they formed for and engaged in a common criminal purpose. Yet, they bristled at the thought that if they deemed an organization criminal, then members of the organization could be punished with any sentence, including death, as membership in that organization would be *per se* criminal. To avoid the unpleasant consequences that would flow by adopting Jackson's interpretation Biddle devised a compromise. To wit, the Tribunal provided members of criminal organizations with escape routes by exempting coerced and ignorant members from prosecution. At this stage, Jackson also had come to have reservations over the severe penalties for mere membership in an organization, but Jackson's own compromise came too late. Biddle's maneuvering left Jackson's modified position without a hearing. Biddle effectively pulled the teeth out of the Tribunal's finding an organization criminal as granting an exemption precluded ever reaching punishment questions. The Tribunal went forward with an investigation into the criminality of organizations, but the results of the investigation had few consequences as the Tribunal also gave individuals wide latitude in excusing their role in a criminal organization.

According to some analysts, the Tribunal's sudden detour undermined the entire enterprise:

> Biddle had killed Bernays's central concept of the trial, supported by Secretary of War Stimson and by Jackson, that the Nazi era represented a conspiracy carried out through the medium of organizations, and that only by a conspiracy indictment could the atrocities the Nazis had committed against their own people be brought before an international tribunal.[17]

In the end, the concept of individual guilt swamped any notion of organizational responsibility for war crimes.

After hearing the charges, the Tribunal acquitted some organizations and upheld charges against other ones. It found the General Staff and High Command not guilty as an organization because of its small size. Nevertheless, although the Tribunal exonerated professional military organizations, it took great pains to emphasize the individual guilt of the German military leaders.[18] The Tribunal dismissed charges against the Reich Cabinet on grounds that it did not constitute an organization after 1937. It also acquitted the SA finding that it had become ineffective as an organization after the 1934 purge. In the end, the Tribunal found that only the SS, Gestapo, and SD qualified as criminal organizations, and it singled out only the upper echelons of the Leadership Corps as legally responsible for war crimes.

In the twelve trials at Nuremberg that followed the main trials of the International Military Tribunal, only nine defendants received convictions solely based on membership in criminal organizations.[19] Only a few of these served any time in prison.[20] The determination of an organization's criminality played little role in other proceedings against Nazis. Mostly, the decisions about the organizations helped denazification tribunals, which, in the US sector alone, had classified 3.5 million criminal organization members.[21] Denazification resulted in "most of the collaborationist elite in administration, justice, education, the economy, remaining in or reentering positions held under the Nazi regime."[22] Denazification was "a process that had begun with wholesale incriminations turned in the direction of wholesale exemptions and then ended in wholesale exonerations."[23] Instead of punishment or restitution, most former Nazi officials and organization members were exonerated and purged of their former Nazi connections. Those responsible for shaping the Tribunal accepted this strategy because they feared the toll, that a policy of widespread and severe retribution would take.

With the exception of former Nazis achieving high positions of power, historians agree that the failure to remove (lustrate) former Nazis from positions of power did not adversely affect post-war Germany.[24] Nevertheless, the failure even to consider organizations as criminal in contemporary debates over war crime tribunals supports the claim that we have learned the wrong lessons from Nuremberg. Although this goes ahead of the story, consider the following possibility. Tribunals that held organizations and their members responsible for war crimes could require the members of criminal organizations to perform governmental and other forms of service. The form of justice that stems from actualizing this possibility goes beyond predicating punishment on individual criminal guilt. Membership in the organization (and not individual criminal guilt) would be a sufficient condition for imposing the performance of a community service. Further, unlike the dominant retributive approach, which concentrates on the criminal guilt of a few leaders, this restorative justice perspective does not rid, *de facto*, members of any moral taint. Rather, it provides members of criminal organizations with a means of restitution. Accordingly, members of criminal organizations have committed wrongs that are akin to the civil wrongs of tort law, but they have not committed wrongs that rise to the level of criminal liability.

A critical dissimilarity between Germany after World War II and Rwanda after the 1994 genocide strengthens the case for a restorative justice approach. After World War II, Nazi criminal organizations were almost completely disbanded. After the Rwandan genocide, organizations that should have qualified as criminal continued to wreak havoc in the region. Today, these organizations (e.g., the *Interahamwe*) still play a major role in destabilizing Central Africa through their operation in the Democratic Republic of the Congo. The failure to confront the responsibility of organizations for war crimes has had and will continue to have disastrous consequences. Before applying a restorative justice model to these current difficulties, let us unearth the conceptual flaws in the dominant retributive justice approach to legal responsibility.

CRIMINAL RESPONSIBILITY OF ORGANIZATIONS

Before proceeding, we must emphasize that we have not set out to survey the literature on criminal responsibility. We are well aware of the vast amount of material on the legal liabilities of corporations and other organizations. We have not attempted to provide an exhaustive and in-depth critique of these analyses. Instead, we seek to highlight the trends underlying these analyses so that we might better situate our recommendations. Moreover, we have not provided an exhaustive survey of relevant case law. Rather, we have carefully selected a few cases to help lay the foundation for our normative proposals.

Critiques

Who should international law hold accountable and for what? Two international relations scholars described the challenge as follows:

> Nuremberg raised several questions which have yet to be answered according to some kind of reliable international criminology: How comprehensive can the list of guilty individuals be?[25]

If we would view the glass as half full, we would note that international legal scholars and activists have made great strides particularly in the area of criminal responsibility. To cite just one of many examples of a progressive expansion of the "list of the guilty," tribunals now can hold state officials responsible for rapes committed under their watch during armed conflicts (see Chapter 3). As codified in the statutes to create an International Criminal Court, rape has become a matter of state responsibility, a war crime. The list of the potential guilty has grown.

Philosophers, like their counterpart in international law, have followed a trend to spread out responsibilities to an increasing number and variety of agents. Business ethicists, for example, have entertained models ranging from those that hold only a few agents responsible to those that argue for spreading the blame to many agents. In his seminal work, Peter French placed primary responsibility on the corporation itself.[26] Many critics rejected French's arguments for treating the corporation as a moral person. There has been a noticeable countervailing trend to develop diffuse models of corporate responsibility.[27]

A similar tendency to adopt models that spread out responsibility has emerged among philosophers concerned with social responsibility. These theorists have argued that responsibility for some social harms should extend far beyond those individuals who directly engaged in the wrongful acts.[28] Some philosophers have argued for shared responsibility for social problems such as racism and sexism. Larry May, for example, claimed that those who hold racist views should share responsibility for racial harms.[29] He proposed to extend moral responsibility even to those who did not directly perpetuate racial harms. May also argued for assigning collective responsibility for rape to men because men who are similar in critical ways to rapists benefit from the crime even though they never engaged in it.[30]

These examples roughly divide into two categories, horizontal (from a few to many individuals) and vertical diffusions of responsibility (from agent to leader). Both categories contain individuals, but they say little about organizations. However, returning to the issue of corporate responsibility, French's intuitions (to place considerable responsibility onto the corporate entity itself) seem largely correct. Indeed, there is something missing in any individualistic model. Organizations must play a role. What responsibilities should we ascribe to the collectivities that operate between the level of individual citizens and the level of a society and a state? In any investigation of genocide, those intermediary collectivities that function as state organizations or have close ties with the state keep coming to the forefront as primary actors in the commission of grave injustices. Ironically, one now famous dispute (Goldhagen) has reached the stage where analysts debate the responsibility of the entire German society for the Holocaust. Yet, these discussions have largely lost sight of questions about the legal and moral responsibility of intermediary entities (between individuals and the state), namely organizations such as the SS. Do these organizations have any responsibilities for war crimes? On the analysis provided in this chapter, the jurisdiction of war crimes' tribunals should extend beyond natural persons to include, as it did in Nuremberg, organizations.

Before assessing the role of organizations in crimes of grave injustice such as genocide, we need to clarify the idea of collective responsibility. Collective criminal responsibility poses a difficult problem because of the framework within which analysts consider it. Discussions of collective responsibility take place within an individualist criminal framework. An uncritical acceptance of the framework leads to a misleading focus on individual guilt, an uncritical acceptance of a criminal law model, and a conflation of guilt and responsibility. As we have repeatedly seen, drafters of international laws transplant notions of national criminal law, such as intent, into global criminal codes (see Chapter 4). It, then, appears quite natural to require intent as an element of criminal liability, including the crime of genocide. It seems natural to require intent because the individualistic framework remains largely unquestioned. The individualist framework has embedded itself so deeply that the absurdity of requiring proof of individual intent for the crime of genocide sails by without a snicker. How could a single individual such as Yugoslavia's former leader Slobodan Milošević have intentionally planned the crime of genocide of which he stood accused? Milošević does not fit the caricature of the Mafia boss who orders selective killings. We trivialize genocide when we treat it as a subcategory of premeditated murder. In cases where the presumptions of individual criminal law predominate, questions about an individual's state-of-mind trump questions about a state's machinery of horror. To function within the individualistic framework, organizations must take on human-like characteristics. Yet, organizational structures and human qualities do not make a good fit. The idea of intent attaches readily to individuals and only awkwardly to collectivities. An individualistic framework forces us to accept convoluted phrases such as "the mind of the organization."

Indeed, collective responsibility becomes problematic not because of its inherent conceptual difficulties (as Nuremberg's Justice Biddle maintained) but because of the questionable individualistic presumptions that keep the framework for criminal responsibility intact while remaining outside the realm of serious critique. In summary, those constructing an international criminal code work largely under the mistaken presumption that a global criminal code should be a national one writ large. The overall result for international law has been to increase the numbers of individuals responsible and to enlarge the types of crimes for which individuals are responsible. However, this has also had the effect of ignoring questions about the organizations within which the individuals carried out previously unfathomable crimes such as genocide.

Proposals

Rather than challenge and dismiss the entire framework, let us work within it by casting the liability of organizations within individualist criminal theories of punishment. The framework's emphasis on individual guilt pushes issues into the criminal law arena where the theory of retribution reigns supreme. Retributive justice has a backward-looking perspective on punishment. Retributivists look back to the crime and ask what justice requires to atone for the past wrong. Alternatively, if we edge the analysis away from criminal law and move it more toward civil law, then a restitution theory of punishment becomes more plausible. Restitution theorists demand a reorientation away from the wrongdoer's *actus reus* and *mens rea*. Restitution theorists turn the spotlight from the perpetrator to the victim.

Developing codes and jurisprudence for an ICC offers opportunities to construct approaches that are not dominated by individualist criminal models. A framework that combines the best from the criminal and civil models provides a robust, realistic, and viable alternative. Consider, for example, a tribunal punishing members of criminal organizations by "sentencing" or requiring them to do community service. This would retain the individualist underpinnings of legal liability while at the same time it would address an organization's role in the acts. Then, we only need to take one more important step. A tribunal should also have the power to order the banning of an organization.

The categories operative within national law do not always carry over to the international arena. National law makes relatively sharp distinctions between civil (tort) and criminal law. Tort law covers largely private matters. Criminal law dominates the public sphere. The criminal system transforms seemingly private matters among individuals into public ones. Punishment of a child within the privacy of a home becomes public when the act turns into criminal abuse. Within national criminal law systems, a legal finding of guilt also involves a moral determination of guilt. Criminal law's public nature goes beyond collective concerns to moral concerns. Criminal law reflects society's morals. Tort law also has moral elements, often expressed as "blameworthiness." Tort law casts blame on a wrongdoer. Tortuous wrongs, however, generally pale in comparison to criminal ones. A list of criminal acts represents a codification of what society regards as the most morally reprehensible ones. A *tortfeasor* (individual who commits a tort, a civil wrong) deserves blame. Given that a criminal stands guilty of immorality, the criminal supposedly deserves greater moral condemnation than a *tortfeasor*. If an individual murders someone, the murderer, obviously, directed the wrong at an individual. However, the murderer also committed a crime against the state (society). Murder constitutes more than a private wrong; it is a public wrong. Although a certain individual or specific individuals experience the direct and immediate effects of a criminal act, crime also has a collective element, a societal dimension. Criminal acts indirectly harm other individuals. Criminal acts threaten collective security and violate society's morality. As an assault on the collectivity (i.e., on society), a criminal act becomes a matter of collective moral concern.

War crimes and genocide, as crimes against society, have a collective moral dimension analogous to that of individual crimes. Yet, society's moral outrage at genocide begins to diminish if the legal process directs it at the guilt of a few individuals. Often, the legal process of ascribing responsibility for war crimes or genocide stops after a few leaders have received their punishments. The process should not stop there. We should want to know the structural roots that bred the horror not only for historical reasons but also for moral ones (see Chapter 4). Genocide constitutes a crime against civilization itself, against the international society. Each incident of genocide or grave injustice on a mass scale erodes the prospects of creating a global moral community. The dominant concepts of criminal responsibility do not suffice for meeting the challenges to humanity posed by these grave injustices. The large numbers of individuals who participate in genocide do not have the requisite criminal intent, namely, the planning capacity, for a prosecutor to charge them with the criminal act of genocide (see Chapter 3). Nevertheless, the participants, minimally, should shoulder some responsibility. In most cases, the participants belonged to organizations, whose structures proved critical to carrying out genocide or a grave injustice. Courts must aid in the removal of those structure by disbanding the organization.

By diverting the focus away from an individual's mental state (*mens rea*), the tort concept of blameworthiness has distinct advantages over the criminal concept of guilt. Yet, "blameworthiness" is too strong. A tort law model yields judgments that would be too harsh. Within tort law, members of criminal organizations are wrongdoers and deserve blame (*per se*) as members of criminal organizations. However, other than doing things for purposes of membership, most members of criminal organizations perform few actions that would qualify as acts of genocide. Most members of criminal organizations do not commit any overt criminal acts. Nevertheless, members of Asahara's Aum Shinrikyo, Butler's Church of the Aryan Nation, Hale's World Church of the Creator, the Nazis SS, Arkan's Tigers, and the Hutu *Interahamwe* contributed, in formal and in other ways, to their respective criminal organizations. As members of criminal organizations, they should shoulder some legal and moral responsibility. The warnings (against taking pre-emptive measures against suspect organizations), issued in the first section, bear repeating. Contrary to the policies adopted by many nations, members of criminal organizations should not stand *guilty by association*. However, they should be held *responsible by association* for grave injustices committed on behalf of their organizations. Finally, although organizations should not be subject to prior restraint, they should be subject to banishment after a finding of their criminality.

During the Nuremberg trials, German defense lawyers asked whether group members could have prevented the injustices carried out by the organization. With this question, the defense effectively placed a shield of immunity around almost all members of the indicted criminal organizations. Few individuals, if any, could have prevented the Holocaust and its associated horrors.

A dramatic example from the context of national law helps to show that the defense set the moral and legal threshold too high. In 1964, thirty-eight neighbors, who heard Kitty Genovese's cries for help, refused to call the police during the prolonged period that it took the killer to murder her outside her New York City apartment building. We may not want to pin legal guilt or blame on the neighbors, but we would be highly remiss if we did not at least consider ascribing moral irresponsibility to them. The success of a moral responsibility case would not hinge (as it did for the defense's arguments at Nuremberg) on whether someone's action could have prevented the murder. Even if the police had arrived too late, the neighbors (individually and collectively as an unorganized association) had a moral duty (and perhaps should have had a legal duty as well) to call the police.

There is a roughly analogous case for holding witnessing members of criminal organizations morally and legally responsible for the genocide acts of participating members of the organization. However, the Genovese case and the genocide case part company here. In the Genovese case, questions about non-witnessing neighbors never arise. In the genocide case, the responsibility ascribed to the organization's members should extend beyond the witnessing members to all members of the organization. All members of the criminal organization (except, perhaps, those intentionally deceived by the group's leaders) have some moral responsibility, and they should have some legal responsibility for the grave injustices undertaken by the organization. In addition to questioning the truth of the excuses, the response to claims of innocence by members of Aum Shinrikyo, the Church of the Aryan Nation, the World Church of the Creator, the Nazis SS, Arkan's Tigers, and the Hutu *Interahamwe* should be weighed against the presumption that all members should have known about their organization's criminal activities. The legal and moral inquiry should not stop at this point. It should continue until the issue of whether to ban the organization altogether has been decided. In a sense, this last determination is the one that fully addresses organization responsibility.

Organizational responsibility differs from collective guilt as the following examples illustrate. In one medieval German town, the act of hiding a "war criminal" opened the possibility of the slaughter of everyone in the town.[31] Daniel Goldhagen provides the most recent example of someone making a case for widely disseminating responsibility among all members of a collectivity (the diffuse model).[32] He has achieved celebrity status as an advocate for diffusing responsibility throughout an entire nation. For Goldhagen, the German people, a diffuse collectivity, should bear considerable responsibility for the anti-Semitism that pervaded their society before and during the Nazi period. He, then, concludes that they (the diffuse collectivity) should also accept responsibility for the Holocaust.

Organization responsibility occupies a more realistic and more defensible middle position between Goldhagen's holding an entire nation morally responsible and Nuremberg Tribunal's ultimately holding only a few leaders criminally guilty. Whatever the complicity of the nation's population might be, atrocities on a mass scale are carried out, generally, not by the population as a whole but through organizations within a nation state. Further, the execution and often the planning of mass atrocities are not the product of an individual mind or a few individual minds but rather a complex array of events that includes the policies and activities of organizations. The Nazi Final Solution for the Jewish problem did not spring from the minds of a few individuals. It unfolded through a series of policies adopted by a few key organizations and implemented under the bureaucratic cover of these and other organizations.

RESTORATIVE JUSTICE

How would a restorative justice model work in legal practice? In our attempt to meet that challenge, please note that we are not offering merely an idealization, but an ideal with realistic prospects. A tribunal, modeled on the original Nuremberg procedures would make a two-stage determination. First, it would follow the precedent set by Nuremberg and give priority to determining the criminality of organizations. The tribunal would investigate all aspects of the organization and activities associated with it. The tribunal would examine the decision procedures and policies as implemented and carried out within and on behalf of the organization. The tribunal would then focus on the links between activities associated with the organization and acts of genocide to determine the criminality of the organization. The tribunal's conclusion that an organization was criminal is tantamount to a strict liability determination. Members become liable by mere (*per se*) membership in the organization. By not differentiating among types of members, it might seem that a tribunal would violate principles of fairness. The first stage of the procedure, however, does not involve a determination of individual criminal guilt. In the first stage, the tribunal only evaluates whether an organization was criminal.

In the second stage, the tribunal would determine punishments for all members of an organization and for the organization itself. At the punishment stage (and not at the liability determination), the tribunal would entertain claims that differentiate among types of members. The Nuremberg Tribunal, at the behest of Judge Francis Biddle, exonerated those who professed no knowledge of the organization's criminal deeds and those who claimed that they performed the acts involuntarily. However, on a strict liability approach, which underlies the finding of an organization's criminality, each member of the organization assumes the moral taint carried by finding the organization criminal. The strict liability model does not permit defenses or excusing pleas by any members of the organization. The punishment imposed on the members of the organization does not depend upon a prior finding of guilt on the part of any individual member of the organization. Minimally, members have responsibilities for acts of their organization and should provide means of restitution for the horrific acts to which they had an institutional or organizational connection.

The tribunal would have a variety of remedies available, including the performance of public service. The degree of restitution imposed by the tribunal would depend upon factors such as a member's knowledge of the acts and involuntariness in performing the acts. If an organization is found criminal and thereby responsible for helping to destroy a nation, then the organization's members have a responsibility as members of the organization (not simply as citizens) to help restore the nation. The "repayment" could come in a variety of forms, including the performance of public services needed to rebuild the nation. Ironically, given the failure of the denazification program, many ex-Nazis ended up performing valuable public services in post World War II Germany.[33] A restorative justice model adds elements of realism to the process. Instead of these individuals pretending that they have been exonerated from past misdeeds (because of a botched denazification procedure), members of criminal organizations would serve in public and other service capacities because of (not in spite of) their membership in morally reprehensible criminal organizations.

The final aspect of the punishment phase of the procedure would address the organization itself. The tribunal would determine whether it should ban the organization and what the scope of a ban should be. If the tribunal finds an organization deeply implicated in genocide, then it should place a temporary or permanent ban on the organization. If the tribunal decides to ban an organization where a genocide took place, it (or some comparable national court) should also have jurisdictional powers to ban the organization elsewhere. These concerns about the organization are not idle academic ones. An organization responsibility model has direct and profound applications, as the following brief analysis of the Rwanda genocide demonstrates.

CASE STUDY: THE RWANDAN GENOCIDE

> The denial of justice is preparing the graves of the future.[34]

Media Inciters: RTML

Again, it bears repeating that the prosecution of organizations should not open the door to a movement to eradicate organizations whenever they come under suspicion of carrying out evil deeds. However, this general rule has an important exception. Concerns about prior restraints dissolve in cases of incitement to genocide.[35] Worries over prior restraints apply to situations where the government perceives an individual or a group as posing a potential threat. Incitement cases, in contrast, involve individuals and groups that take actual steps to instigate genocide. Past and current war crimes tribunals have had some success in convicting individuals who promote genocide. The Nuremberg Tribunal sentenced Julius Streicher to death. Streicher published *Der Stürmer*, a virulently anti-Semitic weekly. Future tribunals need to decide whether promoting is the same as inciting.

The Rwanda Tribunal's mandate prevented the indictment of Leon Mugesera, an avowed hate propagandist. Mugesera's incitement activities took place in 1992 and the ICTR's jurisdiction extended only to acts committed during the 1994 genocide. However, the ICTR recently sentenced Hassan Ngeze, the owner, founder, and editor of *Kangura*, as well as Ferdinand Nahimana and Jean-Bosco Barayagwiza, owner and founder, respectively, of *Radio-Télévision Libre des Mille Collines* (RTML), to life imprisonment.[36] The hate propaganda cases from Germany and Rwanda differ in important ways. *Der Stürmer* represented one of many tentacles of a hate machine that had already amassed a tremendous amount of power before it came into the limelight. The RTML, in contrast, functioned as a primary engine, previously hidden underground, that blasted onto the surface to direct the Rwandan genocide.

It proves instructive to understand RTML's role in the Rwanda genocide. In 1993, RTML began operating and issuing hate vendettas. Although RTML had private funding, it had intimate personnel and operational ties with the Habyarimana government. In fact, RTML was created as a way around restrictions, imposed shortly before by the Arusha Accords, on government-owned media. RTML called on Hutus to avenge the April 6, 1994 death of Rwanda's President Habyarimana:

> The graves are not yet quite full. Who is going to do the good work and help us fill them completely? You *inyenzi* (cockroaches) must know you are made of flesh! We won't let you kill! We will kill you![37]

NGOs, including Human Rights Watch and the US Committee for Refugees, called for Western powers and the United Nations to jam RTML's transmitters. UN officials found that radios under the control of Hutu extremists played a pernicious role in several mass killings of Tutsis in 1993. Major-General Roméo Dallaire, the UN commander charged with overseeing enforcement of the Arusha Peace Accords, claimed that shutting down the main transmitter of hate would have spared countless lives in Rwanda.[38] "Reach for the top part of the house" was a coded signal broadcast over RTML to begin the genocide by reaching for the machetes typically kept above the doors of rural Rwandan homes.[39]

International justice has pursued individual owners of media hate devices because of their leadership positions. However, if the focus shifts (or equally emphasizes) the organization's structure, the role of the leaders in one organization provides leads to other organizations. For example, a former Director of Public Affairs in the Rwandan Foreign Ministry, Jean Bosco Barayagwiza not only owned RTML, he also created the *Coalition pour de la Défense de la Républic* (CDR), the main extremist Hutu organization. After the Tutsi-led Rwandan Patriotic Front (RPF) stopped the genocide, Barayagwiza and his CDR masterminded the exodus (the largest mass exodus in history) of millions of Hutus across Rwanda's borders, mostly into neighboring Zaire (now, the Democratic Republic of the Congo; hereinafter, the Congo). During that flight and in refugee camps provided by the UN, the CDR "monopolized the distribution of humanitarian aid."[40]

The ICTR Appeals Court caused a stir when it ordered the release of Barayagwiza based on the egregious procedural errors committed by the prosecution. The Appeals Court later reversed itself, and the ICTR has since tried and convicted Barayagwiza. Whatever injustices accompany a botched individual prosecution, the focus on individuals has resulted in missed opportunities for achieving some semblance of justice. Barayagwiza should stand accused of inciting genocide through hate radio. In addition, he represents other, arguably more significant, organizations whose alleged crimes continued after the genocide. The "after-genocide" crimes had and have a direct bearing on the 1994 genocide. The exodus, which received a grossly disproportionate amount of global attention, and the subversion of international humanitarian efforts have helped to dissipate the global community's reaction to the genocide. At the time, the world did not see the Hutu exodus as having a direct link to the Hutu perpetrators of the genocide. At first, a largely unquestioned consensus formed that took Hutu fears of atrocities from the new Tutsi regime as the cause of the mass exodus. Now, most analysts accept the following alternative hypothesis: Barayagwiza and his CDR (and not the acts of the RPF) were largely responsible for inducing these mass fears in the Hutus. This alternative hypothesis situates the exodus as part of a scheme to commit further genocide. It becomes most plausible when we focus on the role of organizations within a restorative justice model. However, instead of pursuing this interpretation, the Tribunal extended the reach of international law only to an individual genocide inciter who owns a now defunct radio station.

The international community often has ignored the role of the media organizations in fomenting grave injustices. In the Goma region of the Congo, "Gaspard Gahigi, a former head of RTML, created an Association of Rwandan Journalist in Exile and a newspaper *Amerizo*."[41] Hassan Ngeze, editor of *Kangura*, infamous for its publication of the Hutu Ten Commandments, fled to Kenya. In exile, he continued to publish his hate newspaper until his arrest at the behest of the Tribunal in 1997. The failure to disband media organizations in exile from Rwanda has resulted in the continuation of a lethal propaganda system fueled by hate.

Militia Perpetrators: The *Interahamwe*

Extremist Hutus organized the *Interahamwe* ("those who attack together"), which largely carried out the genocide of 800,000 in Rwanda. By not dealing with organizations, international law fails to address the continuing misdeeds carried out by these organizations. As noted above, the lives of the Nazi organizations ended shortly after World War II. Three months before the Rwandan genocide began, the UN Force Commander Roméo Dallaire sent a warning cable to his superiors.[42] The UN Department of Peacekeeping Operations, headed by the future UN Secretary General Kofi Annan, refused to grant Dallaire's request to disarm and disband the *Interahamwe* militia.[43] The life of the *Interahamwe* did not end at the termination of Rwanda's genocide. Not only did the *Interahamwe* recruit and launch attacks on Rwanda from the UN refugee camps in the former Zaire, but also the *Interahamwe* continues to operate today in the newly formed Democratic Republic of the Congo, where six nations, including Rwanda, until recently, had troops engaged in warfare. No court has ever branded the *Interahamwe* as a criminal organization.

Church Aiders and Abettors: Seventh Day Adventists

A strong case exists for considering extending the scope of responsibility for genocide to religious organizations, such as the Seventh Day Adventist Church. Pastor Elizaphan Ntakirutimana was president of the Adventist Church in the province of Kibuye, with a population of about 30 percent Tutsis (compared to a national population of 15 percent Tutsis) before the genocide. Few Kibuye Tutsis survived the genocide.

The Catholic and Anglican churches expended considerable resources on trying to contend with their role in Rwanda's genocide. Ntakirutimana is the first religious leader that the Tribunal has convicted.[44] The Rwanda Tribunal's individualistic premises assured that they would not examine the role of Ntakirutimana's church. The Catholic and Anglican churches have expended considerable resources in trying to contend with the role of these churches in the genocide. The Seventh Day Adventist Church like its Catholic and Anglican counterparts, at least, should face inquiries into its role as an organization in the 1994 genocide.

An established religious organization has a radically different purpose than a militia. However, justice must address the role of even presumably benign organizations. Tutsis took refuge in Ntakirutimana's church and hospital compound not simply because of Ntakirutimana's authoritative assurances of safety but also because the place of refuge was a church. Philip Gourevitch's book title, *We Wish to Inform you that by Tomorrow My Family and I will be Dead*, proves telling, for it contains the words of an appeal for safety from a minister lower in the church hierarchy than his superior Ntakirutimana.[45] Church members who were not targeted also occupy a position with moral implications. As members of these churches, people are no longer simply morally neutral members of a presumably benign organization. The genocidal nature of the organization's goals and acts, committed at the behest of a leader of an organization, transforms membership in that organization into a moral issue. The Seventh Day Adventist Church at least the part of it operating in the *Kibuye* province in Rwanda, at some point should have become a suspect criminal organization.

An international tribunal's successful indictment, guilt determination, and sentencing of an established religious organization seem highly unlikely. Yet, an indictment of an organization and its subdivisions issues a demand for accountability from the organization. Perhaps there are better ways to address these issues. At present, however, there are no other proposed or plausible accountability mechanisms.

CONCLUSION

When international criminal law begins to focus on organizations, many things begin to fall into place. The sheer enormity and unspeakable horror of genocide become understandable once we accept that only organizations such as a state have the means and power to carry out genocide. The idea of organizational responsibility breaks the stranglehold that the idea of individual criminal guilt has had on international criminal law. The intent element of international criminal law embeds in inner sanctums and policies of organizations and not within the inner recesses of individual minds. Rather than ask how individuals can carry out such horrendous hateful acts, international law needs to address how organizations provide support and rationales for genocide. Organizations, through regulations and laws, institutionalize an extremely sinister form of hate through regulations, rulings, strategies, and laws. Organizations transform passionate individual hatreds into sanctioned collective ones that can motivate genocide. Only organizations could foment and sustain the sweeping judgments about groups that nourish genocide.

Further, the idea of organizational responsibility helps to resolve some important historical disputes generated by Hannah Arendt's *Eichmann in Jerusalem*. First, critics charged that Arendt's analysis of the trial lent itself to exonerating Eichmann. In response, we can now see that Arendt did not excuse Eichmann; she simply did not have the conceptual tools supplied by notions of organizational responsibility. In Arendt's and our analysis, Eichmann stands guilty of genocide not because of his criminal mind or despicable motives but because of his prominent role in the organizational structure that carried out the Holocaust. Second, critics complained about Arendt making judgments about the complicity of Jewish organizations during the Holocaust. The Nazis established Jewish organizations called *Judenrats* (Jewish Councils) and *Aeltestenrats* (Councils of Elders) throughout their occupied territories. Each organization had its own history and operated in peculiar circumstances. Some of these (the Lodz *Judenrat*) did aid the Nazi brutality by providing lists and persuading mothers to relinquish their children. Others (the Warsaw *Judenrat*) tried to resist Nazi demands for Jews to deport while still others (the Tuchin *Judenrat*) attempted armed resistance. Even for those *Judenrats* that fully cooperated, however, their lack of corporate intent and motive clearly exonerated them from organizational criminal responsibility.

A focus on organizations lays a firm foundation for the future of international criminal law. Overall, the idea of organizational criminal responsibility helps to make sense of: why international law should hold leaders responsible for crimes they did not directly commit; why leaders should have greater responsibility for the crimes than even those followers who carried out the criminal acts; why the actors and non-actors from among the followers should share the responsibility; and why organizations should bear criminal responsibility. Without the emphasis on organizations, international criminal law will repeat the mistakes made in Rwanda, perhaps becoming an accomplice through its omission in furthering grave injustices.

The international community must address the terror that criminal organizations continue to unleash in Central Africa. The statutes governing the Ad Hoc War Crimes Tribunal for Rwanda could be amended to extend jurisdiction over organizations. More realistically, policy analysts could discern politically effective avenues in international relations for branding criminal organizations, such as the *Interahamwe*, as rogue. These criminal organizations have better qualifications for membership in the *Axis of Evil* than nation states do. While it might prove difficult to rectify past gaps in implementing an international criminal justice system, it is imperative that policy analysts and jurists do not repeat past omissions. Minimally, efforts should be undertaken to give the ICC jurisdiction over organizations.

Historians may choose to rebut our interpretation of the Nuremberg Tribunal. Philosophers (by the nature of their discipline) will find flaws in the legally oriented and philosophically thin analysis of responsibility that we have offered. Undoubtedly, many scholars, jurists, activists, and policy-makers will dispute our interpretation of the genocide in Rwanda and its aftermath in Central Africa. Fortunately, a restorative justice approach does not entirely stand or fall on these disputes. Further, the claims made in this study need not depend only on the weak defense that at least the right questions have been asked. The failure to raise and answer questions about criminal organizations within international relations has relatively few repercussions for most of us. However, it has enormous implications for victims, past and future, of organized mass violence. Neo Nazi organizations probably have little prospects of having a global impact, and probably too much time has elapsed to investigate the role of the Special Organization (*Teskilati Mahsusa*) in the 1915 Armenian genocide. The *Interahamwe*, however, has already managed to threaten world (or at least African) peace.

It seems only fitting to end with a paraphrase of Justice Robert Jackson's arguments at Nuremberg:

> It seems beyond controversy that to punish a few top leaders but to leave this web of organized bodies in the midst of postwar society would be to foster the nucleus of further group conflicts. These organizations are the carriers from this generation to the next of the infection of aggressive and ruthless violence. The next organized violence and the next genocides will be hatched in the nest of these organizations as surely as we leave their membership with its prestige and influence undiminished by condemnation and punishment.

Conclusion

International Justice and Universal Morality

The film *Calling the Ghosts* chronicles the painful path that a judge and a lawyer had to endure during and after the Bosnian war. These Bosnian Muslims suffered unspeakable indignities while imprisoned in the Omarska concentration camp. After their release, the long-time friends do not talk about the terror they had experienced—even to each other. The film traces their struggle to make the personal political, to give public voice to private pain. When they realize how many other women had suffered similar brutalities, they decide to lead a campaign to bring Omarska into full public view. They force their tormentors to answer accusations of rape and other brutalities. In one recorded interview, the commander of Omarska brushes aside the allegations noting that he would not have even leaned his bicycle against these women to say nothing of having sex with them. Surprisingly, Omarska's rape victims did not seek revenge. Instead, these women organize a movement to achieve justice. The film follows their journey from the private confessions at their kitchen tables to the public hearings before The Hague's international court, the Ad Hoc International Criminal Tribunal for the Former Yugoslavia.

Survivors of grave injustices typically seek "sweet justice" rather than "sour revenge." For example, a Rwandan Diaspora group, led by Benjamin Mwangachuchu, pursued Pastor Elizaphan Ntakirutimana (whose name means "nothing is greater than God"), former president of the Seventh Day Adventist mission at Mugonero Complex in Rwanda's Kibuye prefecture. They had accused this Hutu minister as responsible for the slaughter, within his Seventh Day Adventist church, of 8,000 Tutsis, including some of their relatives. According to the testimonies they gathered, Pastor Ntakirutimana and his physician son Gerard, formerly a doctor at the Mugonero Complex had lured fleeing Tutsis into their compound only to summon the feared *Interahamwe* to exterminate them. Before April 1994, Kibuye had the highest Tutsi population of any Rwandan prefecture (252,000). African Rights estimated that as of July 1994 only 7–8,000 Tutsis remained in Kibuye.

These survivors of Rwanda's genocide did not plan protests against their enemies; they did not engage in shouting matches with the murderers of their loved ones; they did not wallow in their private grief and sorrow. Instead, like the unsung heroes chronicled in *Calling the Ghosts*, they led a successful campaign to have Pastor Ntakirutimana brought before a court of law. After the genocide, Pastor Ntakirutimana fled to Laredo, Texas to live with his son, Eliel, a cardiac anesthesiologist, and a naturalized American citizen who has lived in the United States since 1980. The Rwandan refugees resisted attempts to extradite Pastor Ntakirutimana from the United States to Rwanda, where he would have faced an almost certain death. Instead, with admirable dignity, these survivors sought justice before Arusha's international court, the Ad Hoc International Criminal Tribunal for Rwanda, which did not have the death penalty and, more importantly, which had fair procedures. US authorities arrested him on September 29, 1996. After awaiting trial for fourteen months in the infirmary of the Webb County jail, US Magistrate Marcel Notzon ordered Pastor Ntakirutimana's release.[1] He was rearrested on February 26, 1998 in a case before Federal District Judge John Rainey.[2] After the US Supreme Court denied his appeal, the US government transferred Pastor Ntakirutimana to Arusha on March 31, 2000.[3] On February 21, 2003, the tribunal found Pastor Ntakirutimana guilty of genocide and other crimes and, taking into account his age, sentenced him to ten years in prison.[4]

Overall, the survivors from the Former Yugoslavia and Rwanda did not find any psychological closure through their struggles for justice. Further, they did not finish their legal journeys completely satisfied. However, neither psychological closure nor plaintiff satisfaction should serve as the measures of success. The cases of Omarska's rape victims and Rwanda's genocide survivors dramatize the critical importance of the journey taken relative to the destination reached. These victims and so many others like them admirably chose roads *of justice* and not necessarily roads *to justice*. Their pioneering paths helped to build some of the first roads of an interconnecting global justice system.

The road improvement process continues. The dirt roads of justice built by previous victims are currently being paved with international codes, permanent courts, and universal morality. International criminal codes form the base of these road improvement projects. Criminal justice systems need criminal codes. Societies decide what actions to criminalize. Of course, people seldom have an opportunity to make decisions directly about their nation's criminal code. Imagine having the chance to formulate a nation's criminal code that decriminalized marijuana use and criminalized corporate abuse. A nation's citizens do have moments when they can change pieces of their country's criminal code. To think of creating a criminal code from the beginning seems beyond imagination. However, as repeatedly emphasized in this book, global citizens now have a rare opportunity to influence the direction of the on-going process of constructing an international criminal code.

When President George W. Bush unsigned the Rome Statute, which established the International Criminal Court, the United States excluded itself from the process of formulating an international criminal code at a time when it might help US policy the most. Answers to some critical questions lie within formulations of an international criminal code. How should we define terrorism? What crimes did Saddam Hussein commit? Were the US actions in Afghanistan and Iraq justified? By uninviting itself to the code-creation table, the US government has limited its options primarily to military ways of answering these questions.

The US government has had a schizophrenic relationship to international treaties and codes. It has a dismal record on international treaties. The number of international human rights treaties not ratified by the United States makes a long list.[5] Most notoriously, the United States joined its close ally Somalia as the only countries that have not ratified the International Convention on the Rights of the Child. Perhaps, Somalia has an excuse in that it lacks a central government.

Despite the US government's lackluster performance in adopting international human rights treaties, it has played a key role in formulating them. The 1998 Rome Statute aptly illustrates these conflicting tensions in US policy. Although the United States joined a list of rogue states that refused to sign the Rome Treaty, the United States also played an instrumental role in creating the permanent international criminal tribunal. In fact, it is probably fair to say that without the official and unofficial role of the United States, the International Criminal Court (ICC) would not exist as it does today. Still, considerable public pressure could stimulate the United States to play a more central role in formulating international laws, a role worthy of the leading superpower.

Of course, the roads of justice need more than a foundation layer of laws. Victims would not travel these roads without courts to interpret the laws, that is, without a judiciary to inform the world's citizens what lies at the road's foundation. The establishment of institutions designed to carry out procedures to adjudicate grievances, resolve disputes, and rectify wrongs should have first priority in the making of any governing structure. When people feel aggrieved, they need to know that they can turn to an adjudicatory body that will hear and rule on their complaints. From organizational formation to nation building, the role of adjudicatory structures and devices is perilously undervalued. The likelihood of individuals turning to harmful acts as a way of expressing their grievances increases astronomically without the availability of courts and other adjudicatory institutions designed to hear their claims.

The establishment of a permanent war crimes tribunal marks a stage of considerable progress in international law. Overall, the Nuremberg trials have withstood the charge of victor's justice. Although the plaintive cry of "Never again!" proclaimed after the Holocaust seems naïve in retrospect, Nuremberg bequeathed the basic principles that the ad hoc tribunals have used to deal with the mass slaughters in the Former Yugoslavia and Rwanda.[6] Even though hopes for permanent peace seem to have vanished, the establishment of a permanent non-military court represents a natural progression from the military tribunal at Nuremberg through the ad hoc civilian courts in Arusha and The Hague. While permanent peace may be a far-fetched hope, a distant dream, a global system of justice lies within reach. The newly formed ICC does not sit atop a hierarchy of regional and national courts. The ICC does not review any lower court decisions; it operates as a complement to national criminal law systems. However, by accepting a permanent court, the international community has taken a critical step toward the construction of a truly international judicial order.

Even if others do not share optimism about what the codification of international criminal law and the institution of a permanent international criminal court portend for international law, no one would sensibly deny that these developments with laws and courts mark a considerable achievement. However, the most significant achievement of all remains largely unnoticed. The stones and gravel of laws and courts make a rough yet still usable road of justice. The international community has begun to pave the road with universal morality. The international community has reached a near consensus. Certain wrongs have become universal prohibitions, and genocide lies at the center of those universal wrongs.

Given the central place that genocide holds in the international criminal code and in a global ethics, we must have a clear and precise definition of it. To avoid an array of conflicting claims where almost any egregious wrong could qualify as genocide, we need to carefully limit the range of acts that constitute genocide. Again, the strategy of finding something that almost everyone could agree on proves beneficial. Mass killing serves as the obvious candidate as the central act of genocide. An important lesson emerges from any attempt to specify the other elements of the crime of genocide. National criminal law systems do not serve as an optimal model for an international criminal law system. The intent and motive elements of the crime of genocide are nothing like the intent and motive aspects of the crime of murder. If we think of intent and motive as applying solely to individuals as they do in national criminal law systems, we will seriously distort the idea of genocide. A sole individual does not and cannot carry out genocide in the way that an individual does and can commit murder. By seriously thinking through the nature of genocide, we start to acknowledge the critical role that organizations play in genocide. Individuals typically commit genocide within and as part of organizations. Organizational policies and directives in international criminal law play a parallel role to individual intent and motive in national criminal law systems. The inclusion of organizations does not entail replacing the idea of individual responsibility, which admittedly lies at the heart of the ICC, with some notion of corporate responsibility. It does mean that we should rethink the dominant ways of thinking about responsibility and punishment in international criminal law.

In short, jurists need to exercise considerably more creativity than they have in the past. For example, the specific language of the Rome Statute gives the ICC jurisdiction over only natural persons and not over groups or organizations. This should challenge legal creativity rather than serve as a formidable obstacle. As a first step, consider that the US Constitution's Bill of Rights applies primarily to persons, but the courts have managed to treat corporations as persons under the Constitution. This does not imply an acceptance of the idea of corporation as persons or the advocacy of complete interpretative flexibility. The example simply shows that a legal code lives and changes.

By its nature, jurisprudence serves as an agent of change for law. Philosophy of law tries to bring wisdom to bear on the law. This does not mean that philosophers of law have any particular corner on the wisdom market. A philosophical approach to law should become more widely practiced by all those concerned with law. The jurisprudence of international criminal law is in a nascent state. Jurists have just begun to reflect on the jurisprudence embedded in the decisions of the ad hoc tribunals for the Former Yugoslavia and Rwanda. Jurisprudential reflection does not need to await judicial decisions. Jurisprudence can serve as a normative guide for future decisions of an international criminal court.

International jurists not only need to think outside the confines of national criminal law systems, they also should challenge sacred distinctions such as the divide between criminal and tort law. Imagine a system of punishment that combined criminal punishment for leaders and participants with civil liability for members of criminal organizations. These are not just idle speculations; they have real life consequences. National criminal law systems want to get and keep individual offenders off the streets. Similarly, international criminal law should have ways to keep criminal organizations from ever functioning on any nation's territory.

It may prove difficult if not impossible to stop hate in its early stages. Historians have no conclusive answer to the hypothetical questions about when, what, and how Hitler's rise to power could have been prevented. This does not mean that future efforts to prevent hate are futile. One can make a strong case for the importance of minority protection. Efforts to protect disadvantaged and oppressed groups take on a serious light when seen as part of a strategy to prevent genocide. While the composition of future groups targeted for genocide remains somewhat uncertain, past victim groups fit into a relatively small classification of group types. The laws of genocide try to capture the historical lesson that teaches that it is racial, ethnic, national, and religious groups that have been particularly vulnerable. A study of past cases of genocide shows that among the vulnerable groups any protective measure should be particularly focused on racial and ethnic groups.

However uncertain and debatable preventative and protective measures might be, there is one policy that should be beyond dispute. The international community should have the resolve to stop genocide soon before or immediately after it begins. Further, whatever else international law does, it should have the wherewithal to bring legal proceedings against the perpetrators. If we cannot move forward on the crime of genocide, then we should succumb to hopelessness. Indeed, despair is a choice not inevitability.

Appendix A

Articles of the International Criminal Court

GENOCIDE

Article 6 (a) Genocide by Killing

1. The perpetrator killed one or more persons.
2. Such person or persons belonged to a particular national, ethnical, racial or religious group.
3. The perpetrator intended to destroy, in whole or in part, that national, ethnical, racial or religious group, as such.
4. The conduct took place in group in the conduct of a manifest pattern of similar conduct directed against that group or was that could itself effect such destruction.

Article 6 (b) Genocide by Causing Serious Bodily or Mental Harm

1. The perpetrator caused serious bodily or mental harm to one or more persons.
2. Such person or persons belonged to a particular national, ethnical, racial or religious group.
3. The perpetrator intended to destroy, in whole or in part, that national, ethnical, racial or religious group, as such.
4. The conduct took place in the context of a manifest pattern of similar conduct directed against that group or was conduct that could itself effect such destruction.

Article 6 (c) Genocide by Deliberately Inflicting Condition of Life Calculated to Bring about Physical Destruction

1. The perpertrator inflicted certain condition of life upon one or more persons.
2. Such person or persons belonged to a particular national, ethnical, racial or religious group.

3. The perpetrator intended to destroy, in whole or in part, that national, ethnical, racial or religion group, as such.
4. The conditions of life were calculated to bring about the physical destruction of that group, in whole or in part.
5. The conduct took place in the context of a manifest pattern of similar conduct directed against that group or was conduct that could that itself effect such destruction.

Article 6 (d) Genocide by Imposing Measures Intended to Prevent Births

1. The perpetrator imposed certain measures upon one or more persons.
2. Such person or persons belonged to a particular national, ethnical, racial or religious group.
3. The perpetrator intended to destroy, in whole or in part, that national, ethnical, racial or religious group, as such.
4. The measures imposed were intended to prevent births within that group.
5. The conduct took place in the context of a manifest pattern of similar conduct directed against that group or was conduct that could itself effect such destruction.

Article 6 (e) Genocide by Forcibly Transferring Children

1. The perpetrator forcibly transferred one or more persons.
2. Such person or persons belonged to a particular national, ethnical, racial or religious group.
3. The perpetrator intended to destroy, in whole or in part, that national, ethnical, racial or religious group, as such.
4. The transfer was from that group to another group.
5. The person or persons were under the age of 18 years.
6. The perpetrator knew, or should have known, that the person or persons were under the age of 18 years.
7. The conduct took place in the context of a manifest pattern of similar conduct directed against that group or was conduct that could itself effect such destruction.

Appendix B

Articles of the International Criminal Court

CRIME AGAINST HUMANITY

Article 7 (1) (a) Crime Against Humanity of Murder

1. The perpetrator killed one or more persons.
2. The conduct was committed as part of a widespread or systematic attack directed against a civilian population.
3. The perpetrator knew that the conduct was part of or intended the conduct to be part of a widespread or systematic attack against a civilian population.

Article 7 (1) (b) Crime Against Humanity of Extermination

1. The perpetrator killed one or more person, including by inflicting conditions of life calculated to bring about the destruction of part of a population.
2. The conduct constituted, or took place as part of, a mass killing of members of a civilian population.
3. The conduct was committed as part of a widespread or systematic attack directed against a civilian population.
4. The perpetrator knew that the conduct was part of or intended the conduct to be part of a widespread or systematic attack directed against a civilian population.

Article 7 (1) (c) Crime Against Humanity of Enslavement

1. The perpetrator exercised any or all of the powers attaching to the right of ownership over one or more persons, such as by purchasing, selling, lending or bartering such a person or persons, or by imposing on them a similar deprivation of liberty.
2. The conduct was committed as part of a widespread systematic attack directed against a civilian population.
3. The perpetrator knew that the condut was part of or intended the conduct to be part of a widespread or systematic attack directed against a civilian population.

Appendix C

Genocides: Actual and Purported

A. GENOCIDES BY RANK?

1. Holocaust (1939–1945)
   a. Jews
   b. Gypsies
2. Tutsis (1994)
3. Armenians (1915)
4. Cambodians (1975–1979)?
5. Hereroes (1904)
6. Bosnians (1992–1995)

B. NON-GENOCIDES: GROUPS (PERPETRATORS)?

Native Americans (Colonialists)
Central Africans (Belgium)
Peasants (USSR)
Male Homosexuals (Nazis)
Albanian Kosovars (Yugoslavia/Serbia)
Hutus (Burundi, Rwanda, Congo)

C. NON-GENOCIDES: ACTIONS?

Non-Killing Genocide Acts
- Destruction of a Culture
- Destruction of a Group
- Ethnic Cleansing
- Systematic Rape

Abortion
Democide

Appendix D

Comparative Cases: Phases of Institutionalizations of Group Hatred

	Designation	Discrimination	Brutalization
Third Reich Jews	YES	YES	YES
Bosnian Muslims	NO	No	YES
Albanian Kosovars	No	Yes	Yes
Rwandan Tutsis	Yes	Yes	YES

Note
Capitalizations indicate strong cases; affirmative or negative, of embedded hatreds in the respective phases.

NOTES

INTRODUCTION

1. Interview from archives of Galvin Library of the Illinois Institute of Technology. In 1946, David Boder made the first interviews of Holocaust survivors before there was even a term to describe them. In 1946, he interviewed 109 "displaced persons." David Boder published eight of the interviews in *I Did Not Interview the Dead* (Urbana: University of Illinois Press, 1949). In 1998, researchers found seventy more transcribed and translated interviews, now published at http://voices.iit.edu/.

2. Winston S. Churchill, *The Churchill Papers: The Ever-Widening War*, Martin Gilbert, ed., vol. 3 (New York: W. W. Norton, 1941, 2000).

CHAPTER 1: GENOCIDE: LEGAL CONTEXT

1. Francis Edward Smedley, *Frank Farleigh*, 1850.

2. The 1929 Geneva Convention specifically outlaws reprisal killings of prisoners-of-war. The 1949 Geneva Conventions extended this protection to civilians.

3. Henry Steiner and Philip Alston, *International Human Rights in Context* (Oxford: The Clarendon Press, 1996), p. 70.

4. Terry Nardin, ed., *The Ethics of War and Peace: Religious and Secular Perspectives* (Princeton: Princeton University Press). The selections in this work purportedly cover the territories on the religious map needed to survey international ethics, but it includes essays that cover only the three western monotheistic religions of Judaism, Christianity, and Islam.

5. Paul Christopher, *The Ethics of War and Peace: An Introduction to Legal and Moral Issues*, Second Edition (Upper Saddle River: Prentice Hall, 1999), p. 8.

6. Lao Tzu, *Tao TeChing: The Way of Virtue*. Patrick Michael Byrne, trans. (Square One Publishers, Inc., 2002).

7. Marcus Tullius Cicero, *De Re Publica* 3, XXIII, trans. Clinton Walker Keyes (New York: G. P. Putnam's Sons, 1928), p. 211.

8. Christopher, *The Ethics of War and Peace*, p. 13.

9. President George W. Bush described more than 600 detainees at Guantanamo Bay as "illegal non-combatants picked up off of the battlefield."

10. It also helps to resolve an important historical dispute. An appreciation of the sophisticated structure and power of Roman law defuses the force of a historical interpretation that has played a significant factor in the development of genocide. The historical

debate is over whether the Jews or the Romans killed Jesus of Nazareth. To help resolve the issue consider the following three rather innocuous claims. First, Roman state power ruled the Roman Empire. Second, the rule of law played a central role in the Empire. Third, the governing law of the Empire was Roman. These claims appear obvious and uninformative until they become part of an answer to the question "Who killed Jesus?" If we grant the power and force of ancient Roman law, it becomes difficult not to attribute the death of Jesus to the Romans. Yet, the claim that "The Jews killed Christ" has played a central role in two thousand years of anti-Semitism. Indeed, "Every misfortune that subsequently befell the Jews—from the destruction of Jerusalem to Auschwitz—carried an echo of that invented blood pact from the trial." "The Jews" would have had to have considerable political and legal power within the Roman Empire to be held responsible for the death of Jesus. Yet, the Romans clearly wielded the power in Judea. Pontius Pilate served as a direct emissary of the Roman Emperor Tiberius and not the Roman Senate, and he used the typical Roman form of punishment of crucifixion to kill Jesus. The most reasonable conclusion to draw from these factors is that "The Romans and not the Jews killed Christ." Although this diverges from the survey, it merits attention given the general focus on the topic of genocide.

11. In this section, I shall largely follow the analysis given by Christopher in *The Ethics of War and Peace*.

12. Neil Chippendale, *Crimes against Humanity* (Philadelphia: Chelsea House Publishers, 2000), p. 26.

13. T. L. H. McCormack, "From Sun Tzu to the Sixth Committee: The Evolution of an International Criminal Regime," in T. L. H. McCormack and G. J. Simpson, eds., *The Law of War Crimes: National and International Approaches* (Kluwer, 1997). The English parliament in 1649 was the first to try a head of state, Charles I, with war crimes against his own people (Geoffrey Robertson, *Crimes against Humanity, The Struggle for Global Justice* (London: Penguin Press, 1999, revised edition, New York: New Press, 2003), p. 5).

14. Hiller B. Zobel, *The Boston Massacre* (New York: W. W. Norton, 1970).

15. Raphael Lemkin, author of the *Genocide Convention* (1948) represents another largely unsung hero of humanitarian law. See Samantha Powers, *"A Problem from Hell," America and the Age of Genocide* (New York: Harper Perennial, 2003), chapters 2–5, 13.

16. Henry Dunant, *A Memory of Solferino* (Geneva: International Committee of the Red Cross, 1939, 1959), p. 19.

17. Dunant, *A Memory of Solferino*, pp. 19, 32.

18. Dunant graciously included a footnote attribution to Florence Nightingale, whose 1859 proposal to form groups to aid the wounded had been readily dismissed by most of her contemporaries (Dunant, *A Memory of Solferino*, p. 124, fn 1).

19. Sidney Axinn, *A Moral Military* (Philadelphia: Temple University Press, 1989), p. 65.

20. Peter Maguire, *Law and War, An American Story* (New York: Columbia University Press, 2001), p. 36.

21. The doctrine of military necessity plays a central role in the Leiber Code. While Walzer and others have provided many illustrations of the misuse of this doctrine, there are instances where the doctrine has proved effective. For example, during the Korean War, the commander of the US Air Force refused to approve the bombing of North Korean irrigation dams that would have destroyed its rice crops. Burrus M. Carrahan, "Lincoln, Leiber and the Laws of War: The Origins and Limits of the Principle of Military Necessity," *The American Journal of International Law* 92 (1998), p. 229.

22. The Chemical Weapons Convention, ratified by the United States in 1997, bans the production and stockpiling of chemical weapons. Due to delays from indecision over disposal methods, the United States will probably not meet its 2007 deadline for disposing of tens of thousands of tons of chemical weapons. See Powers, *Problem from Hell*, p. 545, fn. 10.

23. Even the US Supreme Court began to see itself in an international context. In its opinion in *The Paquete Habana*, for example, the Court painted a picture of "a humane world in which if war occurs, the fighting should be as compassionate in spirit as possible" (*The Paquete Habana*, 175 US 677). See Henry Steiner and Philip Alston, *International Human Rights in Context* (Oxford: The Clarendon Press, 1996), p. 69.

24. Jackson Nyamuya Maogoto, *War Crimes and Realpolitik: International Justice from World War I to the 21st* Century (Boulder, London: Lynne Rienner Publishers, 2004), p. 40.

25. Steven R. Ratner and Jason S. Abrams, *Accountability for Human Rights Atrocities in International Law: Beyond the Nuremberg Legacy* (Oxford: Clarendon Press, 1997), p. 46.

26. Some jurists have charged that NATO's bombing campaign in Kosovo violated international law by not falling under either exception in the Charter.

27. Jackson Nyamuya Maogoto, *War Crimes and Realpolitik*, p. 83.

28. Oddly, concerns over *nullen crimen* objections did not arise during any war crimes trials held in the United States. In 1780, General George Washington had Major John Andre tried for violations of the "laws of war" even though the US legislature had not criminalized Andre's acts. A similar situation arose in the 1865 trial of Lincoln's assassins.

29. Edward M. Wise, "The Significance of Nuremberg," *War Crimes: The Legacy of Nuremberg*, Belinda Cooper, ed. (New York: TV Books, 1999), p. 57.

30. Gary Jonathan Bass, *Stay the Hand of Vengeance* (Princeton, New Jersey: Princeton University Press, 2000), p. 144.

31. Bass, *Stay the Hand of Vengeance*, p. 194.

32. Charles E., Wyzanski, Jr. (April 1946). "Nuremberg: A Fair Trial?" *Atlantic Monthly*, pp. 66–70.

33. Robert H. Jackson, "Opening Address for the United States, Nuremberg Trials," *The Case against the Nazi War Criminals* (New York: Knopf, 1946).

34. Not all states make genocide a crime in their national criminal codes. Australia, for example, ratified the Genocide Convention, but it does not have its own laws against genocide.

35. *Prosecutor v. Jeslisic*, IT-95-10-T (1999), para. 60.

36. M. Cherif Bassiouni, "From Versailles to Rwanda in Seventy-Five Years: The Need to Establish a Permanent International Criminal Court," *Harvard Human Rights Journal* 10 (1997), p. 11.

37. Jackson Nyamuya Maogoto, *War Crimes and Realpolitik*, pp. 20–24.

CHAPTER 2: GENOCIDE: GLOBAL CONTEXT

1. Perhaps, Somalia should not count since, at the time, it did not have a central government capable of representing the nation.

2. Article 123 Review of the Statute.

> 1. Seven years after the entry into force of this Statute, the Secretary-General of the United Nations shall convene a Review Conference to consider any amendments to this Statute. Such review may include, but is not limited to, the list of crimes

contained in article 5. The Conference shall be open to those participating in the Assembly of States Parties and on the same conditions.

2. At any time thereafter, at the request of a State Party and for the purposes set out in paragraph 1, the Secretary-General of the United Nations shall, upon approval by a majority of States Parties, convene a Review Conference. *Rome Statute of the International Criminal Court*, U.N. Doc. A/CONF.183/9.

3. Raimond Gaita, *A Common Humanity* (New York: Routledge, 2002), p. xxviii.

4. Jones, John R. W. D. *The Practice of the International Criminal Tribunals for the Former Yugoslavia and Rwanda* (Ardsley, NY: Transnational Publishers, 1998, 2000, 2003), p. 115.

5. James Alan Fox and Jack Levin, *Overkill: Mass Murder and Serial Killing Exposed* (New York: Plenum Press, 1994), pp. 201–206.

6. James Alan Fox and Jack Levin, *Overkill*, p. 225.

CHAPTER 3: GENOCIDE ACT: MASS KILLINGS

1. *Rome Statute of the International Criminal Court*, U.N. Doc. A/CONF.183/9.

2. Raphael Lemkin, "The Importance of the Convention" as quoted in Samantha Powers, *"A Problem from Hell," America and the Age of Genocide* (New York: Basic Books, 2002), p. 51.

3. As quoted in Powers, Samantha Powers, *"A Problem from Hell," America and the Age of Genocide* (New York: Basic Books, 2002), p. 70.

4. As quoted in Arieh J. Kochavi, *Prelude to Nuremberg* (Chapel Hill, NC: The University of North Carolina Press, 1998), p. 221.

5. Steven R. Ratner and Jason S. Abrams, *Accountability for Human Rights Atrocities in International Law*. Second Edition (Oxford: Oxford University Press, 2001), pp. 47–48.

6. Mathew Lippman, "Genocide: The Crime of the Century," 23 *Houston Journal of International Law* (Spring 2001), p. 467.

7. As later analyses will show, the prosecutors were on solid grounds in charging Milošević with genocide only for the war in Bosnia and not for the wars in Croatia and Kosovo. These distinctions are not merely academic as a determination of an on-going genocide provides stronger grounds for humanitarian intervention (however, in this discussion, retrospectively) than do the finding of war crimes.

8. Admittedly, these sweeping historical judgments about genocide already assume a particular definition of genocide, but this should not undermine our claims about the trends.

9. Jack Nusan Porter, "Introduction," in Jack Nusan Porter, editor, *Genocide and Human Rights: A Global Anthology* (Washington, DC: University Press of America, 1982), pp. 9–10.

10. R. J. Rummel, "The Holocaust in Comparative and Historical Perspective." Paper delivered to the Conference on "The 'Other' as a Threat: Demonization and Antisemitism," (June 12–15, 1995) at Hebrew University of Jerusalem.

11. As quoted in Philip Gourevitch, *We Wish to Inform You that Tomorrow We will be Killed with our Families* (New York: Picador, 1998), p. 153.

12. The United States had less trouble using the "g" word for Kosovo than it did for Rwanda. On June 25, 1999, President Clinton defended the bombing of Kosovo as a way to stop "deliberate, systematic efforts at... genocide." Recently, the United States overcame another period of reluctance to use the word when on September 9, 2004 US Secretary of State Colin Powell labeled the 18-month attack on largely black citizens in the Darfur region of Sudan as "genocide." The Clinton and Bush administrations refused to use a precise legal sense of the word "genocide" to avoid taking forceful action to stop mass killings.

13. Raphael Lemkin, *Axis Rule in Occupied Europe* (Washington, DC: Carnegie Endowment for International Peace, 1944).

14. Natan Lerner, *Group Rights and Discrimination in International Law* (Dordrecht, The Netherlands: Martinus Nijhoff Publishers, 1991).

15. *Report of the Committee on Foreign Relations, US Senate, on 'The Genocide Convention,'* Sen. Exec. Rpt. 99–2, 99th Cong., 1st Sess., July 18, 1985, at pp. 18, 19, 26–27. In ratifying the Genocide Convention, the US Senate passed a reservation at the insistence of Senator Jesse Helms that effectively prevents the International Court of Justice from exercising jurisdiction over the United States under this article.

16. "CRIMES AGAINST HUMANITY: namely, murder, *extermination*, enslavement, deportation, and other inhumane acts committed against any civilian population, before or during the war, or persecutions on political, racial, or religious grounds in execution of or in connection with any crime within the jurisdiction of the Tribunal, whether or not in violation of domestic law of the country where perpetrated [italics added]." *Texts of the Agreement for the Establishment of an International Military Tribunal and Annexed Charter*, United Nations Treaties Series, 5, 251.

17. A narrow definition of genocide distinguishes genocide from civilian war deaths. Unfortunately, space does not permit a defense of this important distinction.

18. *Convention on the Prevention and Punishment of the Crime of Genocide* December 9, 1948, art. I, 78 United Nations Treaty Series 277, 280 [hereinafter Genocide Convention] as collected in *International Documents on Human Rights*, Satish Chandra, ed. (New Delhi: Mittal Publications, 1990).

19. *The Prosecutor versus Jean Kambanda*, ICTR 97-23-S (1998).

20. Genocide Convention in *International Documents*, pp. 171–174.

21. We address the issue of how many killings constitute genocide in the next section.

22. As quoted in Patrick Thornberry, *International Law and the Rights of Minorities* (Oxford: Clarendon Press, 1991), p. 72.

23. To show how far the concept of genocide can go consider Lemkin's typography of genocides that included moral debasement of the population through, for example, exposure to pornography. Lemkin, *Axis Rule in Occupied Europe*, p. 90.

24. "Its [AUM's] members can claim the distinction of being the first group in history to combine ultimate fanaticism with ultimate weapons in a project to destroy the world." Robert Jay Lifton, *Destroying the World to Save It: Aum Sinrikyo and the New Global Terrorism* (New York: Henry Holt and Company, 1999), pp. 345, 343.

25. In 1999, the Japanese Diet passed one law that put AUM under close police scrutiny and another law that required AUM to turn over its assets to its victims. In 2000, the government discovered that AUM-owned companies had developed the software used by the police for surveillance. Lifton, *Destroying the World to Save It*, pp. 345–346.

26. On AUM's anti-Semitism see David Goodman, "Antisemitism in Japan: Its History and Current Implications," in *The Construction of Racial Identities in China and Japan*, Frank Dikötter, ed. (Honolulu: University of Hawaii Press, 1997).

27. Note that AUM's action (analogous to those of Cruse discussed in Chapter 2) would not qualify as genocide, according to the analysis given in Chapter 6, because AUM, as far as we know, did not single out members of any specific group.

28. See Alison Palmer, "Ethnocide," *Genocide in Our Time*, Michael N. Dobkowski and Isidor Walliman, eds. (Ann Arbor, Michigan: Pierian Press, 1992), pp. 1–22.

29. We have taken this account of Rabe's life largely from the late Iris Chang's *Rape of Nanking: The Forgotten Holocaust of WW II* (1997), pp. 191–194.

30. Chang, *Rape of Nanking*, p. 119.

31. Chang, *Rape of Nanking*, p. 102.

32. *Rape of Nanking* by Iris Chang is subtitled *The Forgotten Holocaust of WW II*. Chang, *Rape of Nanking*, p. 215.

33. Catherine MacKinnon, "Rape, Genocide and Women's Human Rights," *Harvard Women's Law Journal, 17* (Spring 1994), pp. 5–16.

34. *Prosecutor v. Jean-Paul Akayesu*, Judgment, No. ICTR-96-4-T (1998), hereinafter referred to as *Akayesu*, available on-line at http://www.un.org/ictr/english/judgments/akayesu.html. Summary of the Judgment in the Jean-Paul Akayesu Case, ICTR 96-4-T, para. 13 (1998), available on-line at http://www.un.org/ictr/english/singledocs/jpa_ summary.html.

35. The original indictments against Akayesu did not contain rape charges. After the testimonies of two witnesses, the prosecutor succeeded in amending the indictment to include charges of rape and sexual violence.

36. Pauline Nyiramasuhuko, Rwandan Minister for Family and Women's Development during the genocide period, is the first woman charged with genocide in an international court (ICTR-97-21-AR72). Prosecutors also charged she and her son Shalom Ntahobali, a former militia leader, with mass rape.

37. A Sarajevo joke, circa 1994, as quoted in Geoffrey Robertson. *Crimes against Humanity: The Struggle for Global Justice* (New York: The New Press, 2000), p. 303.

38. Dylan Thomas, "A Refusal to Mourn the Death, by Fire, of a Child in London."

39. Raphael Lemkin, *Axis Rule in Occupied Europe*, p. 71.

40. Gourevitch, *We wish to inform*, p. 201.

41. Astri Suhrke and Bruce Jones "Preventative Diplomacy in Rwanda," in *Opportunities Missed, Opportunities Seized*, Bruce W. Jentleson, ed. (New York: Carnegie Corporation, 2000), p. 256.

42. John F. Murphy, "The Quivering Gulliver: U.S. Views on a Permanent International Criminal Court," *International Lawyer* 34 (Spring 2000), p. 53.

CHAPTER 4: GENOCIDE MIND: ORGANIZATIONAL POLICIES

1. *Rome Statute of the International Criminal Court*, U.N. Doc. A/CONF.183/9.

2. *Prosecutor v. Jeslisic*, IT-95–10-T (1999), para. 66.

3. Geoffrey Robertson, *Crimes against Humanity: The Struggle for Global Justice*. Revised Edition (New York: The New Press, 2002), p. 305.

4. *Prosecutor v. Tadić*, IT-94-1-I. Initial Indictment (February 13, 1995).

5. Mary Williams Walsh, "A Tribunal in a Time of Atrocities," *Los Angeles Times* (August 30, 1995). See chapter 7 for a distinction between individual and organizational responsibility.

6. Samantha Powers, "The World of Radovan Karadžić," *U. S. News & World Report* (July 24, 1995).

7. *Prosecutor v. Karadžić and Mladic*, (Case No. IT-95-5, IT-95-5-R61, IT-95-18-R61) Initial Indictment, July 24, 1995 and Rule 61 Decision of (1996).

8. Donald G. McNeil, "Its Past on Its Sleeve, Tribe Seeks Bonn's Apology," *The New York Times*, International Section (May 31, 1998), p. 3. Trotha signed the proclamation as "The great General of the mighty German Kaiser." Some scholars have questioned the existence of the extermination order, but Trotha's letters and other contemporaneous accounts support the existence of the document. Jan-Bart Gewald, "Imperial Germany and the Herero of Southern Africa: Genocide and the Quest for Recompense," in *Genocide,*

War Crimes and the West, ed., Adam Jones (New York: Zed Books, 2004), pp. 59–77, 61–62.

9. Raul Hilberg, *The Destruction of the European Jews*, Student Edition (New York: Holmes & Meier, 1985), p. 265.

10. Charles W. Sydnor, Jr., "Executive Instincts, Reinhard Heydrich and the Planning for the Final Solution," *The Holocaust and History*, Michael Berenbaum and Abraham J. Peck, eds. (Bloomington, IN: Indiana University Press, 1998), pp. 159–186, 175.

11. Hilberg, *The Destruction of the European Jews*, p. 263.

12. Syndor, "Executive Instincts," *The Holocaust and History*, pp. 176–177.

13. Israel Charny, "Review of Helen Fein's *Genocide: A Sociological Perspective*" *Internet on the Holocaust and Genocide*, nos. 30–31 (February 1991), pp. 5–6.

14. *Union Carbide Corporation v. Union of India, Supreme Court of India*, Civil Appeal Nos. 3187–89.

15. Tyagi YK, Rosencranz A., "Some International Law Aspects of the Bhopal Disaster," *Social Science Medicine* 27 (1988), pp. 1105–1112.

16. As quoted in Robert Conquest, *The Harvest of Sorrow: Soviet Collectivization and the Terror-Famine* (New York: Oxford University Press, 1986).

17. Robert C. Tucker, *Stalin in Power: The Revolution From Above, 1928–1941* (New York: W. W. Norton, 1990), pp. 190, 195.

18. Lynne Viola, "The Gray Zone," *The Nation* (October 13, 2003), pp. 25–29, 26. A review of Anne Applebaum, *Gulag: A History* (New York: Doubleday, 2002). Viola claims that Western scholars unwittingly followed the lead of Alexander Solzhenitsyn in blaming the Communist system and not any particular leader or leaders for the mass atrocities.

19. Irving Louis Horowitz, *Taking Lives: Genocide and State Power* (New Brunswick, NJ: Transaction Books, 1980), p. 17.

20. William Eckhart and Gernot Köhler, "Structural and Armed Violence in the 20th Century: Magnitudes and Trends," *International Interactions* 6:4 (1980), pp. 347–375, 348.

21. Eric Markusen, "Genocide and Modern War," *Genocide in Our Time*, Michael N. Dobkowski and Isidor Walliman, eds. (Ann Arbor, MI: Pierian Press, 1992), p. 119.

22. Isidor Wallimann and Michael Dobkowski, eds. *Genocide and the Modern Age* (Westport, CT: Greenwood Press, 1987), pp. xvi–xvii.

23. Tony Barta, "Realties of Genocide: Land and Lives in the Colonialization of Australia," in *Genocide and the Modern Age*, Isidor Wallimann and Michael Dobkowski, eds. (New York: Greenwood Press, 1987), p. 238.

24. *The People v. Englebrecht*, California Court of Appeal, Fourth Appellate District, Super. Ct. No. NO76625. *People v. Acuna*, Supreme Court of California Super. Ct. No. 729322.

25. See Barnabas Gero, "The Role of the Hungarian Constitutional Court," *Institute on East Central Europe* (March, 1997).

26. Berel Lang, *Act and Idea in the Nazi Genocide* (Chicago: University of Chicago Press, 1990).

27. *Jelisic*, TC, para. 100.

28. *Jelisic*, TC, para. 101. The Appeals Chamber diluted the Trial Chamber insistence on proof of a plan and organization by indicating that "the existence of a plan or policy may become an important factor in most cases" (*Jelisic*, AC, para. 48). We claim that proof of an organizational plan should be a necessary element of the *mens rea* component of the crime of genocide.

29. *Jelisic*, Appeals, para. 42.

30. However, the Appeals Chamber retained an individual intent element by indicating its willingness to accept that, absence an actual plan, Jelisic still "believed he was following a plan sent down by superiors to eradicate the Muslims in Brcko." (*Jelisic*, para. 66).

31. Sylvia Moreno, "Unresolved Murders of Women Rankle in Mexican Border City," *Washington Post* (December 16, 2005).

32. Bundy was convicted of the first-degree murder of twelve-year-old Kimberly Leach and sentenced to death. The conviction and sentence were affirmed in *Bundy v. State*, 471 So.2d 9 (Fla. 1985), cert. denied, 479 U.S. 894, 93 L. Ed. 2d 269, 107 S. Ct. 295 (1986). After the governor signed a death warrant, Bundy filed a motion for post conviction relief, which was denied. The Supreme Court of Florida affirmed and at the same time denied a petition for writ of habeas corpus in *Bundy v. State*, 497 So.2d 1209 (Fla. 1986). Bundy then filed a petition for habeas corpus in the federal district court, which was also denied. However, the court of appeals stayed Bundy's execution pending appeal from the denial of his petition for habeas corpus in *Bundy v. Wainwright*, 805 F.2d 948 (11th Cir. 1986). That court later directed the district court to hold an evidentiary hearing on Bundy's claim that he was incompetent to stand trial in *Bundy v. Dugger*, 816 F.2d 564 (11th Cir.), cert. denied, 484 U.S. 870, 108 S. Ct. 198, 98 L. Ed. 2d 149 (1987). After holding such a hearing, the district court ruled that Bundy was competent to stand trial in *Bundy v. Dugger*, 675 F. Supp. 622, 635 (M.D. Fla. 1987). This order was affirmed by the court of appeals in *Bundy v. Dugger*, 850 F.2d 1402 (11th Cir. 1988). The US Supreme Court denied Bundy's petition for writ of certiorari in *Bundy v. Dugger*, 488 U.S. 1034, 102 L. Ed. 2d 980, 109 S. Ct. 849 (1989). On January 17, 1989, the governor signed a second death warrant and scheduled Bundy's execution for January 24, 1989. The Florida Supreme Court affirmed the order denying Bundy's motion for post conviction relief and Bundy's application for stay of execution in *Theodore Robert Bundy v. State of Florida*, 538 So. 2d 445 (1989, Supreme Court of Florida). Subsequent appeals were denied in *Theodore Robert Bundy v. State of Florida*, 541 So. 2d 1172 (1989, Supreme Court of Florida).

33. See Katherine Ramland, *The Human Predator: A Historical Chronicle of Serial Murder and Forensic Investigation* (Berkley, 2005).

34. Helen Fein, "Genocide, Terror, Life integrity, and War Crimes: The Case of Discrimination," *Genocide: Conceptual and Historical Dimensions*, George J. Andreopoulos, ed. (Philadelphia: University of Pennsylvania Press, 1994).

35. *Karadžić and Mladic*, Rule 61 Decision of July 11, 1996.

36. The requirement of an authoritative, organizational structure, operating within or outside the state apparatus, would generally rule out a single individual committing genocide.

37. The *UN Commission of Experts* submitted to the Security Council (December 4, 1994), para 1.14.

38. Adam Hochschild, *King Leopold's Ghost* (New York: Houghton Mifflin, 1998), p. 225.

39. Hochschild, *King Leopold's Ghost*, p. 282.

40. I want to thank Bill Frelick of the US Committee on Refugees for raising this complex problem.

41. Unfortunately, however, since the September 11, 2001 attack on the Twin Towers, the international community has lost sight of a critical distinction between state and non-state terrorist organizations.

42. René Lemarchand, "Burundi: The Politics of Ethnic Amnesia," *Genocide Watch*, Helen Fein, ed. (New Haven, CT: Yale University Press, 1992), pp. 70–86, 80.

43. Amnesty International, *Burundi: Killings of Children by Government Troops*, AFR. 16/04 (1988), p. 3.

44. Lamarchand, *Genocide Watch*, p. 79.

45. *The United Nations Commission of Experts* submitted to the Security Council (December 4, 1994), para 7.15

46. Astri Suhrke and Bruce Jones, "Preventative Diplomacy in Rwanda: Failure to Act or Failure of Actions?," *Opportunities Missed, Opportunities Seized: Preventive Diplomacy in Post-Cold War World* (Lanham: Rowman & Littlefield, 2000), p. 256.

47. *The United Nations Commission of Experts* submitted to the Security Council (December 4, 1994), para 7.16.

48. *The United Nations Commission of Experts* (December 4, 1994), para 7.7.

49. *The United Nations Commission of Experts* (December 4, 1994), para 7.2.

50. *The United Nations Commission of Experts* (December 4, 1994).

51. *Africa Rights* (1995), p. 1126.

52. *International Herald Tribune* (June 13, 1994).

53. *International Herald Tribune* (June 14, 1994).

54. *Prosecutor v. Delalic*, Judgment (November 16, 1998), para. 175.

CHAPTER 5: GENOCIDE MOTIVE: INSTITUTIONALIZED HATRED

1. Robert D. Kaplan, *Balkan Ghosts: A Journey Through History* (New York: Vintage, 1993), p. xviii.

2. Jurists sometimes address motive issues under the guise of intent, and in genocide cases, they think about motive under something called "special intent."

3. *Prosecutor v. Jelisic* (Case No. IT-95-10-T), Judgment, December 14, 1999), para. 79.

4. *Jelisic*, para. 49.

5. Hurst Hannum and David Hawk, "The Case Against the Standing Committee of the Communist Party of Kampuchea, Draft Memorial for the International Court of Justice," (1986) as reprinted in *International Law: Norms, Actors, Process*, Jeffrey L. Dunoff et al., eds. (New York and Gaithersberg, MD: Aspen Publishers, 2002), p. 572.

6. Raul Hilberg, *The Destruction of the European Jews* (New York: Holmes & Meier, 1995).

7. Milton J. Easman, *Ethnic Politics* (Ithaca, NY: Cornell University Press, 1994), pp. 13–14.

8. Hilberg, *The Destruction of the European Jews*, p. 267.

9. Hilberg, *The Destruction of the European Jews*, p. 305.

10. Miranda Vickers, *Between Serb and Albanian: A History of Kosovo* (New York: Columbia University Press, 1998), p. 217.

11. Group designations can become quite absurd when the situation enters the brutalization phase. The underling absurdity of group designations appears in the more severe phases of brutalization. The Nazis exterminated Jewish vermin. In the Balkans, Arkan's thugs imposed fantasized identities on their Bosnian Muslim victims, and the *genocidaires* in Rwanda murdered Tutsi cockroaches. In a sense, these perpetrators kill their bizarre visions of groups.

12. B. Jenkins and S. A. Sofos S.A. *Nation and Identity in Contemporary Europe* (London: Routledge, 1996), p. 272.

13. Malcolm, *Kosovo*, p. 351.

14. Mahmood Mamdani, *When Victims Become Killers: Colonialism, Nativism, and the Genocide in Rwanda* (Princeton: Princeton University Press, 2002), p. 38.

15. Avishai Margalit and Gabriel Motzkin, "The Uniqueness of the Holocaust," *Philosophy and Public Affairs* (Winter 1996), pp. 65–83.

16. In April 2002, the Dutch coalition government of Prime Minister Wim Kok resigned over reports of the role of Dutch troops in the Srebrenica massacre. After the assassination of national party candidate Pim Fortuyn, a right-wing coalition government briefly took power in the Netherlands.

17. Jackson Nyamuya Maogoto, *War Crimes and Realpolitik: International Justice from World War I to the 21st Century* (Boulder, London: Lynne Rienner Publishers, 2004), pp. 168–169, fn 39.

18. Gourevitch, *We Wish to Inform You*, p. 169.

CHAPTER 6: GENOCIDE VICTIMS: PERPETRATOR DEFINED

1. Israel W. Charny, "Toward a Generic Definition of Genocide," *Genocide: Conceptual and Historical Dimensions*, ed., George J. Andreopoulos (Philadelphia: University of Pennsylvania Press, 1994), p. 71.

2. Charny, *Genocide*, pp. 70–71.

3. Tim Cole, *Selling the Holocaust* (New York: Routledge, 1999), p. 162. The numbers of identity cards for each victim group are as follows: Jews (364), Polish prisoners (47), Jehovah's Witnesses (20), homosexuals (9), Gypsies (3), and euthanasia victims (2).

4. GAOR, 3rd Session, Part 1, Sixth Committee and Annexes (1948–9), 63rd–69th meetings, 71st–81st meetings, 91st–110th meetings, and 128th–134th meetings.

5. Patrick Thornberry, *International Law and the Rights of Minorities* (Oxford: Clarendon Press, 1991), p. 57.

6. As a corollary to the intra-group animosity thesis, consider that the more direct and immediate a group member's experience is to harm directed at the group, the less animosity that group member will have later to members of the perpetuator's group. Correlatively, the further removed the person is from the group conflict, the deeper and more long lasting will be the animosity.

7. See my "Minorities in International Law" *Canadian Journal of Law and Jurisprudence* 10 (1997), pp. 1–13. The problem of how to define groups not only creates difficulties for the laws of genocide, it also creates obstacles in many other areas of international law such as minority rights. For example, international jurists have debated whether to adopt a subjective or objective definition of a minority. On a subjective view, group identity depends upon what group members say it is. A subjective analysis is over-inclusive since, theoretically, people could self-identity with any group. On an objective analysis of a minority, group identity turns on external features of a group. The objective approach faces problems finding agreement on these objective characteristics for any one group. Further, an objective approach is under-inclusive. No matter how meticulous and careful we are in the search for definitively distinguishing group characteristics, the standards we come up with are doomed to failure. Instead of adopting a subjective or an objective definition of minority, we should look at how those who discriminate against minorities provide the basis for determining those groups entitled to legal protection. What works for identifying minorities susceptible to discrimination works for identifying the group types vulnerable to acts of genocide.

8. *Prosecutor v. Jean-Paul Akayesu*, Judgment, No. ICTR-96-4-T (September 2, 1998). International Criminal Court for Rwanda, Judgment of the Trial Chamber, para. 170.

9. Nigel Eltringham, *Accounting for Horror: Post-Genocide Debates in Rwanda* (London: Pluto Press, 2004), p. 28. *Akayesu* Judgment, the Trial Chamber, ICTR (1998), para. 511.

10. *The Prosecutor v. Clément Kayishema* Judgment, ICTR (ICTR-95-1) (1999), para. 98.

11. Frank Chalk and Kurt Johanassohn, *The History and Sociology of Genocide: Analyses and Case Studies* (New Haven: Yale University Press, 1990), p. 23.

12. In an earlier proposal that also broadens the kinds of groups included, Drost defined genocide as "the deliberate destruction of physical life of individual human beings by reason of their membership of any human collectivity as such." Pieter Drost, *The Crime of State*, vol. 2, *Genocide* (Leyden: A. W. Sythoff, 1959), p. 125.

13. *Prosecutor v. Jelisic* (Case No. IT-95-10-T), Judgment, Trial Chamber (14 December 1999), para. 70.

14. I shall use the expression "Pol Pot's regime" interchangeably with "Democratic Kampuchea." The survivors of 1975–1979 refer to the 1975–1979 era as "the era of the contemptible Pot." Pol Pot's co-leaders, in turn, called him "Brother Number One." David P. Chandler, *Brother Number One, A Political Biography of Pol Pot* (Boulder: Westview Press, 1999, revised edition), p. 113.

15. As quoted in Michael J. Bazler, "Reexamining the Doctrine of Humanitarian Intervention in Light of the atrocities in Kampuchea and Ethiopia," *Stanford Journal of International Law* 23:2 (1987), p. 552.

16. "Outside of the Jews no other coherent group was so intensively persecuted in the Hitler period [as Jehovah Witnesses]." Michael H. Kater, "Die Ernsten Bibelforscher im Dritten Reich," *Vierteljahrshefte fur Zeitgeschichte* 17 (1969), pp. 181–218, 181. As quoted in Eric A. Johnson, *Nazi Terror* (New York: Basic Books, 1999), p. 239.

17. John Roth pointedly challenges us to consider the following proposition: "If more people practiced versions of what the Jehovah's Witnesses preach and practice, the Holocaust could have been prevented and genocide would scourge the world no more." John K. Roth, *Holocaust Politics* (Louisville, KY: Westminster John Knox Press, 2001), p. 236.

18. In the United States, Jehovah Witnesses also suffered persecution during the same period. In 1939, a Jewish-American jurist, Felix Frankfurter wrote the majority opinion that upheld by an 8 to 1 vote a school district ban on Jehovah's Witness attending school because they refused to salute the flag. The decision was later overturned in *Minersville School District v. Gobitis* (1942).

19. Ben Kiernan, "The Cambodian Genocide" *Genocide: Conceptual and Historical Dimensions*. George J. Andreopoulos, ed. (Philadelphia: University of Pennsylvania Press, 1994), pp. 197–198.

20. *The United Nations Group of Experts for Cambodia Report*, para. 64.

21. David Hawk, "International Human Rights Law and Democratic Kampuchea," *The Cambodian Agony*. David A. Ablin and Marlowe Hood, eds. (Armonk: M. E. Sharpe, 1990), p. 131.

22. Mathew Lippman, "The 1948 Convention on the Prevention and Punishment of the Crime of Genocide," *Temple International and Comparative Law Journal* 8 (1985), p. 4.

23. Richard C. Lukas, "The Polish Experience during the Holocaust," in *A Mosaic of Victims*, ed., Michael Berenbaum (New York: New York University Press, 1990), pp. 88–95, 90.

24. Israel Gutman, "The Victimization of the Poles," in *A Mosaic of Victims*. Michael Berenbaum, ed. (New York: New York University Press, 1990), p. 98.

25. For a defense of dropping the bomb, see Robert James Maddox, *Weapons for Victory: The Hiroshima Decision Fifty Years Later* (Columbus, MO: University of Missouri Press, 1995). For the case against dropping the bomb, see Gar Alperovitz, *The Decision to Use the Atomic Bomb* (New York: Vintage Press, 1996). For a balanced account, see J. Samuel Walker, *Prompt and Utter Destruction: President Truman and the Use of the Atomic Bomb Against Japan* (Chapel Hill, NC: University of North Carolina Press, 1997).

26. Kiernan in *Genocide*, p. 198.

27. *The United Nations Group of Experts for Cambodia Report*, para. 71.

28. Bohdan Vitvitsky, "Slavs and Jews: Consistent and Inconsistent Perspectives on the Holocaust," *A Mosaic of Victims: Non-Jews Persecuted and Murdered by the Nazis*. Michael Berenbaum, ed. (New York: New York University Press, 1990), pp. 101–108, p. 106.

29. Aharon Weiss, The Holocaust and the Ukrainian Victims," *A Mosaic of Victims: Non-Jews Persecuted and Murdered by the Nazis*. Michael Berenbaum, ed. (New York: New York University Press, 1990), pp. 109–115.

30. Ben Kiernan, "The Cambodian Genocide: Issues and Ropers," *Genocide: Conceptual and Historical Dimensions*, George J. Andreopoulos, ed. (Philadelphia: University of Pennsylvania Press, 1994), p. 201.

31. For a contrary analysis see George J. Andreopoulos, "Introduction: The Calculus of Genocide," *Genocide: Conceptual and Historical Dimensions*, ed., George J. Andreopoulos (Philadelphia: University of Pennsylvania Press, 1994), p. 24, n. 13.

32. For example, Brenda Davis Lutz and James M. Lutz, "Gypsies as Victims of the Holocaust," *Holocaust and Genocide Studies* 9 (1995), pp. 346–359.

33. Ian Hancock, "Responses to the Porrajmos: The Romany Holocaust," *Is the Holocaust Unique?*, Alan S. Rosenbaum, ed. (Boulder: Westview Press, 1996), p. 54.

34. Gunther Lewy, *The Nazi Persecution of the Gypsies* (New York: Oxford University Press, 2000), pp. 52–55.

35. Margalit and Motzkin, "The Uniqueness of the Holocaust," *Is the Holocaust Unique?* Alan S. Rosenbaum, ed. (Boulder: Westview Press, 1996), p. 79.

36. Gunther Lewy, *The Nazi Persecution of the Gypsies*, p. 38.

37. Gunther Lewy, *The Nazi Persecution of the Gypsies*, p. 223. See cases of Auschwitz SS block leader Ernst-August König (ZSL Ludwigsburg, 402, AR-Z 47/84, Bd., 3) and Ruth Kellermann of the Research Institute for Racial Hygiene and Population Biology (ZSL Ludwigsburg, 414 AR 540/83, Bd., 4).

38. John A.S. Grenville, "Neglected Holocaust Victims," *The Holocaust in History*. Michael Berenbaum and Abraham J. Peck, eds. (Indiana University Press, 1998), p. 321.

39. Steven R. Ratner and Jason S. Abrams, *Accountability for Human Rights Atrocities in International Law*. Second Edition (Oxford: Oxford University Press, 2001), p. 286.

40. Michael Vickery, *Cambodia: 1975–1982* (Boston: South End Press, 1984).

41. As evidence that the Khmer Rogue treated the Chinese as a race, Elizabeth Becker cites the use of "politically sanctioned racist taunts," such as "chalk faced," that Cambodians hurled at the Chinese. Elizabeth Becker, *When the War Was Over* (New York: PublicAffairs, 1998), pp. 244–245. Yet, Ben Kiernan (who, ironically, critics charge with placing too much emphasis on racism) claims that the Chinese "were not targeted for execution because of their race [sic?], but like other evacuated city dwellers they were made to work harder and in much more deplorable conditions than rural dwellers."

Ben Kiernan, *The Pol Pot Regime: Race, Power, and Genocide in Cambodia under the Khmer Rouge, 1975–1979* (New Haven and London: Yale University Press, 1996).

42. Historians and political commentators sometimes confuse group types. Becker, for example, conflates culture, nationality, and race. She speaks about how the Chinese who visited Cambodia from China ignored the Chinese who were born in Cambodia as if "there was no cultural or racial loyalty." Her surprise at the gap between the two groups stems from her assumption that the members of both groups have the same ethnicity or come from the same race. She also links race to politics: "The question of racial purity seemed of a piece with the superiority the Khmer Rouge felt toward other communists and other countries." To the contrary, race does not function on the same conceptual plane as political and territorial affiliations. From the alleged fact that the Khmer Rouge thought that they were better and purer communists than China's Communist Party, it does not follow that the Khmers thought of the Chinese as an inferior race. Elizabeth Becker, *When the War Was Over* (New York: PublicAffairs, 1998), p. 245.

43. We purposefully ended the analysis in this section by using the label *Chinese Cambodians* instead of *Cambodian Chinese* as the latter implies a racial group (which we argued against) and the former an ethnic group (which we argued for).

44. Primo Levi, *The Drowned and the Saved* (New York: Summit Books, 1988), p. 125.

45. See Susan Neiman, *Evil in Modern Thought: An Alternative History of Philosophy* (Princeton: Princeton University Press, 2002).

46. Eric A. Johnson. *Nazi Terror*. (New York: Basic Books, 1999), p. 484.

47. "The intent to destroy the Cham and other ethnic minorities appears evidenced by such Khmer Rouge actions as their announced policy of homogenization, the total prohibition of these groups' distinctive cultural traits, their dispersal among the general population and the execution of their leadership." *The United Nations Group of Experts for Cambodia Report*, para. 64.

48. In the case of the Muslim Chams, questions concerning the extent of the mass killings, the *actus reus*, also have caused controversy. Kiernan, emphasizing the high proportion of Cambodia's Cham population killed, quickly concludes that they suffered genocide at the hands of Pol Pot. Vickery, however, sees the loss of 20,000 Muslim Chams as falling below a threshold needed for genocide. Even if we dispute Vickery's figures as an underestimation, numbers count (as we have seen see in Chapter 3) when deciding whether genocide took place. While it is almost impossible to defend any specific number of killings where it becomes appropriate to invoke the term "genocide," the number of killings is a relevant factor in assessing whether the acts constitute genocide. The burden of proof should fall on those who claim that a considerable number of killings do not exceed the threshold. In the absence of any coherent analysis of why 20,000 deaths fall below the mark, we must reject Vickery's dismissal. Contrary to Vickery's analysis, then, 20,000 victims from one group should qualify as a genocide act assuming that the other requirements also are fulfilled. Admittedly, it remains an open question whether the Cham case meets the other requirements for the crime of genocide.

49. Vickery, *Cambodia: 1975–1982*, p. 182.

50. Lyman H. Letgers, "The Soviet Gulag: Is It Genocide?" *Toward the Understanding and Prevention of Genocide*, Israel W. Chaney, ed. (Boulder: Westview Press, 1984), p. 65.

51. "Outside of specially targeted groups like Jews, Communists, and staunch religious opponents, there was considerable measure of grumbling and nonconformity on the part of the ordinary German population but very little protest or serious opposition" (Johnson, *Nazi Terror*, p. 283).

52. Johnson, *Nazi Terror*, p. 297. "The Gestapo's treatment of the majority of the population stood in sharp contrast to its treatment of these targeted groups" (Johnson, *Nazi Terror*, p. 284).

53. David P. Chandler, *The Tragedy of Cambodian History* (New Haven: Yale University Press, 1991), pp. 263–265.

54. David P. Chandler, *Brother Number One: A Political Biography of Pol Pot* (Boulder: Westview Press, 1992), p. 4.

55. Ben Kiernan, *The Pol Pot Regime* (New Haven: Yale University Press, 1996), p. 26.

56. Craig Etcheson, "Mapping Project 1999: The Analysis," *Document Center of Cambodia*, p. 2.

57. Ibid, p. 3.

58. Ibid.

59. Serge Thion "Genocide as a Political Commodity," *Genocide and Democracy in Cambodia* (New Haven: Yale University Southeast Asia Studies, 1993), p. 172.

CHAPTER 7: GENOCIDE PERPETRATORS: ORGANIZED BARBARITY

1. Robert Jay Litton, *Destroying the World to Save It: Aum Shinrikyo, Apocalyptic Violence, and the New Global Terrorism* (Metropolitan Books, 1999).

2. In 2004, a US district court found Hale guilty of one count of soliciting to murder a federal judge who had ruled against his organization in a trademark case.

3. See the articles collected in *Collective Responsibility: Five Decades of Debate in Theoretical and Applied Ethics*. Larry May and Stacey Hoffman, eds. (Lanham, MD: Rowman & Littlefield, 1991).

4. There is considerable controversy over the Thugs. While many scholars see the Thugs as a distinct Muslim/Hindu religious group with a distinct set of rituals and practices relating to the goddess Kali that flourished between the thirteenth and the nineteenth centuries, others dismiss the Cult of Thuggee as a product of British colonial imagination. See, van Woerkens, Martine, *The Strangled Traveler: Colonial Imaginings and the Thugs of India*. Translated by Catherine Tihanyi (2002).

5. At Nuremberg, Justice Jackson used these examples to dispel the objection that the Nuremberg Charter had introduced entirely new concepts.

6. Rafael Lemkin, *Axis Rule in Occupied Europe* (Washington, DC: Carnegie Endowment for International Peace, 1944).

7. As quoted in Robert E. Conot, *Justice at Nuremberg* (New York: Harper & Row, 1983), p. 12.

8. As quoted in Whitney R. Harris, *Tyranny on Trial: The Evidence at Nuremberg* (New York: Barnes & Noble, 1954, 1995), p. 13.

9. Whitney R. Harris, *Tyranny on Trial: The Evidence at Nuremberg* (New York: Barnes & Noble, 1954, 1995).

10. Joseph E. Persico, *Nuremberg: Infamy on Trial* (New York: Penguin Books, 1994), p. 180.

11. Ibid.

12. Ibid, p. 181.

13. It is important to underscore just how many Nazi suspects the United States held. The figure of 200,000 indicates that the Allies thought that the complicity in war crimes spread widely among the German population. Until recently, Rwanda held Hutus in prison as suspects for committing genocide and other war crimes. The international community took

the figure of 130,000 Hutus held in Rwanda's jail as *prima facie* evidence of wrongdoing by the Rwanda government. Human rights groups harshly criticized Rwanda for, among other things, holding that many people in prison.

14. As quoted in Conot, *Justice at Nuremberg*, p. 455. According to Persico, Jackson resorted to the concept of group guilt because of the overwhelming numbers of potential war criminals (Persico, *Nuremberg: Infamy on Trial*, p. 180). However, Jackson's words alone show that he agreed with Bernays that the organizational indictment spread responsibility for the horrors more widely.

15. Conot, *Justice at Nuremberg*, p. 456.

16. Eugene Davidson, *The Trial of the Germans* (Columbia, Missouri: University of Missouri Press, 1966), p. 561.

17. Conot, *Justice at Nuremberg*, p. 485.

18. For the case against the German professional military see *The German Army and Genocide: Crimes against War Prisoners, Jews, and Other Civilians, 1939–1944*. Hamburg Institute for Social Research (New York: The New Press, 1999), and Omer Bartov, "The Wehrmacht Exhibition Controversy: The Politics of Evidence," in *Crimes of War: Guilt and Denial in the Twentieth Century*. Omer Bartov et al., eds (New York: The New Press, 2002), pp. 41–60.

19. Yet, Persico claims, "No member of a convicted organization . . . was punished solely on the strength of the IMT verdicts" (Persico, *Nuremberg: Infamy on Trial*, p. 396).

20. Harris, *Tyranny on Trial*, p. 545.

21. About 13 million in the US occupation zone registered. Of these, local boards processed about 3 million. The Military Governor granted amnesty to 2.5 million without any trial. Fewer than 10 percent of those originally registered as Nazis underwent a trial, and of the few convicted, almost all received minor sentences. See John Dornberg, *Schizophrenic Germany* (New York: Macmillan, 1961) as reprinted in *Transitional Justice*, Neil Kritz, ed. (Washington, DC: United States Institute of Peace, 1995), p. 26. Of the 930,000 tried by denazification tribunals, "1,549 were classified as major offenders, 21,000 as offenders, 104,000 as lesser offenders, and 475,000 as followers. Over 500,000 people were fined for various criminal offenses, 122,000 suffered restrictions on employment, 25,000 were subject to confiscation of property, 22,000 were declared ineligible to hold public office, 30,000 were required to perform special labor, and 9,000 were given prison sentences." Norman E. Tutorow, *War Crimes, War Criminals, and War Crimes Trials* (Westport, CT: Greenwood Publishing Group, 1986), pp. 7–8.

22. John H. Herz, "Denazification and Related Policies," in *From Dictatorship to Democracy*. John H. Herz, ed. (Westport, CT: Greenwood, 1982) as reprinted in *Transitional Justice*. Vol. II. Neil Kritz, ed. (Washington, DC: United States Institute of Peace, 1995), p. 41. Not all former Nazi party members fared well even when exonerated. During the horrifying Rape of Nanking (1938), John Rabe, while working for the German industrial giant Siemens, saved 250,000 Chinese as head of the International Committee of the Nanking Safety Zone. After his return to Germany, the Gestapo interrogated him. After the war, a German acquaintance denounced him as a member of the NSDAP, the Nazi party. His appeal for de-nazification was first rejected but then granted by the de-nazifying commission of the British sector. The legal ordeal had impoverished him. Survivors of the massacre raised money and sent food to Rabe, who died in 1950. See Iris Chang, *The Rape of Nanking* (New York: Basic Books, 1997), pp. 191–194.

23. Herz, "Denazification and Related Policies," p. 40.

24. The charge against former Nazis comes more in the form of moral outrage than it does as a claim that the former Nazis either continue to promote hate or that they govern ineffectively. The same holds true of former war criminals in Japan.

25. Jarat Chopra and Thomas G. Weiss, "Sovereignty is no Longer Sacrosanct: Codifying Humanitarian Intervention." *Ethics and International Affairs* 6 (1992), pp. 95–117.

26. Peter A. French, *Collective and Corporate Responsibility* (New York: Columbia University Press, 1984).

27. David T. Risser, "The Social Dimension of Moral Responsibility: Taking Organizations Seriously," *Journal of Social Philosophy* 27:1 (Spring 1996), pp. 189–207. Massey had made a case for holding those who made small or *de minimus* contributions to harm legally and morally responsible.

28. Larry May, *The Morality of Groups* (Notre Dame: Notre Dame University Press, 1987).

29. Larry May, *Sharing Responsibility* (Chicago: University of Chicago Press, 1992).

30. Larry May and Robert Strikwerda, "Men in Groups: Collective Responsibility for Rape," *Hypatia*, 9:2 (Spring 1994), pp. 134–151.

31. As cited in Davidson, *The Trial of the Germans*, p. 556.

32. Daniel Goldhagen, *Hitler, and His Willing Executioners* (New York: Alfred A. Knopf, 1996).

33. Of course, some ex-Nazis have served in roles of highly questionable value. As judges, for example, they have assured a great deal of continuity with the Third Reich. See Ingo Müller, *Hitler's Justice: The Courts of the Third Reich* (Cambridge, MA: Harvard University Press, 1991).

34. André Siboman, *Hope for Rwanda* (Sterling, VA: Pluto Press, 1997), p. 116.

35. Jamie Frederic Metzl, "Rwandan Genocide and the International Law of Radio Jamming," *American Journal of International Law* 91 (October 1997), p. 628.

36. *The Prosecutor v. Ferdinand Nahimana Jean-Bosco Barayagwiza Hassan Ngeze* Case No. ICTR-99-52-T, Trial Chamber (13 December 2003). Despite the difficulties the US government has in carrying out the extradition of individuals wanted for criminal prosecution for genocide, civil suits against *genocidaires*, although seemingly unrelated, have achieved some success in US courts. The US District Court, Southern District of New York, for example, granted compensatory and punitive damages against Jean Bosco Barayagwiza, owner of RTML, under the 1798 Alien Tort Act. *Mushikiwabo v. Barayagwiza*, United States District Court, Southern District of New York (9 April 1996), unpublished report.

37. Gérard Prunier, *The Rwanda Crisis: History of Genocide* (New York: Columbia University Press, 1995), p. 224.

38. *The International Panel of Eminent Personalities to Investigate the 1994 Genocide in Rwanda and the Surrounding Events*, Organization of African Unity, Chapter 15, 1999.

39. Prunier, *The Rwanda Crisis*, p. 211.

40. Prunier, *The Rwanda Crisis*, p. 314.

41. Siboman, *Hope for Rwanda*, p. 116.

42. For an attempt to understand the issues from a UN bureaucratic perspective see Michael Barnett, *Eyewitness to a Genocide: The United Nations and Rwanda* (Ithaca, NY: Cornell University Press, 2002).

43. Kathleen Berry, "Rwanda and the United Nations: A Case of Active Indifference," *International Network on Holocaust and Genocide*, 14: 2–3, pp. 10–20, 12.

44. *The Prosecutor v. Elizaphan And Gérard Ntakirutimana* Cases No. ICTR-96-10 & ICTR-96-17-T, Trial Chamber (21 February 2003).

45. Philip Gourevitch, *We Wish to Inform You that by Tomorrow My Family and I will be Dead* (New York: Farrar, Straus and Giroux, 1998).

CONCLUSION: INTERNATIONAL JUSTICE AND UNIVERSAL MORALITY

1. *In the Matter of Surrender of Elizaphan Ntakirutimana*, US Dist. Ct. Southern Dist. of TX, Laredo Div., Civil Act. No. L-98-43. (August 7, 1998).

2. *In the Matter of Surrender of Elizaphan Ntakirutimana*, US Dist. Ct. Southern Dist. of TX, Laredo Div., Misc. No. L-96-5 (December 17, 1997).

3. *Elizaphan Ntakirutimana v. Janet Reno* et al., 184 F.3d 419 (United States Court of Appeal, Fifth Circuit, 5 August 1999); and 528 U.S. 1135 (Supreme Court, 24 January 2000), *certiorari* denied.

4. *The Prosecutor v. Elizaphan and Gérard Ntakirutimana*, Cases No. ICTR-96-10 & ICTR-96-17-T (February 21, 2003).

5. The US government has not signed the following international treaties (conventions): Convention on the Law of the Sea; Convention on the Prohibition of the Use, Stockpiling, Production and Transfer of Anti-Personnel Landmines; International Convention against the Recruitment, Use, Financing and Training of Mercenaries; Convention for the Suppression of the Traffic in Persons; International Convention on the Suppression and Punishment of the Crime of Apartheid. It has signed but not ratified: Convention on the Elimination of all Forms of Discrimination against Women; Kyoto Protocol to the UN Framework Convention on Climate Change; Convention on Biological Diversity; Comprehensive Nuclear Test-Ban Treaty; International Covenant on Economic, Social and Cultural Rights; Convention against Transnational Organized Crime.

6. "During the first session of the UN General Assembly in 1946, the United States sponsored Resolution 95(I), which affirmed 'the principles of international law recognized by the Charter of the Nuremberg Tribunal and the judgment of the tribunal.'" Jackson Nyamuya Maogoto. *War Crimes and Realpolitik: International Justice from World War I to the 21st Century* (Boulder, London: Lynne Rienner Publishers, 2004), p. 204.

BIBLIOGRAPHY

THEORY

Evil

Baumeister, Roy F. *Evil: Inside Human Violence and Cruelty*. New York: W. H. Freeman and Company, 1997, 1999.

Bernstein, Richard J. *Radical Evil: A Philosophical Interrogation*. Cambridge: Polity Press, 2002.

Card, Claudia. *The Atrocity Paradigm: A Theory of Evil*. New York: Oxford University Press, 2002.

Copjec, Joan, ed. *Radical Evil*. London: Verso, 1996.

Lara, Maria Pia, ed. *Rethinking Evil*. Berkeley: University of California Press, 2001.

Larrimore, Mark, ed. *The Problem of Evil, a Reader*. Oxford: Blackwell, 2001.

Neiman, Susan. *Evil in Modern Thought: An Alternative History of Philosophy*. Princeton: Princeton University Press, 2002.

Osiel, Marc. *Mass Atrocity, Ordinary Evil, and Hannah Arendt*. New Haven, CT: Yale University Press, 2001.

Peterson, Michael L. *God and Evil: An Introduction to the Issues*. Boulder, CO: Westview Press, 1998.

——, ed. *The Problem of Evil: Selected Readings*. Notre Dame, IN: University of Notre Dame Press, 1992.

Petman, Jarna. "The Problem of Evil in International Law." In Jana Petman and Jan Klabbers, eds. *Nordic Cosmopolitanism*. Leiden: Martinus Nijhoff, 2002.

Rorty, Amelie Oksenberg, ed. *The Many Faces of Evil: Historical Perspectives*. New York: Routledge, 2001.

Seeskin, Kenneth. "What Philosophy Can and Cannot Say about Evil." In Alan Rosenberg and Gerald E. Myers, eds. *Echoes from the Holocaust: Philosophical Reflections on a Dark Time*. Philadelphia, PA: Temple University Press, 1988, pp. 91–104.

Simon, Thomas W. "Expunging Evil," *Free Inquiry* 20 (December 2005/January 2006): 40–44.

Staub, Ervin. *The Roots of Evil: The Psychological and Cultural Origins of Genocide*. London and Cambridge: Cambridge University Press, 1992.

Thomas, Lawrence Mordekhai. *Vessels of Evil*. Philadelphia, PA: Temple University Press, 1993.

Woodruff, Paul and Harry A. Wilmer. *Facing Evil: Confronting the Dreadful Power behind Genocide, Terrorism, and Cruelty*. Chicago and La Salle, IL: Open Court, 1988.

Justice and Injustice

Arendt, Hannah. *Origins of Totalitarianism*. New York: Harcourt, 1951.
Bass, Gary Jonathan. *Stay the Hand of Vengeance*. Princeton, NJ: Princeton University Press, 2000.
Gaita, Raimond. *A Common Humanity*. New York: Routledge, 1998.
Gioseffi, Daniela, ed. *On Prejudice: A Global Perspective*. New York, Anchor, 1993.
Glover, Jonathan. *Humanity: A Moral History of the Twentieth Century*. New Haven, CT, and London: Yale University Press, 1999.
Juergensmeyer, Mark. *Terror in the Mind of God: The Global Rise of Religious Violence*. Third Edition. Berkeley: University of California Press, 2003.
Kritz, Neil, ed. *Transitional Justice: How Emerging Democracies Reckon with Former Regimes*. Three Volumes. Washington, DC: US Institute of Peace, 1995.
Minow, Martha. *Between Vengeance and Forgiveness: Facing History after Genocide and Mass Violence*. Boston, MA: Beacon Press, 1998.
Neicr, Ayreh. *War Crimes: Brutality, Genocide, Terror, and the Struggle for Justice*. New York: Times Books, 1998.
Shklar, Judith. *The Faces of Injustice*. New Haven, CT: Yale University Press, 1990.
——. *Ordinary Vices*. Cambridge, MA: Harvard University Press, 1984.
Simon, Thomas. *Democracy and Social Injustice*. Lanham, MD: Rowman & Littlefield, 1995.
Woozley, A. D. "Injustice," *Studies in Ethics* 7 (1973): 109–110.

Ethics and Justice of War

Axinn, Sidney. *A Moral Military*. Philadelphia, CT: Temple University Press, 1989.
Barry, J. *The Sword of Justice: Ethics and Coercion in International Politics*. London: Praeger, 1998.
Beitz, Charles et al., eds. *International Ethics*. Princeton, NJ: Princeton University Press, 1985.
Best, G. *Humanity in Warfare*. New York: Columbia University Press, 1980.
——. *War and Law since 1945*. Oxford: Clarendon, 1994.
Christopher, Paul. *The Ethics of War and Peace*. Englewood Cliffs, NJ: Prentice Hall, 1999, 2004.
Elshtain, Jean Bethke, ed. *Just War Theory*. Oxford: Basil Blackwell, 1992.
Frey, R. G. and C. W. Morris, eds. *Violence, Terrorism, and Justice*. Cambridge: Cambridge University Press, 1991.
Hedges, Chris. *War Is a Force that Gives Us Meaning*. New York: Anchor, 2003.
Holmes, R. *On War and Morality*. Princeton, NJ: Princeton University Press, 1989.
Howard, M. *The Laws of War: Constraints on Warfare in the Western World*. New Haven, CT: Yale University Press, 1994.
Human Rights Watch. *Slaughter among Neighbors*. New Haven, CT: Yale University Press, 1995.
Huntington, Samuel. *The Soldier and the State*. Cambridge, MA: Harvard University Press, 1957.
Johnson, J. T. *The Just War Tradition and the Restraint of War*. Princeton, NJ: Princeton University Press, 1981.
——. *Morality and Contemporary Warfare*. New Haven, CT: Yale University Press, 1999.

Jokic, Aleksandar, ed. *War Crimes and Collective Wrongdoing: A Reader*. Oxford: Blackwell, 2001.

May, Larry and Stacey Hoffman, eds. *Collective Responsibility: Five Decades of Debate in Theoretical and Applied Ethics*. Lanham, MD: Rowman & Littlefield, 1991.

Nardin, T, ed. *The Ethics of War and Peace: Religious and Secular Perspectives*. Princeton, NJ: Princeton University Press, 1996.

——. *Law, Morality, and the Relations of States*. Princeton, NJ: Princeton University Press, 1983.

Nardin, T. and D. Mapel, eds. *Traditions of International Ethics*. Cambridge: Cambridge University Press, 1992.

Norman, R. *Ethics, Killing, and War*. Cambridge: Cambridge University Press, 1995.

Ramsey, Paul. *The Just War: Force and Political Responsibility*. New York: Charles Scribner's Sons, 1968.

Rawls, J. *The Law of Peoples*. Cambridge, MA: Harvard University Press, 1999.

Regan, R. *Just War: Principles and Cases*. Washington, DC: Catholic University of America Press, 1996.

Russell, Frederick. *The Just War in the Middle Ages*. London: Cambridge University Press, 1975.

Waltz, K. *Man, The State and War*. Princeton, NJ: Princeton University Press, 1978.

Walzer, Michael. *Arguing about War*. New Haven, CT: Yale University Press, 2006.

——. *Just and Unjust Wars*. New York: Basic Books, 1977, 1992, and 2006.

Wasserstrom, Richard, ed. *War and Morality*. Belmont, CA: Wadsworth, 1970.

Wells, D. A. *An Encyclopedia of War and Ethics*. Westport, CT: Greenwood, 1996.

INTERNATIONAL CRIMES

Founet, Caroline. *International Crimes—Theories, Practice, and Evolution*. London: International Law Publishers, 2006.

Passas, Nikos, ed. *International Crimes*. Dartmouth: Ashgate, 2003.

Rummel, R. J. *Statistics of Democide, Genocide, and Mass Murder since 1900*. Charlottesville, VA: Center for National Security Law, University of Virginia, 1997.

Crime of Genocide

General

Alvarez, Alex. *Governments, Citizens, and Genocide: A Comparative and Interdisciplinary Perspective*. Bloomington, IN: Indiana University Press, 2001.

Andreopoulos, George J., ed. *Genocide: Conceptual and Historical Dimensions*. Philadelphia: University of Pennsylvania Press, 1994.

Bartov, Omer. *Mirrors of Destruction: War, Genocide, and Modern Identity*. Oxford: Oxford University Press, 2000.

Bartov, Omer and Phyllis Mack, eds. *In God's Name: Genocide and Religion in the 20th Century*. Oxford: Berghahn Books, 2000.

Chalk, Frank and Kurt Johanassohn. *The History and Sociology of Genocide: Analyses and Case Studies*. New Haven, CT: Yale University Press, 1990.

Charny, Israel W. *Genocide: A Critical Bibliographic Review*. New York: Facts on File Publications, 1988.

Charny, Israel W. *Genocide: A Critical Bibliographic Review, Volume 2*. New York: Facts on File Publications, 1991.

Charny, Israel et al., eds. *Encyclopedia of Genocide*. Santa Barbara, CA: ABC-CLIO, 1999.

Eckhart, William and Gernot Köhler, "Structural and Armed Violence in the 20th Century: Magnitudes and Trends," *International Interactions* 6:4 (1980): 347–375.

Fein, Helen. *Accounting for Genocide*. New York: The Free Press, 1979.

——. *Genocide: A Sociological Perspective* (Newbury Park, CA: Sage Publications/International Sociological Association, 1993). Reviewed by Israel Charny, "Review of Helen Fein's *Genocide: A Sociological Perspective*" *Internet on the Holocaust and Genocide*, nos. 30–31 (February 1991): 5–6.

Hewitt, William. *Defining the Horrific: Readings on Genocide and Holocaust in the 20th Century*. Englewood Cliffs, NJ: Prentice Hall, 2003.

Hinton, A. L., ed. *Annihilating Difference: The Anthropology of Genocide*. Berkeley: University of California Press, 2002.

——, ed., *Genocide: An Anthropological Reader*. Malden, MA: Blackwell Publishers, 2000.

Horowitz, Irving Louis. *Taking Lives: Genocide and State Power*. Fifth Edition, Revised. New Brunswick, NJ: Transaction Books, 2002.

Jensen, S. L. B. *Genocide: Cases, Comparisons, and Contemporary Debates*. Danish Center for Holocaust and Genocide Studies, 2003.

Jentleson, Bruce W., ed. *Opportunities Missed, Opportunities Seized*. New York: Carnegie Corporation, 2000.

Jonassohn, Kurt and K. S. Björnson. *Genocide and Gross Human Rights Violations in Comparative Perspective*. New Brunswick, NJ: Transaction Books, 1998.

Jones, Adam. *Genocide: A Comprehensive Introduction*. London: Routledge, 2006.

——, ed. *Genocide, War Crimes and the West*. New York: Zed Books, 2004.

Kimenyi, Alexandre and Otis L. Scott. *Anatomy of Genocide: State-Sponsored Mass-Killings in the Twentieth Century*. New York: Edwin Mellen, 2001.

Koff, Clea. *The Bone Woman: A Forensic Anthropologist's Search for Truth in the Graves of Rwanda, Bosnia, Croatia, and Kosovo*. New York: Random House, 2004.

Kressel, Neil Jeffrey. *Mass Hate: The Global Rise of Genocide and Terror*. New York: Plenum Press, 1996.

Kuper, L. *Genocide: Its Political Use in the Twentieth Century*. Harmondsworth: Penguin, 1981.

Lemkin, Raphael. *Axis Rule in Occupied Europe*. Washington, DC: Carnegie Endowment for International Peace, 1944.

Lifton, Robert J. and Markusen, E. *The Genocidal Mentality: Nazi Holocaust and Nuclear Threat*. New York: Basic Books, 1988.

Lippman, Mathew. "Genocide: The Crime of the Century," *Houston Journal of International Law* 23 (2001).

Melson, Robert. *Revolution and Genocide: On the Origins of the Armenian Genocide and the Holocaust*. Chicago: University of Chicago Press, 1992.

Porter, Jack Nusan, ed. *Genocide and Human Rights: A Global Anthology*. Washington, DC: University Press of America, 1982.

Powers, Samantha. *"A Problem from Hell," America and the Age of Genocide*. New York: Basic Books, 2002.

Roth, John K., ed. *Genocide and Human Rights: A Philosophical Guide*. New York: Palgrave, 2005.

Sartre, Jean Paul. *On Genocide*. Boston: Beacon Press, 1968.
Simon, Thomas W. "Defining Genocide," *Wisconsin International Law Review* (1996): 243–256.
——. "Genocide: Normative Comparative Studies." In John K. Roth and Elisabeth Maxwell-Meynard, eds. *Remembering for the Future: The Holocaust in the Age of Genocide*. London: Macmillan, 2001, pp. 1–23.
Smithy, R., ed. *Genocide: Essays toward Understanding, Early Warning, and Prevention*. Williamsburg, VA: Association of Genocide Scholars, 1999.
Totten, Samuel and M. I. Sherman, eds. *Genocide at the Millennium: A Critical Bibliographic Review*. New Brunswick, NJ: Transaction Books, 2005.
Totten, Samuel and Steven Jacobs, eds. *Pioneers of Genocide Studies*. New Brunswick, NJ: Transaction Books, 2002.
Totten, Samuel, William S. Parsons, and Israel Charny, eds. *Century of Genocide: Eyewitness Accounts and Critical Views*. New York and London: Garland Publishing Inc., 1997.
Valentino, B. A. *Final Solutions: Mass Killing and Genocide in the Twentieth Century*. Ithaca, NY: Cornell University Press, 2004.
Wallimann, Isidor and Michael Dobkowski, eds. *Genocide and the Modern Age*. New York: Greenwood Press, 1987.
——. *Genocide in the Modern Age: Etiology and Case Studies of Mass Death*. Syracuse, NY: Syracuse University Press, 2000.

CASES OF GENOCIDE

Herero Genocide

Anderson, Rachel. "Redressing Colonial Genocide under International Law: The Hereros' Cause of Action against Germany," *California Law Review* 93 (2005): 1135–1189.
Bridgman, J. M. *The Revolt of the Hereros*. Berkeley and Los Angeles: University of California Press, 1981.
Drechsler, Horst. *Let Us Die Fighting: The Struggle of the Herero and the Nama against German Imperialism*. London: Zed Press, 1980.
Gewarld, Jan-Bart and James Currey. *Herero Heroes: A Socio-Political History of the Herero of Namibia 1890–1923*. Oxford and Athens, OH: Ohio University Press, 1999.
Powers, Donald G. "Its Past on Its Sleeve, Tribe Seeks Bonn's Apology," *New York Times*, International Section (May 31, 1998).

Armenian Genocide

Akcam, Taner. *A Shameful Act: The Armenian Genocide and the Question of Turkish Responsibility*. New York: Henry Holt, 2006.
Balakian, Peter. *The Burning Tigress: The Armenian Genocide and America's Response*. New York: Harper Collins, 2003.
Dadrian, Vahakn N. "Genocide as a Problem of National and International Law: The World War I Armenian Case and its Contemporary Legal Ramifications," *Yale Journal of International Law* 14 (1989): 321–334.
——. *The History of the Armenian Genocide: Ethnic Conflict from the Balkans to Anatolia to the Caucasus*. Providence, RI: Berghahn Books, 1995.

Dadrian, Vahakn N. *Warrant for Genocide: Key Elements of Turko-Armenian Conflict*. New Brunswick, NJ: Transaction Books, 1999.
Hovannisian, Richard G., ed. *The Armenian Genocide: History, Politics, Ethics*. New York: St. Martin's Press, 1992.
——, ed. *The Armenian Genocide in Perspective*. New Brunswick, NJ: Transaction Books, 1986.
——, ed. *The Armenian Holocaust: A Bibliography Relating to the Deportations, Massacres, and Dispersion of the Armenian People, 1915–1923*. Cambridge, MA: Armenian Heritage Press (and NAASR), 1978.
——, ed. *Remembrance and Denial: The Case of the Armenian Genocide*. Detroit: Wayne State University Press, 1998.
Libaridan, Gerald J., ed. *A Crime of Silence: The Armenian Genocide*. Permanent Peoples' Tribunal. New York: Zed Books, 1985.
Yeghiayan, Vartkes, ed. *The Armenian Genocide and the Trials of the Young Turks*. La Verne, CA: American Armenian International College Press, 1990.

Nazi Holocaust

Bauer, Y. *The Holocaust in Historical Perspective*. Seattle: University of Washington Press, 1978.
Bauman, Z. *Modernity and the Holocaust*. Cambridge: Polity Press, 1989.
Berenbaum, Michael, ed. *A Mosaic of Victims*. New York: New York University Press, 1990.
Berenbaum, Michael and Abraham J. Peck, eds. *The Holocaust in History*. Indiana: Indiana University Press, 1998.
Boder, David. *I Did Not Interview the Dead*. Urbana: University of Illinois Press, 1949.
Browning, Christopher. *Ordinary Men*. New York: Harper Collins, 1993.
——. *The Origins of the Final Solution: The Evolution of Nazi Jewish Policy, September 1939–March 1942*. Lincoln, NE: University of Nebraska Press, 2004.
Bullock, Allan. *Hitler: A Study in Tyranny*. New York: Harper & Row, 1962.
Cole, Tim. *Selling the Holocaust*. New York: Routledge, 1999.
Fackenheim, Emile. *To Mend the World*. New York: Schoken Books, 1982.
Goldhagen, Daniel J. *Hitler and His Willing Executioners*. New York: Alfred A. Knopf, 1996.
Habermas, Jürgen. "A Kind of Indemnification: The Tendencies toward Apologia in German Research on Current History," *Yad Vashem Studies* 19 (1988): 75–92.
Hancock, Ian "Responses to the Porrajmos: The Romany Holocaust." In Alan S. Rosenbaum, ed. *Is the Holocaust Unique?* Boulder, CO: Westview Press, 1996.
Herz, John H. "Denazification and Related Policies." In John H. Herz, ed. *From Dictatorship to Democracy*. Westport, CT: Greenwood, 1982.
Hilberg, Raul. *The Destruction of the European Jews*. Student Edition. New York: Holmes & Meier, 1985.
Johnson, Eric A. *Nazi Terror*. New York: Basic Books, 1999.
Katz, S. T. *The Holocaust in Historical Context. Volume 1: The Holocaust and Mass Death before the Modern Age*. New York: Oxford University Press, 1994.
Lang, Berel. *Act and Idea in the Nazi Genocide*. Chicago, IL: University of Chicago Press, 1990.
——. *The Future of the Holocaust: Between History and Memory*. Ithaca, NY: Cornell University Press, 1999.

——. *Holocaust Representation: Art within the Limits of History and Ethics*. Baltimore: Johns Hopkins University Press, 2000.
——. *Writing and the Holocaust*. New York: Holmes & Meier, 1988.
Laqueur, Walter and Judith Tydor Baumel, eds. *Holocaust Encyclopedia*. New Haven, CT: Yale University Press, 2001.
Levi, Primo. *The Drowned and the Saved*. New York: Summit Books, 1988.
Lewy, Gunther. *The Nazi Persecution of the Gypsies*. New York: Oxford University Press, 2000.
Lipstadt, Barbara. *Beyond Belief: The American Press and the Holocaust 1933–1945*. New York: Free Press, 1986.
——. *Denying the Holocaust: The Growing Assault on Truth and Memory*. New York: Penguin, 1994.
Lutz, Brenda Davis and James M. Lutz. "Gypsies as Victims of the Holocaust," *Holocaust and Genocide Studies* 9 (1995): 346–359.
Margalit, Avishai and Gabriel Motzkin. "The Uniqueness of the Holocaust," *Philosophy and Public Affairs* (Winter 1996): 65–83.
Markusen, E. and D. Kopf. *The Holocaust and Strategic Bombing*. Boulder, CO: Westview Press, 1995.
Nolte, Ernst. "A Past Will Not Pass Away—A Speech It Was Possible to Write, But Not to Present," *Yad Vashem Studies* 19 (1988): 65–73.
Rosenbaum, Alan S. and Israel S. Charny, eds. *Is the Holocaust Unique?: Perspectives on Comparative Genocide*. Boulder, CO: Westview Press, 1997.
Roth, John K. *Holocaust Politics*. Louisville, KY: Westminster John Knox Press, 2001.
Rubenstein, Richard. *The Cunning of History: The Holocaust and the American Future*. New York: Harper & Row, 1975.
Simon, Thomas W. "The Holocaust's Moral Uniqueness?" In Alan Rosenberg et al., eds. *Contemporary Portrays of Auschwitz and Genocide: Philosophical Challenges*. New York: Humanity Press, 2000, pp. 76–94.
Staub, Ervin. *The Roots of Evil: The Origins of Genocide and Other Group Violence*. Cambridge: Cambridge University Press, 1989.
Vogel, Lawrence, ed. *Mortality and Morality: A Search for the Good after Auschwitz*. Evanston, IL: Northwestern University Press, 1996.
Wiesel, Elie. *Night*. Stella Rodway, trans. New York: Hill & Wang, 1961.

Grave Injustices in Former Yugoslavia

Bacevich, Andrew J. and Eliot A. Cohen, eds. *War Over Kosovo*. New York: Columbia University Press, 2001.
Branka, Maga. *The Destruction of Yugoslavia: Tracking the Break-up 1980–92*. London: Verso, 1993.
Bringa, Tonc. *Being Muslim the Bosnian Way*. Princeton: Princeton University Press, 1995.
Davis, G. S. *Religion and Justice in the War over Bosnia*. New York: Routledge, 1996.
Doubt, Keith "Intellectual Betrayal and Agony of Bosnia and Herzegovina," *Centre For Historical Studies* (May 22, 2001).
Gutman, Roy. A *Witness to Genocide: The 1993 Pulitzer Prize-Winning—Dispatches on the "Ethnic Cleansing" of Bosnia*. New York: Macmillan, 1993.
Ignatieff, Michael. *Virtual War, Kosovo and Beyond*. New York: Picador, 2000.

Kaplan, Robert D. *Balkan Ghosts: A Journey through History*. New York: Vintage, 1993.

Lampe, John R. *Yugoslavia as History*. Cambridge: Cambridge University Press, 1996.

Malcolm, Noel. *Bosnia, A Short History*. New York: New York University Press, 1994, 1996.

——. *Kosovo: A Short History*. Washington Square, NY: New York University Press, 1998.

Powers, Samantha. "The World of Radovan Karadžić," *U. S. News & World Report* (July 24, 1995).

Sells, Michael A. *The Bridge Betrayed: Religion and Genocide in Bosnia*. Berkeley: University of California Press, 1996.

Sofos, Keith. *Sociology after Bosnia and Kosovo: Recovering Justice*. Lanham, MD: Rowman & Littlefield, 2000.

Vickers, Miranda. *Between Serb and Albanian: A History of Kosovo*. New York: Columbia University Press, 1998.

Rwandan Genocide

Adelman, Howard and Astri Suhrke, eds. *The Path of a Genocide: The Rwanda Crisis from Uganda to Zaire*. New Brunswick, NJ: Transaction Books, 1999.

African Rights. *Rwanda: Death, Despair, and Defiance*. London: African Rights, 1995.

——. *Rwanda: Killing the Evidence: Murders, Attacks, Arrests, and Intimidation of Survivors and Witnesses*. London: African Rights, 1996.

Amnesty International. *Burundi: Killings of Children by Government Troops*, AFR. 16/04, 1988.

Barnett, Michael. *Eyewitness to a Genocide: The United Nations and Rwanda*. Ithaca, NY: Cornell University Press, 2002.

Berry, John A. and Carol Pott Berry, eds. *Genocide in Rwanda, A Collective Memory*. Washington, DC: Howard University Press, 1999.

Dallaire, Roméo A. *Shake Hands with the Devil: The Failure of Humanity in Rwanda*. New York: Avalon, 2004.

Des Forges, A. *"Leave None to Tell the Story": Genocide in Rwanda*. New York: Human Rights Watch, 1999.

Destexhe, Alain. *Rwanda and Genocide in the Twentieth Century*. New York: New York University Press, 1995.

Eltringham, Nigel. *Accounting for Horror: Post-Genocide Debates in Rwanda*. London: Pluto Press, 2004.

Gourevitch, Philip. *We Wish to Inform You That Tomorrow We Will Be Killed with Our Families*. New York: Picador, 1998.

Lemarchand, René. "Burundi: The Politics of Ethnic Amnesia." In Helen Fein, ed. *Genocide Watch*. New Haven, CT: Yale University Press, 1992, pp. 70–86.

Mamdani, Mahmood. *When Victims Become Killers: Colonialism, Nativism, and the Genocide in Rwanda*. Princeton: Princeton University Press, 2002.

Melvern, L. *A People Betrayed: The Role of the West in Rwanda's Genocide*. London & New York: Zed Books, 2000.

Metzl, Jamie Frederic. "Rwandan Genocide and the International Law of Radio Jamming," *American Journal of International Law* 91 (1997): 628.

Organization of African Unity. *The International Panel of Eminent Personalities to Investigate the 1994 Genocide in Rwanda and the Surrounding Events*, Organization of African Unity, 1999.
Prunier, Gérard. *The Rwanda Crisis: History of Genocide*. New York: Columbia University Press, 1995.
Roth, Carol and John K. Roth, eds. *Genocide in Rwanda: Complicity of the Churches?* New York: Paragon House, 2004.
Siboman, André. *Hope for Rwanda*. Sterling, VA: Pluto Press, 1997.
Straus, Scott. *The Order of Genocide: Race, Power, and War in Rwanda*. Ithaca, NY: Cornell University Press, 2006.
Suhrke, Astri and Bruce Jones. "Preventative Diplomacy in Rwanda: Failure to Act or Failure of Actions?" In Bruce W. Jentleson, ed. *Opportunities Missed, Opportunities Seized: Preventive Diplomacy in Post-Cold War World*. Lanham, MD: Rowman & Littlefield, 2000.

Cambodian Killing Fields

Ablin, David A. and Hood, Marlowe, eds. *The Cambodian Agony*. Armonk: M. E. Sharpe, 1990.
Becker, Elizabeth. *When the War Was Over, Cambodia and the Khmer Rouge Revolution*. New York: Public Affairs, 1986, 1998.
Blazer, Michael J. "Reexamining the Doctrine of Humanitarian Intervention in Light of the Atrocities in Kampuchea and Ethiopia," *Stanford Journal of International Law* 23:2 (1987): 552.
Chandler, David P. *Brother Number One, a Political Biography of Pol Pot*. Revised Edition. Boulder, CO: Westview Press, 1999.
——. *A History of Cambodia*. Third Edition. Boulder, CO: Westview Press, 2000.
——. *The Tragedy of Cambodian History*. New Haven, CT: Yale University Press, 1991.
Etcheson, Craig. *After the Killing Fields: Lessons from the Cambodian Genocide*. New York: Praeger, 2005.
——. "Mapping Project 1999: The Analysis," *Document Center of Cambodia*.
Hannum, Hurst. "International Law and the Cambodian Genocide: The Sounds of Silence," *Human Rights Journal* (1989): 82.
Kiernan, Ben. *Genocide and Democracy in Cambodia*. New Haven, CT: Yale University Southeast Asia Studies, 1993.
——. *The Pol Pot Regime: Race, Power, and Genocide in Cambodia under the Khmer Rouge, 1975–1979*. New Haven, CT, and London: Yale University Press, 1996.
Mills, Nicolaus and Kira Brunner, eds. *The New Killing Fields, Massacre and the Politics of Intervention*. New York: Basic Books, 2002.
Vickery, Michael. *Cambodia: 1975–1982*. Boston: South End Press, 1984.

Genocide, Other Candidates

Rummel, R. J. *Death by Government*. New Brunswick, NJ: Transaction Books, 1994.
Stannard, David E. *American Holocaust: The Conquest of the New World*. New York: Oxford University Press, 1992.

CRIMES AGAINST HUMANITY

General

Bassiouni, M. Cherif. *Crimes against Humanity in International Criminal Law*. Second Revised Edition. Cambridge, MA: Kluwer Law International, 1999.

Chippendale, Neil. *Crimes against Humanity*. Philadelphia, PA: Chelsea House Publishers, 2000.

Lattimer, Mark and Philippe Sands, eds. *Justice for Crimes against Humanity*. Hart, 2003.

Luban, David. "A Theory of Crimes against Humanity," *Yale Journal of International Law* 29 (2004): 85–167.

May, Larry. *Crimes against Humanity, A Normative Account*. New York: Cambridge University Press, 2005.

Robertson, Geoffrey. *Crimes against Humanity: The Struggle for Global Justice*. New York: The New Press, 2000.

Shelton, Dinah, ed. *Encyclopedia of Genocide and Crimes against Humanity*. New York: Macmillan, 2004.

Cases of Crimes against Humanity

Famine

Applebaum, Anne. *Gulag: A History*. New York: Doubleday, 2002. Reviewed by Viola, Lynne. "The Gray Zone," *The Nation* (October 13, 2003): 25–29.

Conquest, Robert. *The Harvest of Sorrow: Soviet Collectivization and the Terror-Famine*. New York: Oxford University Press, 1986.

Letgers, Lyman H. "The Soviet Gulag: Is It Genocide?" In Israel W. Chaney, ed. *Toward the Understanding and Prevention of Genocide*. Boulder, CO: Westview Press, 1984.

Marcus, D. "Famine Crimes in International Law," *American Journal of International Law* 97 (2003): 245–281.

Tucker, Robert C. *Stalin in Power: The Revolution from Above, 1928–1941*. New York: W. W. Norton, 1990.

Rape

Askin, K. D. "Prosecuting Wartime Rape and Other Gender-Related Crimes under International Law: Extraordinary Advances, Enduring Obstacles," *Berkeley Journal of International Law* 21 (2003): 288–349.

——. "Sexual Violence in Decisions and Indictments of the Yugoslav and Rwandan Tribunals: Current Status," *American Journal of International La*w 93 (1999): 97–123.

——. *War Crimes against Women. Prosecution in International War Crimes Tribunals*. The Hague: Martinus Nijhoff, 1997.

Chang, Iris. *The Rape of Nanking*. New York: Basic Books, 1997.

Meron, Theodore, "Rape as a Crime under International Humanitarian Law," *American Journal of International Law* 87 (1993): 424.

Miller, A. A. "From the International Criminal Tribunal for Rwanda to the International Criminal Court: Expanding the Definition of Genocide to Include Rape," *Penn State Law Review* 108 (2003): 349–373.

Russell-Brown, S. L. "Rape as an Act of Genocide," *Berkeley Journal of International Law* 21 (2003): 350–374.
Stiglmayer, Alexandra, ed. *Mass Rape: The War against Women in Bosnia-Herzegovina.* Lincoln, NE: University of Nebraska Press, 1994.

Terrorism

Bassiouni, M. C. *International Terrorism: A Compilation of U.N. Documents (1972–2001).* Ardsley, NY: Transnational Publishers, 2002.
Chadwick, E. *Self-determination, Terrorism, and the International Humanitarian Law of Armed Conflict.* The Hague and Boston, MA: Martinus Nijhoff, 1996.
Elagab, Omer Y., comp. *International Law Documents Relating to Terrorism.* Second Edition. London: Cavendish Publishers, 1997.
Han, Henry H., ed. *Terrorism & Political Violence: Limits & Possibilities of Legal Control.* New York: Oceana, 1993.
Heere, Wybo P., ed. *Terrorism and the Military: International Legal Implications.* The Hague: T.M.C. Asser Press.
Higgins, Rosalyn and Maurice Flory, eds. *Terrorism and International Law.* London and Florence, KY: Routledge, 1997.
Levie, H. *Terrorism in War: The Law of War Crimes.* Dobbs Ferry, NY: Oceana, 1993.
Lifton, Robert Jay. *Destroying the World to Save It: Aum Sinrikyo and the New Global Terrorism.* New York: Henry Holt and Company, 1999.
Sterba, James P. ed. *Terrorism and International Justice.* New York: Oxford University Press, 2003.
United Nations. *International Instruments Related to the Prevention and Suppression of International Terrorism.* New York: United Nations, 2001.

War Crimes

Bartov, Omer et al., eds. *Crimes of War: Guilt and Denial in the Twentieth Century.* New York: New Press, 2002.
Dunant, Henry. *A Memory of Solferino.* Geneva: International Committee of the Red Cross, 1939, 1959.
Gutman, Roy and David Rieff, eds. *Crimes of War: What the Public Should Know.* W. W. Norton & Company, 1999.

LAW

http://www.jurist.law.pitt.edu/
http://diana.law.yale.edu/

International Criminal Law

http://www.un.org/
http://www.hrw.org/hrw/

Bassiouni, M. C., ed. *International Criminal Law.* Second Edition. Ardsley, NY: Transnational Publishers, 1998.

Bassiouni, M. C. *Introduction to International Criminal Law*. Ardsley, NY: Transnational Publishers, 2003.

Cassese, A. *International Criminal Law*. New York: Oxford University Press, 2003.

Dörmann, K. et al., eds. *Elements of War Crimes under the Rome Statute of the International Criminal Court: Sources and Commentary*. New York: Cambridge University Press, 2003.

Maogoto, Jackson Nyamuya. *War Crimes and Realpolitik: International Justice from World War I to the 21st* Century. Boulder, CO and London: Lynne Rienner Publishers, 2004.

Ratner, Steven R. and Jason S. Abrams, eds. *Accountability for Human Rights Atrocities in International Law: Beyond the Nuremberg Legacy*. Oxford: Clarendon Press, 1997.

Shklar, Judith. *Legalism*. Cambridge, MA: Harvard University Press, 1986.

Steiner, Henry and Philip Alston. *International Human Rights in Context*. Oxford: Clarendon Press, 1996.

Sunga, L. S. *The Emerging System of International Criminal Law, Developments in Codification and Implementation*. La Haye: Kluwer, 1997.

Werle, Gerhard, ed. *Principles of International Criminal Law*. The Hague: T.M.C. Asser Press, 2005.

Laws of War

Carrahan, Burrus M. "Lincoln, Leiber and the Laws of War: The Origins and Limits of the Principle of Military Necessity," *The American Journal of International Law* 92 (1998): 213–229.

Dinstein, Yoram and Mala Tabory. *War Crimes in International Law*. The Hague, Boston, and London: Martinus Nijhoff, 1996.

Grotius, Hugo. *On the Law of War and Peace*. J. B. Scott, ed. London: Carnegie Endowment for International Peace, 1925.

Hartigan, R. S. *Lieber's Code and the Law of War*. Chicago: Precedent, 1983.

Lauterpacht, H. *International Law. Volumes. 3 and 4: The Law of Peace*. Cambridge: Cambridge University Press, 1977–1978.

Maguire, Peter. *Law and War, an American Story*. New York: Columbia University Press, 2001.

McCormack, T. L. H. and G. J. Simpson, eds. *The Law of War Crimes: National and International Approaches*. The Netherlands: Kluwer, 1997.

Meron, Theodore. *War Crimes Law Comes of Age*. Oxford: Clarendon, 1998.

Reisman, M. and C. Antoniou, eds. *The Laws of War*. New York: Vintage, 1994.

Roberts, Adam and Richard Guelff, eds. *Documents on the Laws of War*. Third Edition. New York: Oxford University Press, 2000.

Stojanovic, Lazar, ed. *International Conference on War-Crimes Trials*. Proceedings of the International Conference on War-Crimes Trials. Belgrade: Humanitarian Law Center, 2000.

Laws of Genocide

Arnold, R. "The *Mens Rea* of Genocide under the Statute of the International Criminal Court," *Criminal Law Forum* 14 (2003): 127–151.

Ball, H. *Prosecuting War Crimes and Genocide: The Twentieth Century Experience*. Lawrence, KS: University of Kansas Press, 1999.

Convention on the Prevention and Punishment of the Crime of Genocide. Dec. 9, 1948, art. I, 78 United Nations Treaty Series 277.

Fraser, D. *Law after Auschwitz: Towards a Jurisprudence of the Holocaust*. Durham, NC: Carolina Academic Press, 2005.

Kim, P. "The Law of Genocide in the Jurisprudence of ICTY and ICTR in 2004," *International Criminal Law Review* 5 (2005): 431–446.

LeBlanc, L. J. "The United Nations Genocide Convention and Political Groups: Should the United States Propose Amendment?" *Yale Journal of International Law* 13 (1988): 268–295.

——. *The United States and the Genocide Convention*. Durham, NC: Duke University Press, 1991.

Lippman, Mathew. "The 1948 Convention on the Prevention and Punishment of the Crime of Genocide," *Temple International and Comparative Law Journal* 8: 4 (1985).

Report of the Committee on Foreign Relations, U.S. Senate, on "The Genocide Convention," Sen. Exec. Rpt. 99–2, 99th Cong., 1st Sass., July 18, 1985.

Ruebner, Ralph. "The Evolving Nature of the Crime of Genocide," *John Marshall Law Review* 38 (2005): 1227–1236.

Schaack, B. van. "The Crime of Political Genocide: Repairing the Genocide Convention's Blind Spot," *Yale Law Journal* 106 (1997): 2259–2291.

Schabas, William. *Genocide in International Law: The Crimes of Crime*. Cambridge: Cambridge University Press, 2000.

Tournaye, C. "Genocidal Intent before the ICTY," *The International and Comparative Law Quarterly* 52 (2002): 447–462.

TRIBUNALS

International Tribunals

http://www.iwpr.net/tribunal/mainpage.htm
http://www.worldlii.org/int/cases/

Chandra, Satish, ed. *International Documents on Human Rights*. New Delhi: Mittal Publications, 1990.

Knoops, Geert-Jan Alexander. *An Introduction to the Law of International Criminal Tribunals: A Comparative Study*. Ardsley, NY: Transnational Publishers, 2003.

Mettraux, G. *International Crimes and the Ad Hoc Tribunals*. New York: Oxford University Press, 2005.

Reichel, Philip, ed. *Adjudicating International Crimes, Handbook of Transnational Crime & Justice*. Thousand Oaks, CA: Sage, 2005.

Sands, P., ed. *From Nuremberg to the Hague: The Future of International Criminal Justice*. New York: Cambridge University Press, 2003.

War Crimes Tribunals

International Military Tribunal (Nuremberg Tribunal)

http://www.yale.edu/lawweb/avalon/imt.htm

Conot, Robert E. *Justice at Nuremberg*. New York: Harper & Row, 1983.

Davidson, Eugene. *The Trial of the Germans*. Columbia, MI: University of Missouri Press, 1966.
Ginsburgs, George and V. N. Kudriavtsev, eds. *The Nuremberg Trial and International Law*. 42 Law in Eastern Europe. Dordrecht and Boston: Martinus Nijhoff, 1990.
Harris, Whitney R. *Tyranny on Trial: The Evidence at Nuremberg*. New York: Barnes & Noble, 1954, 1995.
Jackson, Robert H. *The Case against the Nazi War Criminals*. New York: Knopf, 1946.
——. *The Judgment of Nuremberg, 1946*. London: The Stationary Office, 1946, 1999.
Kochavi, Arieh J. *Prelude to Nuremberg*. Chapel Hill, NC: University of North Carolina Press, 1998.
Müller, Ingo. *Hitler's Justice, The Courts of the Third Reich*. Deborah Lucas Schneider, trans. Cambridge, MA: Harvard University Press, 1991.
Persico, Joseph E. *Nuremberg: Infamy on Trial*. New York: Penguin Books, 1994.
Smith, B. F. *The American Road to Nuremberg: The Documentary Record, 1944–1945*. Stanford, CA: Hoover Institution Press, 1982.
Taylor, Telford. *The Anatomy of the Nuremberg Trials: A Personal Memoir*. New York: Knopf, 1992.
Tusa, A. and J. Tusa. *The Nuremberg Trial*. New York: Atheneum, 1984.
Willis, J. F. *Prologue to Nuremberg: The Politics and Diplomacy of Punishing War Criminals of the First World War*. Westport, CT: Greenwood, 1982.
Wyzanski, Charles E., Jr. "Nuremberg: A Fair Trial?" *Atlantic Monthly* (April 1964): 66–70.

The International Military Tribunal for the Far East (Tokyo Tribunal)

http://www.yale.edu/lawweb/avalon/imt.htm

Minear, R. H. *Victors Justice: The Tokyo War Crimes Trial*. Ann Arbor, MI: Center for Japanese Studies, The University of Michigan, 2001.
Röling, B. V. A. and C. F. Rüter, eds. *The Tokyo Judgment: The International Military Tribunal for the Far East (I.M.T.F.E)*. Amsterdam: APA—University Press Amsterdam, 1977.
Shiroyama, Saburo. *War Criminal, The Life and Death of Hirota Koki*. John Bester, trans. Tokyo and New York: Kodansha International, 1974.

International Criminal Tribunal for the Former Yugoslavia (ICTY)

http://www.un.org/icty

Ackerman, John E. and Eugene O'Sullivan. *Practice and Procedure of the International Criminal Tribunal for the Former Yugoslavia: With Selected Materials from the International Criminal Tribunal for Rwanda*. The Hague and Cambridge, MA: Kluwer Law International, 2000.
Allain, Jean. *The Practice of the International Criminal Tribunal for the Former Yugoslavia: An Annotation of its Statute. 25 May 1993 Till 1 January 1997*, Genève: Mémoire de DES, IUHEI, 1997.
Boas, G., ed. *International Criminal Law Developments in the Case Law of the ICTY*. The Hague and Boston, MA: Martinus Nijhoff, 2003.

Bohlander, M. "Prosecutor V. Duško Tadić: Waiting to Exhale," *Criminal Law Forum: An International Journal* 11 (2000): 217–248.

Calvo-Coller, Karin N. *The Trial Proceedings of the International Criminal Court: ICTY and ICTR Precedents*. The Hague and Boston, MA: Martinus Nijhoff, 2006.

Hazan, Pierre. *Justice in a Time of War: The True Story behind the International Criminal Tribunal for the Former Yugoslavia*. James Thomas Snyder, trans. Texas: A & M University Press, 2004.

Jones, John R. W. D. *The Practice of the International Criminal Tribunals for the Former Yugoslavia and Rwanda*. Ardsley, NY: Transnational Publishers, 1998, 2000, 2003.

——. *The Practice of the International Criminal Tribunal for the Former Yugoslavia and Rwanda*. Ardsley, NY: Transnational Publishers, 1999.

Klip, André and Göran Sluiter, eds. *Annotated Leading Cases of International Criminal Tribunals, Volume I–IX: International Criminal Tribunal for the Former Yugoslavia 1999–2006*. Intersentia Uitgevers N.V., 1999–2006.

Scharf, M. P. *Balkan Justice: The Story behind the First International War Crimes Trial since Nuremberg*. Durham, NC: Carolina Academy Press, 1997.

Trahan, Jennifer et al., eds. *Genocide, War Crimes, and Crimes against Humanity: Topical Digests of the Case Law of the International Criminal Tribunal for Rwanda and the International Criminal Tribunal for the Former Yugoslavia*. New York: Human Rights Watch, 2004.

Williams, P. R. and M. P. Scharf. *Peace with Justice: War Crimes and Accountability in the Former Yugoslavia*. Lanham, MD: Rowman & Littlefield, 2002.

International Criminal Tribunal for Rwanda (ICTR)

http://www.un.org/ictr

Akhavan, Payam. "The Crime of Genocide in the ICTR Jurisprudence," *Journal of International Criminal Justice* 3 (2005): 989–1006.

Aptel, C. "The Intent to Commit Genocide in the Case Law of the International Criminal Tribunal for Rwanda," *Criminal Law Forum* 13 (2002–3): 273–291.

Klip, André and Göran Sluiter, eds. *Annotated Leading Cases of International Criminal Tribunals, Volume I–IX: The International Criminal Tribunal for Rwanda*. Intersentia Uitgevers N.V., 2001.

Magnarella, Paul J. *Justice in Africa: Rwanda's Genocide, Its Courts and the UN Criminal Tribunal*. Aldershot: Ashgate, 2000.

Morris, Virginia and Michael P. Scharf. *The International Criminal Tribunal for Rwanda*. Ardsley, NY: Transnational Publishers, 1998.

Temple-Raston, Dina. *Justice on the Grass, Three Rwandan Journalists, Their Trials for War Crimes, and a Nation's Quest for Redemption*. New York: Free Press, 2005.

International Criminal Court (ICC)

http://www.icc-cpi.int/home.html&l=en
www.un.org/icc/

Bantekas, Ilias and Susan Nash. *International Criminal Law*. Second Edition. International Specialized Book Service Inc, 2003.

Bassiouni, M. Cherif. "Establishing an International Criminal Court: Historical Survey," *Military Law Review* 149 (1995): 49–57.

——. ed. *The Statute of the International Criminal Court: A Documentary History*. Ardsley, NY: Transnational Publishers, 1998.

Cassese, Antonio. *International Criminal Law*. Oxford: Oxford University Press, 2003.

Cassese, Antonio et al., eds. *International Criminal Law: A Commentary on the Rome Statute*. Oxford: Oxford University Press, 2001.

——, eds. *The Rome Statute for an International Criminal Court: A Commentary*. New York: Oxford University Press, 2002.

Cottier, M., ed., *Handbook on the Draft Statute for an International Criminal Court*. Bruxelles: The European Law Students' Association, 1998.

Dörmann, K. et al., eds. *Elements of War Crimes under the Rome Statute of the International Criminal Court: Sources and Commentary*. Cambridge: Cambridge University Press, 2003.

Driscoll, William et al., eds. *The International Criminal Court: Global Politics and the Quest for Justice*. New York: International Debate Education Association, 2004.

Ferencz, Benjamin. *An International Criminal Court: A Step toward World Peace: A Documentary History and Analysis*. Dobbs Ferry, NY: Oceana Publications, 1990.

Lee, Roy S., ed. *The International Criminal Court: Elements of Crimes and Rules of Procedure and Evidence*. Ardsley, NY: Transnational Publishers, 2001.

——. *The International Criminal Court: The Making of the Rome Statute: Issues, Negotiations, and Results*. Dordrecht: Kluwer Law International, 2000.

MacGoldrick, Dominic et al., eds. *The Permanent International Criminal Court: Legal and Policy Issues*. Oxford: Hart, 2004.

Murphy, John F. "The Quivering Gulliver: U.S. Views on a Permanent International Criminal Court," *International Lawyer* 34 (Spring 2000): 45–53.

Paust, Jordan L. et al., eds. *International Criminal Law: Cases and Materials*. Second Edition. Durham, NC: Carolina Academic Press, 2000.

Schabas, William A. *An Introduction to the International Criminal Court*. Cambridge: Cambridge University Press, 2004.

Shelton, Dinah, ed., *International Crimes, Peace, and Human Rights: The Role of the International Criminal Court*, Ardsley, NY: Transnational Publishers, 2000.

Sunga, Lyal S. *The Emerging System of International Criminal Law: Developments in Codification and Implementation*. Dordrecht: Martinus Nijhoff, 1997.

Weller, M. "Undoing the Global Constitution: UN Security Council Action on the International Criminal Court," *International Affairs* 78 (2002): 693–712.

Other Tribunals

Arendt, Hannah. *Eichmann in Jerusalem: A Report on the Banality of Evil*. New York: Viking Press, 1964.

Ascheim, ed. *Hannah Arendt in Jerusalem*. Berkeley: University of California Press.

Mullins, C. *The Leipzig Trials: An Account of the War Criminals' Trials and a Study of the German Mentality*. London: H.F. & G. Witherby, 1921.

INDEX

About the Author

THOMAS W. SIMON, a philosopher and lawyer, teaches at Illinois State University. His publications include *Democracy and Social Injustice* (1995) and *Law and Philosophy* (2000). He was a Liberal Arts Fellow at Harvard Law School and a founding faculty member of Miyazaki International College in Japan. He also has taught law in Kosovo, Malaysia, and Slovenia. He founded and edited *Injustice Studies*, an electronic journal. He consults for the United Nations (Working Group on Minorities) and the American Bar Association (Central/Eastern European Law Initiative). He served on a drafting committee for Albania's constitution. As a practicing attorney, he has represented a Diaspora Rwandan group.